Protecting Our Future

Protecting Our Future
Educating a Cybersecurity Workforce

edited by

JANE LECLAIR

HUDSON
WHITMAN
EXCELSIOR COLLEGE PRESS

Published in the United States by
Hudson Whitman/ Excelsior College Press
7 Columbia Circle, Albany, NY 12203
www.hudsonwhitman.com

Printed in the United States of America
Book design by Sue Morreale
Cover design by Philip E. Pascuzzo

Library of Congress
Cataloging-in-publication data
Due to the 2013 government shutdown, an LCCN/PCN could not be provided.
ISBN: 978-0-9898451-1-3 (paperback)

Contents

Acknowledgments

No literary work is completed without the assistance and help of a large group of dedicated individuals who often labor tirelessly to move the project forward. Assistance comes in many forms, from inspiration and motivation, to research and work "in the trenches." Many thanks go to Dr. Jeanne Contardo, who contributed greatly to this project with her hard work and motivational efforts. All of the chapter authors need to be thanked for agreeing to participate in this project despite their busy schedules. They were dedicated to this project, provided a great deal of valuable information, and met all their deadlines in a professional and timely manner. The staff in the Excelsior College community also worked hard to bring this work to fruition; without their efforts this project might still be in the works. Special thanks are owed to Hudson Whitman/ Excelsior College Press for steering us through our first publication. Finally, Dr. John Ebersole, president of Excelsior College, must be thanked for his leadership and farsightedness in the formation of the National Cybersecurity Institute.

Foreword

Over the years, America has faced a great many challenges and it has been an honor to serve our country during some of its more challenging times. During my tenures as Secretary of Defense, I experienced firsthand the importance of sharp focus on those who would do our nation harm. I also witnessed the damage that can come when our country lets its guard down and is unprepared to meet our adversaries.

The challenges we face are in a state of constant evolution. For every offense there is a defense and for every defense there is an offense. This is especially true in times of geopolitical change and uncertainty. Currently, one of the greatest challenges we face is the evolving nature of technology and the impact it has on safeguarding our country's sensitive information. I have said in the past that, "Our task, your task, is to try to connect the dots before something happens." That sentiment is as true today as it was then. Much is happening in the cyberworld and we need to stay well ahead of the curve if we are to be able to protect our vital interests.

The topic of cybersecurity has been covered with broad strokes in several books, but this work by the National Cybersecurity Institute at Excelsior College delves into specific areas in considerable detail. We need to prepare on all levels, from individual computers, to business enterprises, to the government, for the looming challenges in the digital domain. This book will help us understand the challenges and better prepare for our future.

Donald Rumsfeld
13th and 21st U.S. Secretary of Defense

Introduction

JANE LECLAIR

In the world of technology, cybersecurity is without a doubt the most important topic of our times. As a society, we are increasingly engaging with cyberspace through the innumerable online, cloud-based, and networked activities in which we take part every day. We have become in many regards digital people, with our entire lives, in one aspect or another, online and open to inspection. The information that traverses these digital networks is of value not only to us as individuals, but to our national security as well. Our personal computers are constantly being assaulted by viruses, the cybersystems of the banking industry are attacked on a daily basis, and every day government agencies such as the Pentagon are attacked as many as ten million times. Cybersecurity is the process by which we guard our personal, business, and government data.

Advancing technologies have given us the ability to transmit vast amounts of information over the Internet, to electronically move billions of dollars in transactions on a daily basis, and to compile increasingly large amounts of data for our business organizations. By some estimates, in 2012, each day there were more than 2.5 quintillion bytes of data generated. In the banking sector, financial institutions increasingly rely on electronic means to transfer monies and increase customer service to achieve higher rates of satisfaction. With regard to the business community, increasingly more businesses are relying heavily on electronic means to improve their performance in all sectors and in some cases, a business may only exist in the digital world. Digital technology easily provides us with the ability to use social media, do our personal banking, shop online, read books, watch the news, and remotely monitor and secure our homes. Americans alone spent more than $200 billion on online shopping in 2011 and are expected to shell out $327 billion in Internet stores by 2016 (Woo 2012).

Much of our national security is entwined with technology as well. All branches of government, including the military and defense contractors, heavily rely on technology. The military is especially concerned with activity over the Internet for protection of our country. While speaking at a forum at the Brookings Institution, Gen. Martin E. Dempsey, chairman of the Joint Chiefs of Staff, noted, "One thing is clear: cyber has escalated from an issue of moderate concern to one of the most serious threats to our national security" (Roulo 2013).

There is no question that many cyber-attacks on critical government assets are being made by the intelligence services of foreign countries and nation-states. As these attacks are well financed, sophisticated, and directed, only the government has the resources readily available to counter them. Cyber warfare is no longer something found in fiction, but is a real, growing and serious threat to our nation's security.

The notion of "cybersecurity" is a relatively new one in both the workforce and among education and training providers. Technologies are rapidly evolving and much has happened in the past decade to create a great sense of urgency to protect our systems. Increasingly, experts are urging that our cyber infrastructure be strengthened to meet these mounting challenges. As we seek to improve our defenses, we also need to recognize the importance of educating our workforce so that there is a seamless transition between educational facilities and industries.

As our reliance on technology has grown, so has our vulnerability. Increasingly, there are individuals and foreign countries that would seek to do us and our systems harm. With seeming regularity there are reports of cyber-attacks on our financial institutions, government agencies, defense contractors, and our own personal computers. Millions of dollars have been lost to cybercrime, increasingly sophisticated malware attack our personal systems, and, alarmingly, there have been increased cyber-attacks on our government systems from foreign countries.

With so much at risk, the security of our data and information is of prime concern. Millions of dollars have been spent to harden computer systems against outside attack. Computers have been upgraded with new virus protection and much has been done to educate those who care for our systems. This effort to safeguard our data has resulted in cybersecurity becoming one of the fastest growing areas in the technology field. The U.S. Department of Labor estimates that in the next decade job growth in the cybersecurity field will exceed 25 percent, with salaries averaging upward of $75,000 (Bureau of Labor Statistics 2012).

Although much has been written about the issue of cybersecurity, there remain gaps to address. There is a scarcity of information about the need to develop the cyber workforce, especially in certain subsectors including national security. Those specific subsectors have unique challenges that need to be addressed. Excelsior College, in conjunction with the National Cybersecurity Institute (NCI) in Washington D.C., has asked experts in those unique sectors to contribute their expertise. This publication seeks to fill those gaps with their knowledge and experience on those specific subsectors. The special sectors that are examined in this publication are cybersecurity in state, local, and federal governments; in the military and national defense; health care; the telecommunications industry; the international community; small businesses and nonprofits; the financial world; the utility industry; the educational community; and the identification of future cybersecurity trends.

In their chapter, Kyle Foley and Melody Balcet from IBM address the unique issues of cybersecurity at the federal, state, and local levels of government. They examine security trends over the past decade and discuss challenges for the future. The security of information entrusted to our governmental agencies is of utmost importance. Data on our incomes, health, and personal lives fill volumes in government data-bases and need to be secure.

Next, Capt. Shana Beach with the U.S. Air Force addresses the importance of cybersecurity to the U.S. military and the implications of the newly coined term *cyber warfare*. Our national security should rank as the prime concern for cybersecurity. Our military's strategy, readiness, and future development efforts need to be closely guarded from potential enemies. Recently, our military systems have been probed by foreign governments seeking vital information.

In chapter 3, Sean Murphy of SAIC examines issues relating to cybersecurity in the health care industry and emphasizes, in particular, the importance of securing patient data. We are at a crucial time of transition in our health care structure system and sensitive patient data needs to be secured and made available only to those with a true need to know.

In the fourth chapter, K. Maman and Tom Conners, both from Deloitte & Touche, discuss cybersecurity and the telecommunications industry. We rely heavily on the telecommunications industry for all our communication needs. Regional disasters interrupting service to cell towers have shown how reliant we are on our cellular telephones. If there is a disruption of communications on a national level, there will no doubt be serious consequences for a huge portion of the U.S. population.

In chapter 5, Anthony Bargar with the Cybersecurity Consulting Group details the critical role of cybersecurity in the financial industry and what a disruption could entail. In the United States, millions of transactions occur on a daily basis with money transferring from one account to another. Financial institutions routinely transfer vast sums of money electronically from one institution to another. Keeping our financial systems safe from cyber-attack has been an ongoing process.

Next, Geoff Schwartz of the Entergy Corporation shares his many years of experience in the utility industry with a discussion of cyber threats to the all-important power grid, and details the steps that have been taken to safeguard our utilities. Regional blackouts have shown us how dependent we are on electricity; without electricity there is very little in the modern world that will function. Not only our power grid, but the very sources of our power, the generating stations themselves, must be protected from cyber-attack.

In chapter 7, Ernest McDuffie of NIST combines his talents in education and cybersecurity to highlight the importance of training and education. He discusses best practices and what the future of cyber education may hold for us all. It takes a good deal of both training and education to be qualified to compete in the ongoing battle in the cyber world. Training establishes a nuts-and-bolts knowledge base, but education provides an inside look as to the reasons for, and relationships of, the cyber world.

In chapter 8, Kai Roer from the Roer Group discusses the state of cybersecurity and the workforce in the international sector and explains the additional challenges faced by organizations abroad in finding their cyber talent. Cyber threats occur not only in the United States, but also across the globe. All nations are vulnerable to cyber-attack and need to defend their assets. This chapter examines these international threats and what is being done to secure systems around the world.

In chapter 9, Greg Keeley of Ariana Partners, and a Fellow with the NCI at Excelsior College, provides his insights regarding the cyber threats faced by the small business and nonprofit communities and his predictions for the future. Small businesses are the backbone of the modern economy in America. They handle countless transactions, order, produce, and deliver products and services to their clients. During each transaction data is created and/or stored and needs to be protected from cyber-attack that might harm the business or its clients.

In the last chapter, James H. Jones, Jr. of SAIC concludes this work with a discussion of future trends in educating a cybersecurity workforce, including the need for a diversified body of knowledge to combat future threats. Cybersecurity, crime, terrorism, and cyber warfare are ongoing issues that are never fully resolved. Like a game of chess, for each move that is made, a countermove occurs. To stay on top of the evolving world of cybersecurity, the workforce needs to constantly upgrade its skills through education. With so much at risk, the arena of cybersecurity needs to take advantage of all available knowledge, dictating a diversified workforce that can provide many differing perspectives toward the solution of a problem.

Cybersecurity is without question one of the most important issues of the twenty-first century. As technology rapidly evolves, increasingly more information is generated and available through digital means. Much of that data is highly sensitive, valuable, and needs to be securely stored. From our personal computers to the most highly sensitive government systems, data needs to be effectively protected. The NCI in Washington, D.C. is dedicated to the research and development of programs and processes that will assist in the ongoing battle against illegal and intrusive activities in cyberspace. The NCI, in conjunction with Excelsior College, is pleased to present this publication with input from experts in the various subsectors that have been underrepresented in the cybersecurity field. Cybercrime, cyber terrorism, and cybersecurity are all important topics in our current society. Those issues have been broadly explored in previous works, but this compilation of subsectors seeks to fill gaps that those works have failed to fully address. A recent article in the *New York Times* noted that "Cybersecurity is not just a matter of blocking bad things a cyber attack can do: it is protecting all the good things that cyberinsecurity can prevent us from doing. Genuine cybersecurity should not be seen as an additional cost, but as an enabler, guarding our digital way of life" (Ilves, 2013). This publication acts as an important guardian at our digital portals.

References

Bharadwaj, Anandhi, Omar A. El Sawy, Paul A. Pavlou, and N. Venkatraman. 2013. "Visions and Voices on Emerging Challenges in Digital Business Strategy." *MIS Quarterly* 37:471–82.

Bureau of Labor Statistics. 2012. "Information Security Analysts, Web Developers, and Computer Network Architects." In *Occupational Outlook Handbook, 2012–13 Edition. United States Department of Labor.* http://www.bls.gov/ooh/computer-and-information-technology/information-security-analysts-web-developers-and-computer-network-architects.htm.

Ilves, Toomas Hendrik. 2013. "Cybersecurity: A View from the Front." *New York Times*, April 11. Accessed August 1, 2013. http://www.nytimes.com/2013/04/12/opinion/global/cybersecurity-a-view-from-the-front.html?pagewanted=all.

Roulo, Claudette. 2013. "DOD Must Stay Ahead of Cyber Threat, Dempsey Says." *American Forces Press Service*, June 27. Accessed July 15, 2013. http://www.defense.gov/news/newsarticle.aspx?id=120379.

Woo, Stu. 2012. "Online-Retail Spending at $200 Billion Annually and Growing." *Wall Street Journal*, February 27. Accessed July 27, 2013. http://blogs.wsj.com/digits/2012/02/27/online-retail-spending-at-200-billion-annually-and-growing/.

Chapter 1

Cybersecurity and Government
Federal, State, and Local

MELODY L. BALCET AND KYLE M. FOLEY

Introduction

Developing and maintaining a deep, high-quality cybersecurity workforce is paramount to the success of federal, state, and local governments. The United States is increasingly reliant on information technology (IT) in government operations. The security and privacy of government systems and data is critical to gaining and retaining public confidence and to the successful delivery of government services. Furthermore, as the threat of attacks on government IT systems increases along with our reliance on IT systems for critical functions, cyber-attacks can be catastrophic to government operations and national security.

The cybersecurity workforce is responsible for the critical task of protecting the nation's IT infrastructure. In order to successfully carry out this important mission, governments must hire, train, and retain a workforce that has the knowledge, skills, and abilities to meet this tremendous challenge. Governments can have policies that stress the importance of protecting the IT infrastructure and sensitive information, but without an educated and well-trained workforce, the security and privacy policies cannot be successfully implemented.

The missions of federal, state, and local governments vary widely, but they all rely on highly sensitive data in their daily operations. Whether it is personal information used in processing tax returns by the Internal Revenue Service, national security information used by the Department of Defense (DoD) to make military decisions, or real estate asset information used by municipalities for tax assessments, the information handled, processed, and stored by these government agencies must be secure in order to maintain public confidence and to reduce the risk for attack from malicious outsiders.

Cybersecurity programs in governments are needed to protect the confidentiality, integrity, and availability of the data that is stored, processed, and transmitted in their IT systems. Confidentiality refers to limiting access to data only to authorized individuals. Integrity refers to the accuracy of the data and its ability to deflect attempts to destroy or modify data without permission. Availability refers to the requirement that data be available to its authorized users when it is needed. Cybersecurity programs develop policies and procedures and use various technologies so that the confidentiality, integrity, and availability of the data are preserved for all authorized users and stakeholders.

As government IT systems become increasingly more interconnected due to the expanded use of the Internet, the risk for cybersecurity attacks increases. Malicious activity over the Internet comes in many shapes and forms. Other governments or nation-states, terrorist organizations, or corporations or individuals can launch cyber-attacks; motivations for the attacks may vary significantly. However, in all cases the perpetrators are motivated to negatively affect the confidentiality, integrity, and availability of government data. Some common forms of cyber-attacks on governments include malicious software (viruses, worms, and Trojan horses), denial of service attacks, and spear phishing. Malicious software programs often are attached to email messages or downloaded from websites. Once present on a computer, malicious software or malware can destroy or modify data or negatively affect the performance of the network. Denial of service attacks occur when cybercriminals send so many messages to an organization that it is unable to respond and becomes unavailable for authorized use. Spear phishing refers to the use of fraudulent email messages that attempt to lure the user into providing access to their system or sharing personal or government information.

A knowledgeable cybersecurity workforce will understand the various types of potential attacks and have the ability to develop and implement defense mechanisms to prevent and respond to these attacks. For example, a government's cybersecurity team must have the knowledge, skills, and abilities to implement firewall technologies to prevent unauthorized access to a government organization's network, or they must have the ability to deploy encryption technologies so the organization's databases can be encrypted in case unauthorized access to the network occurs. Encryption transforms the data into unreadable text unless one has the proper key to decrypt it.

Federal Government Cybersecurity Activities

The U.S. government is a vast enterprise with a wide range of programs and missions that touch all aspects of the U.S. and global economies, including national security and defense, the environment, food safety, transportation, energy, law, and social benefits. There are hundreds of organizations in the executive, legislative, and judicial branches of the federal government that carry out these unique missions; they all have mission-critical IT systems that support their daily operations (USA.gov 2013). These systems store, process, and transfer sensitive information and must be secure in order to protect the confidentiality, integrity, and availability of their data.

Given the breadth and importance of the federal government, the president and Congress have directed the Department of Commerce and the Department of Homeland Security (DHS) to take on the major roles in coordinating cybersecurity guidelines and activities for the federal enterprise. The National Institute of Standards and Technology's (NIST) Information Technology Laboratory (ITL) is the organization within the Department of Commerce that is tasked with establishing cybersecurity standards and guidelines. ITL's mission is "to scale new frontiers in Information Measurement Science to enable international social, economic, and political advancement by collaborating and partnering with industry, academia, and other NIST laboratories to advance science and engineering, setting standards and requirements for unique scientific instrumentation and experiments, data, and communications" (Information Technology Laboratory 2011). The ITL Computer Security Division (CSD) drafts and publishes the federal cybersecurity standards and guidelines. The CSD works closely with federal agencies when drafting its directives and provides consulting services to federal agencies on standards and guidelines implementation.

The DHS also plays a major role with cybersecurity in the federal government. The DHS Office of Cybersecurity and Communications (CS&C) is responsible for enhancing the security of the U.S. cyber and communications infrastructure and works to prevent or minimize disruptions to critical information infrastructure in order to protect the public, the economy, and government services. CS&C leads efforts to protect critical civilian government and private sector networks and it operates the National Cybersecurity and Communications Integration Center (NCCIC), a national point of cyber and communications incident integration (U.S. Department of Homeland Security 2013). The United States Computer Emergency Readiness Team (US-CERT) is the operational arm of the NCCIC, which serves as a 24/7 cyber-monitoring, incident-response, and management center.

Each federal organization is responsible for complying with the NIST standards and guidelines and the DHS directives. These requirements often are very technical and complex, and demand a skilled and knowledgeable cybersecurity workforce to successfully comply with and implement them. The requirements cover a broad array of management, operational, and technical controls and provide a solid foundation for federal agency cybersecurity programs.

There are several initiatives and partnerships with federal organizations to improve the federal cybersecurity workforce. Two of the major initiatives are the National Initiative for Cybersecurity Education (NICE) and the National Science Foundation (NSF) scholarship program.

The NICE program, which is being led by NIST, has three primary goals (National Initiative for Cybersecurity Education 2012):

1. Raise national awareness about risks in cyberspace.

2. Broaden the pool of individuals prepared to enter the cybersecurity workforce.

3. Cultivate a globally competitive cybersecurity workforce.

Each program goal has numerous objectives and strategies. More than twenty federal departments and agencies are involved in the program.

The scope of the NICE program extends beyond the federal workforce to include students in kindergarten through postgraduate school. The four components of the program are:

1. National Cybersecurity Awareness (lead by the DHS)

2. Formal Cybersecurity Education (lead by the Department of Education and NSF)

3. Cybersecurity Workforce Structure (lead by the DHS)

4. Cybersecurity Workforce Training and Professional Development (lead by the DoD, the Office of the Director of National Intelligence [ODNI], and DHS)

NSF's CyberCorps®: Scholarship for Service program has two tracks: scholarships and capacity. The scholarship track provides funding for scholarships that go to students studying cybersecurity. In return, the student recipients are required to work for a federal, state, local, or tribal government for a period equal to the length of their scholarship. The capacity track seeks proposals from colleges and universities for funding for cybersecurity programs that lead to an increase in the college or university's ability to produce cybersecurity professionals (National Science Foundation 2013).

Both of these programs aim to improve cybersecurity awareness and knowledge through education. The NICE program is led by federal agencies and has a broad scope that includes programs at primary and secondary levels of education, whereas the NSF program is focused on postsecondary education at colleges and universities. Both programs will improve the cybersecurity workforce by providing knowledge, skills, and abilities in cybersecurity across the economic spectrum.

Relevant Cybersecurity Laws and Policies

Federal Government

The Federal Information Security Management Act of 2002 (FISMA), also known as Title III of the E-Government Act, is major federal information security legislation passed in 2002 that outlines requirements for federal agencies' management of government information and information systems. The main areas addressed by the regulation are outlined as follows (Computer Security Resource Center 2002):

- Assigns authorities and functions for the director of the Office of Management and Budget (OMB).

- Requires federal agencies to ensure an annual independent evaluation of information security program practices by its inspector general or external auditor.

- Requires the director of OMB to ensure the operation of a federal information security incident center.

- Requires federal agencies to take special precautions for securing national security systems.

- Requires appropriations be made to carry out the requirements of the regulation.

- Assigns responsibilities for federal information systems standards.

- Assigns responsibility to NIST for defining standards and guidelines for information security.

- Implements the Information Security and Privacy Advisory Board as an advisory committee to NIST, the Secretary of Commerce, and OMB.

- Requires federal agencies to maintain an inventory of all major information systems.

To meet the legislative requirements of FISMA, NIST initiated the FISMA implementation project, which continues today under the leadership of CSD. The goal of the FISMA implementation project is to promote the development of key security standards and guidelines including the following:

- Standards for categorizing information and information systems by mission impact.

- Standards for minimum security requirements for information and information systems.

- Guidance for selecting appropriate security controls for information systems.

- Guidance for assessing security controls in information systems and determining security control effectiveness.

- Guidance for the security authorization of information systems.

- Guidance for monitoring the security controls and the security authorization of information systems (Computer Security Resource Center 2013).

The FISMA implementation project has had a major effect on the federal cybersecurity workforce. Its sweeping guidelines covering all aspects of cybersecurity laid the foundation for the knowledge, skills, and abilities needed for federal cybersecurity programs. It also outlines the specific management, operational, and technical controls required in federal agency operations to protect the IT systems and infrastructure. In today's federal cybersecurity environment, the cybersecurity workforce must have detailed knowledge of FISMA and the NIST guidelines for the required controls in federal information systems.

NIST prescribes a risk-based continuous monitoring approach to securing federal information systems. Figure 1.1 illustrates this risk management framework.

NIST issues Federal Information Processing Standards (FIPS) and special publications (SPs) to identify, document, and communicate the required controls and processes for federal information systems security. *NIST SP 800-37: Guide for Applying the Risk Management Framework to Federal Information Systems: A Security Life Cycle Approach*, describes each of the steps in the framework and provides guidance and references for the federal cybersecurity workforce to use when working with federal information systems.

The guidelines for step one of the risk management framework are found in *FIPS 199: Standards for Categorization of Federal Information and Information Systems* (National Institute of Standards and

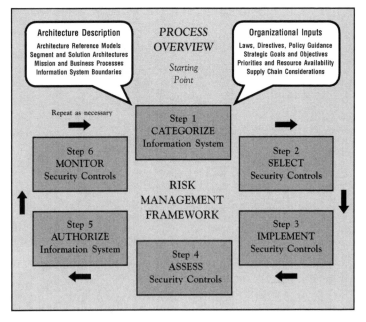

Figure 1.1. Risk management framework (National Institute of Standards and Technology 2011).

Technology 2004). This standard establishes a process for categorizing federal information systems as high, moderate, or low risk based on the data the system processes and the criticality of the system to the federal agency's mission.

Step 2 of the risk management framework uses *NIST SP 800-53: Security and Privacy Controls for Federal Information Systems and Organizations* (National Institute of Standards and Technology 2013b) and *FIPS-200: Minimum Security Requirements for Federal Information and Information Systems* (National Institute of Standards and Technology 2006) to determine the management, operational, and technical controls that will be implemented for the system. NIST established the required and recommended controls based on the system's categorization (high, moderate, or low).

Once the federal agency has implemented the required controls, *NIST SP 800-53A: Guide for Assessing Security Controls in Federal Information Systems and Organizations* (National Institute of Standards and Technology 2010) provides a process for assessing and reporting on the status of the system's controls. If it is determined that the required controls are implemented and operating as intended, the information system is authorized for operation by the senior agency official responsible for the system. *NIST SP 800-37* Section 3.5 lays out the process for authorizing the information system.

When the system is implemented and operating in production, the agency's cybersecurity workforce monitors and reports on the status of the system's information security controls and remediates identified risks as appropriate. The risk management framework is an ongoing process that is followed until the information system is retired.

OMB Circular A-130: Management of Federal Information Resources was first issued in 1985 to designate information resource management requirements in compliance with the Paperwork Reduction Act (PRA) of 1980. Appendix III, entitled *Security of Federal Automated Information Resources*, outlines further requirements for federal agency management of information resources. The current version was released in 2000 and as of mid-2013, a new version is available in draft, but a timeline for completion has not been identified.

State and Local Governments

State and local governments also need strong cybersecurity policies and programs in order to protect the confidentiality, integrity, and availability of the sensitive information they store, process, and transfer in their program operations. Like the federal government, state and local governments heavily rely on IT systems to deliver services to their citizens. State and local government services include first responders such as fire and police departments, utilities, courts, environmental protection, transportation, tax administration, and education. All of these programs collect and store personally identifiable information about their citizens and sensitive information about the businesses that operate in their jurisdictions.

In addition to federal regulations and requirements, each state and local government operates under its own set of local and state laws and regulations. A successful cybersecurity program in each state and local government requires an understanding of the legal and regulatory environment in which the government operates and how the government fits into the larger state and federal security ecosystem. For example, a state may operate a nuclear power plant to provide electricity for its citizens; the plant is required to follow local, state, and federal laws and regulations while conducting its business.

State governments have responded to citizens' concerns about Internet privacy and cybersecurity risks by enacting privacy legislation for business activities operating within their jurisdictions. These laws address a wide range of complex issues including the following:

- Employer access to social media passwords.

- Privacy of online activities.

- Websites or online services that collect personal information.

- False and misleading statements in website privacy policies.

- Privacy of personal information held by Internet service providers.

- Employee email communications and Internet access.

- Privacy policies for government websites (National Conference of State Legislatures 2013).

State and local governments need a strong cybersecurity workforce in order to successfully protect their IT infrastructure and data; this workforce must be knowledgeable about the technologies that its government uses and the laws and regulations with which it must comply. This is a tremendous challenge, and these governments often have difficulty competing in the marketplace for skilled workforce resources due to fiscal pressures.

Recent Federal Initiatives

Although the U.S. Congress has attempted to draft and pass sweeping cybersecurity legislation over the past few years, that legislation has not materialized. As a result, President Obama issued *Executive Order 13636: Improving Critical Infrastructure Cybersecurity*, which directed the NIST to work with public- and private-sector stakeholders to develop a voluntary framework for reducing cyber risks to critical infrastructures. This framework, when completed, will consist of standards, guidelines, and best practices to promote the protection of critical infrastructures. The voluntary framework will provide the operators of U.S. critical infrastructures with a prioritized, flexible, repeatable, and cost-effective approach to managing cybersecurity-related risk while protecting business confidentiality, individual privacy, and civil liberties (National Institute of Standards and Technology 2013a).

The framework currently is being developed through a series of public comment periods and workshops with public- and private-sector participants. This process provides key stakeholders with an opportunity to shape these new guidelines. This project is ongoing and as of the time of writing, a final publication date has not been determined.

Challenging Cybersecurity Threats

That cybersecurity threats have increased exponentially over the past ten years is not surprising, and represents only the beginning of the continued challenges faced by the government sectors and their cybersecurity workforce. Robert S. Mueller (2012), director of the FBI indicated, "in the not too distant future, we anticipate that the cyber threat will pose the number one threat to our country." Studies have shown that the techniques used in current cyber-attacks, even the most sophisticated ones, have not changed much over the years. However, the speed at which technology has improved and the wide availability of basic cyber-attack techniques on the Internet have made it difficult for the cybersecurity workforce to keep up the required knowledge, skills, and abilities to fight our cyber adversaries.

There are three threat types that are a particular challenge for the cybersecurity workforce to address: zero-day attacks, the advanced persistent threat (APT), and the insider threat.

- Zero-day attacks or threats exploit previously unknown vulnerabilities and occur during the vulnerability window that exists between the time a vulnerability is first exploited and when a security patch is developed and made available to address it.

- "[APT] usually refers to a group, such as a government, with both the capability and the intent to persistently and effectively target a specific entity. The term is commonly used to refer to cyber threats, in particular that of internet-enabled espionage, using a variety of intelligence gathering techniques to access sensitive information . . ." (Wikipedia 2013).

- The insider threat refers to a threat to an organization that comes from its own employees or workforce. Insider threats can be intentional—someone internal to the organization who intends to do harm—or unintentional—someone unwittingly or unknowingly does harm to an organization, usually a result of failure to know or follow established policies or best practices. Insider threats are an important consideration, as government agencies build and grow their cybersecurity workforce and posture to prevent a cybersecurity-related incident.

US-CERT provides the federal government with guidelines for reporting a cybersecurity incident and defines security incident categories (CATs). These categories range from CAT 0 through CAT 6 and identify the time period within which security incidents must be reported to US-CERT. US-CERT also provides current activity, alerts, bulletins, and tips to help the federal cybersecurity workforce prevent, detect, and respond to a cybersecurity incident.

The Department of Defense

The threats affecting the federal government also apply within the DoD and similarly have the potential to affect mission activities. Although not unique to DoD, the potential for loss of human life and safety is a consequence that must always be at the forefront of risk management discussions in order to support the warfighter: U.S. soldiers in the field. Furthermore, central to the DoD's mission is protecting and ensuring national security. This is a stark contrast to the bottom-line dollar figures that usually drive risk management decisions in other federal agencies and the commercial sector.

On June 23, 2009, the secretary of defense directed the commander of U.S. Strategic Command to establish the United States Cyber Command (USCYBERCOM), which is located and operated out of Fort Meade, Maryland. A subordinate unified command, USCYBERCOM, under the command of the director of the National Security Agency, "is responsible for planning, coordinating, integrating, synchronizing, and directing activities to operate and defend the Department of Defense information networks and when directed, conducts full-spectrum military cyberspace operations (in accordance with all applicable laws and regulations) in order to ensure U.S. and allied freedom of action in cyberspace, while denying the same to our adversaries" (United States Strategic Command 2011). All combatant commands, services, agencies, and field activities within the DoD perform cyber-defense activities under its direction. USCYBERCOM coordinates and reports incidents on behalf of the DoD, as appropriate, with US-CERT (Chairman of the Joint Chiefs of Staff 2012).

Building a Cybersecurity Workforce in Government

Assessing the current state of the cybersecurity workforce in government is not an easy task. In the federal government, the initial challenge of defining who fits within this subset of the federal labor pool is further complicated by the fact that these definitions do not necessarily align with a specific occupational series. This makes the ability to track progress extremely difficult. In an attempt to better understand the composition and capabilities of the federal IT workforce, DHS, in partnership with the federal CIO Council (the principal interagency forum on federal agency practices for IT management), developed and implemented the IT Workforce Assessment for Cybersecurity (ITWAC). This anonymous and voluntary assessment was intended to assist agencies in implementing the National Cybersecurity Workforce Framework (established by NICE to provide a common understanding of and lexicon for cybersecurity work) as well as collect data to support aforementioned NICE efforts (National Initiative for Cybersecurity Education 2011). More than eighty agencies were invited to participate in the ITWAC and 22,956 IT professionals from fifty-two federal departments and agencies completed the 2012 assessment published on March 14, 2013 (National Initiative for Cybersecurity Education 2013). The assessment, although limited by its participant base, highlighted some key findings:

- The majority of the federal civilian cybersecurity professional population is above the age of forty.

- Although the 2210 occupational series accounts for the largest percentage, cybersecurity professionals are dispersed across other occupational series (Office of Personnel Management 2013).

- Participants from several pay grades and multiple 2210 series parenthetical titles indicated a need for training in Information Assurance (IA) compliance (National Initiative for Cybersecurity Education 2013).

There are certainly a myriad of ways government organizations can build their cybersecurity workforce. According to NICCS, "best in class workforce planning is designed in a repeatable and reliable fashion, highlighting risks and forecasting needs over time." NICCS maintains that there is no cookie-cutter solution and the chosen approach must fit the specific needs of an organization while taking into consideration the unique requirements of the cybersecurity profession. The NICCS guidance highlights three major components to best practice workforce planning:

1. Process: Establishing an integrated and consistent means of diagnosing workforce needs and risks. This includes a defined model, data, and analytics.

2. Strategy: Providing a direct line of sight between business and workforce requirements. This includes a shared vision, governance, and continuous monitoring or performance.

3. Infrastructure: Supporting execution of an effective and repeatable workforce planning process. This includes a healthy workforce of people, collaboration across levels, and enabling technology (National Initiative for Cybersecurity Careers and Studies 2013).

The sample workforce planning process chart shown in Figure 1.2 can help organizations, including federal, state, and local governments, create an effective, long-term staffing strategy that aligns with the mutual need to have a knowledgeable, skilled, and able cybersecurity workforce.

Phase 1	Phase 2	Phase 3	Phase 4
Define and Identify Workforce	**Conduct Supply Analysis**	**Conduct Demand and Gap Analysis**	**Implement Workforce Planning**
• Collect workforce data from Human Resource Information Systems (HRIS) and other sources • Identify functional positions/roles • Develop competency/ skills, proficiency levels • Validate data with HR Managers, Supervisors	• Use statistical tools to conduct a workload analysis to understand work performed • Determine workforce capabilities needed to accomplish work • Create analytical tools to depict characteristics • Validate outputs with organization • Conduct supply analysis to determine strengths, risks, gaps	• Identify future demands for workforce needs • Use historical and current data to analyze trends, and model data • Conduct a gap analysis on current and future supply/ demand • Identify workforce objectives and determine workforce development strategies	• Develop and implement an action plan with a detailed timeline and phased approach • Create feedback mechanisms • Determine which employees will own process and train them to continuously employ workforce planning process

Figure 1.2. Sample workforce planning process (National Initiative for Cybersecurity Careers and Studies 2013).

The Department of Defense

The cybersecurity workforce in the DoD has long been defined in *DoD Directive 8570.01: Information Assurance Training, Certification, and Workforce Management*, published August 15, 2004. Certified current on April 23, 2007, this document has served as the overarching policy document governing the cybersecurity workforce in the DoD. *DoD Directive 8570.01* serves two purposes. First and foremost, it establishes policy and assigns responsibilities for information assurance training, certification, and workforce management for the entire DoD (Department of Defense 2007). Second, it authorizes *DoD 8570.01-M: Information Assurance Workforce Improvement Program*, published December 19, 2005, which establishes formal guidance for building and maintaining a trained, certified, and capable cybersecurity workforce and associated reporting requirements (Department of Defense 2012). The *Information Assurance Workforce Improvement Program* was certified on January 24, 2012 with the publication of *Change 3* and reflects the most current cybersecurity workforce policy for the DoD.

DoD Directive 8570.1 and DoD 8570.01-M are currently under revision under a new name. The newer policy, in its current draft, is called *DoD Directive 8140: Cyberspace Workforce Management Program*, and leverages the NICE construct. The policy will have several accompanying manuals, including the update to the current *DoD 8570.01-M*.

The Road Ahead: Future Trends

Several distinct trends have emerged that affect government cybersecurity workforce needs. It is important to acknowledge these trends and plan accordingly. The recent update to *NIST SP 800-37*, evolution of FISMA reporting requirements in recent years, and the proposed changes to OMB *Circular A-130* highlight a shift in how the federal government conducts business, namely in how federal information systems are monitored and how the information is reported. Specifically, continuous monitoring will play an important role in the future needs and makeup of the government cybersecurity workforce. Another trend worth highlighting is the increasingly blurred line between the cybersecurity workforce and the broader IT workforce that has resulted from the acknowledgment of the broader cybersecurity role each member of the IT workforce plays. How each organization plans for and implements good workforce planning processes that are specific to the cybersecurity needs of that organization will determine the eventual success of building and maintaining a knowledgeable, skilled, and able cybersecurity workforce.

References

Chairman of the Joint Chiefs of Staff. 2012. *Chairman of the Joint Chiefs of Staff Manual 6510.01B.* July 10. http://www.dtic.mil/cjcs_directives/cdata/unlimit/m651001.pdf.

Computer Security Resource Center. 2002. *Federal Information Security Management Act of 2002.* National Institute of Standards and Technology. http://csrc.nist.gov/drivers/documents/FISMA-final.pdf.

———. 2013. "Federal Information Security Management Act (FISMA) Implementation Project." Accessed August 7, 2013. *National Institute of Standards and Technology.* http://csrc.nist.gov/groups/SMA/fisma/index.html.

Department of Defense. 2007. *Directive 8570.01: Information Assurance Training, Certification, and Workforce Management.* http://www.dtic.mil/whs/directives/corres/pdf/857001p.pdf.

———. 2012. *DoD 8570.01-M: Information Assurance Workforce Improvement Program.* Last modified January 24. http://www.dtic.mil/whs/directives/corres/pdf/857001m.pdf.

Information Technology Laboratory. 2011. "What ITL Does." *National Institute of Standards and Technology.* Last modified January 25. http://www.nist.gov/itl/what-itl-does.cfm.

Mueller, Robert S. 2012. "Combating Threats in the Cyber World: Outsmarting Terrorists, Hackers, and Spies." Remarks presented at the *RSA Cyber Security Conference,* March 1, 2012. San Francisco, CA. http://www.fbi.gov/news/speeches/combating-threats-in-the-cyber-world-outsmarting-terrorists-hackers-and-spies.

National Conference of State Legislatures. 2013. "State Laws Related to Internet Privacy." Last modified April 13, 2013. http://www.ncsl.org/issues-research/telecom/state-laws-related-to-internet-privacy.aspx.

National Initiative for Cybersecurity Careers and Studies. 2013. "Cybersecurity Workforce Planning." Accessed August 7, 2013. http://niccs.us-cert.gov/careers/workforce-planning.

National Initiative for Cybersecurity Education. 2011. "National Cybersecurity Workforce Framework." http://csrc.nist.gov/nice/framework/.

———. 2012. "Strategic Plan." http://csrc.nist.gov/nice/documents/nicestratplan/nice-strategic-plan_sep2012.pdf.

———. 2013. "2012 Information Technology Workforce Assessment for Cybersecurity (ITWAC) Summary Report." March 14, 2012. https://cio.gov/wp-content/uploads/downloads/2013/04/ITWAC-Summary-Report_04-01-2013.pdf.

National Institute of Standards and Technology. 2004. *FIPS PUB 199: Standards for Security Categorization of Federal Information and Information Systems.* http://csrc.nist.gov/publications/fips/fips199/FIPS-PUB-199-final.pdf.

———. 2006. *FIPS PUB 200: Minimum Security Requirements for Federal Information and Information Systems.* http://csrc.nist.gov/publications/fips/fips200/FIPS-200-final-march.pdf.

———. 2010. *NIST Special Publication 800-53A: Guide for Assessing the Security Controls in Federal Information Systems and Organizations.* http://csrc.nist.gov/publications/nistpubs/800-53A-rev1/sp800-53A-rev1-final.pdf.

———. 2011. *NIST Special Publication 800-37: Guide for Applying the Risk Management Framework to Federal Information Systems.* http://csrc.nist.gov/publications/nistpubs/800-37-rev1/sp800-37-rev1-final.pdf.

———. 2013a. "Cybersecurity Framework." Last modified July 25, 2013. http://www.nist.gov/itl/cyberframework.cfm.

———. 2013b. *Special Publication 800-53: Security and Privacy Controls for Federal Information Systems and Organizations.* http://nvlpubs.nist.gov/nistpubs/SpecialPublications/NIST.SP.800-53r4.pdf.

National Science Foundation. 2013. "CyberCorps: Scholarship for Service (SFS)." Accessed August 7, 2013. http://www.nsf.gov/funding/pgm_summ.jsp?pims_id=5228.

Office of Personnel Management. 2013. "GS-2210: Information Technology Management Series." Accessed August 7, 2013. http://www.opm.gov/policy-data-oversight/classification-qualifications/general-schedule-qualification-standards/0300/gs-2210-information-technology-management-series/.

United States Strategic Command. 2011. "U.S. Cyber Command." http://www.stratcom.mil/factsheets/Cyber_Command/.

U.S. Department of Homeland Security. 2013. "Office of Cybersecurity and Communications." Accessed August 7, 2013. http://www.dhs.gov/office-cybersecurity-and-communications.

USA.gov. 2013. "A-Z Index of U.S. Government Departments and Agencies."
    Accessed August 7, 2013. http://www.usa.gov/directory/federal/O.shtml.
Wikipedia. 2013. s.v. "advanced persistent threat." Last modified July 19,
    2013. http://en.wikipedia.org/wiki/Advanced_persistent_threat.

Chapter 2

Cybersecurity and the Military

SHANA KAYNE BEACH

Introduction

Over the past several years, we have faced increasing cybersecurity challenges as seen by the number and variety of cyber-attacks against various governments and their infrastructures. However, until recently those challenges were not treated as a threat in terms of military activity response. That changed in November 2011, when the U.S. Department of Defense (DoD) identified cyberspace as an operational domain in which to conduct military activities (Department of Defense 2011a). Since then, we have seen a series of activities and reports by the national security and defense communities that place cybersecurity as one of the top priorities in the international domain.

In April 2012, Frank J. Cilluffo, director of the Homeland Security Policy Institute, detailed to the U.S. House of Representatives Iran's $1 billion investment into cyber operations capabilities, and the Iranian intent to use these capabilities against U.S. interests (U.S. House of Representatives 2012). In August 2012, malicious cyber actors disrupted the operations of more than thirty thousand computers belonging to the Saudi Arabian oil company Aramco (U.S. House of Representatives 2013b). Although oil production was not affected, the attacks sent a powerful message regarding the susceptibility of key resources to cyber-attacks. In January 2013, the information security company Mandiant released a report that detailed cyber espionage activities against more than 140 organizations. Many of the intrusions originated from infrastructures registered to the Pudong New Area of Shanghai, China, the same location as the People's Liberation Army (PLA) Unit 61398, which has been tasked with computer network operations (Mandiant 2013). Shortly afterward, Thomas Donilon, National Security advisor, publicly called on China to cease its cyber intrusions against U.S. businesses, and reiterated that the United States "will take action to protect our economy against cyber threats" (Donilon 2013). In May 2013, a Pentagon report stated that hackers had stolen more than two dozen missile defense, aviation, and naval weapons systems designs (Nakashima 2013a). This attack was corroborated in an annual report to Congress that outlined Chinese computer network exploitation efforts to access U.S. defense data (Office of the Secretary of Defense 2013).

These events are just a few of the publicly available examples of cyber threats in the international context. Whether or not the threats are legitimately imminent and destructive, the U.S. government and the DoD have recognized the need to maintain defensive and offensive cyber capabilities to protect military operations and U.S. critical infrastructure and key resources (CIKR). Funding for cyber resources has increased dramatically in the last few years, and the demand for a cyber-savvy military workforce is at an all-time high. Secretary of Defense Chuck Hagel acknowledges that cyber-attacks "have grown into a defining security challenge" due to the anonymous and worldwide nature of the Internet (Hagel 2013a).

This chapter introduces the cybersecurity concepts that make military operations in the cyber domain particularly distinctive. It also examines how these concepts affect the development of an effective military cybersecurity workforce.

Defining Cyberspace Operations

The DoD relies on a specific vocabulary to ensure consistent communication between its many components. Although the term *cybersecurity* is commonly used in private industry and non-military federal agencies to refer to a broad spectrum of cyberspace disciplines, the DoD uses a specific lexicon when referring to military operations in the cyberspace domain. DoD Joint Publications contain the official definitions related to cybersecurity in the military:

- Cyberspace: A global domain within the information environment consisting of the interdependent network of information technology (IT) infrastructures and resident data, including the Internet, telecommunications networks, computer systems, and embedded processors and controllers.

- Cyberspace Operations: The employment of cyberspace capabilities where the primary purpose is to achieve objectives in or through cyberspace.

- Cyberspace Superiority: The degree of dominance in cyberspace by one force that permits the secure, reliable conduct of operations by that force, and its related land, air, maritime, and space forces at a given time and place without prohibitive interference by an adversary.

- Defensive Cyberspace Operations: Passive and active cyberspace operations intended to preserve the ability to use friendly cyberspace capabilities and protect data, networks, net-centric capabilities, and other designated systems. Also called DCO.

- Defensive Cyberspace Operation Response Actions: Deliberate, authorized defensive measures or activities taken outside of the defended network to protect and defend DoD cyberspace capabilities or other designated systems. Also called DCO-RA.

- Cyber Counterintelligence: Measures to identify, penetrate, or neutralize foreign operations that use cyber means as the primary tradecraft methodology, as well as foreign intelligence service collection efforts that use traditional methods to gauge cyber capabilities and intentions.

- Offensive Cyberspace Operations: Cyberspace operations intended to project power by the application of force in or through cyberspace. Also called OCO.

- Network Operations: Activities conducted to operate and defend the global information grid. Also called NETOPS.

- Information Assurance: Actions that protect and defend information systems by ensuring availability, integrity, authentication, confidentiality, and nonrepudiation. Also called IA.

- Department of Defense Information Network Operations: Operations to design, build, configure, secure, operate, maintain, and sustain DoD networks to create and preserve IA on the DoD information networks. Also called DODIN operations.

These terms will be referenced throughout this chapter as they provide a common lexicon for DoD correspondence, policy, strategy, doctrine, and planning documents (Department of Defense 2013c). Additionally, although the rest of the chapters in this book refer to a "cybersecurity workforce," this chapter will use the DoD's term of *cyberspace workforce*.

Even with these official definitions in place, the defense and intelligence communities continue to refine the characterization of cyberspace. In his remarks during a conference, Deputy Secretary of Defense Carter described three aspects of cyber in which the DoD plays a role. The first is "defense of our own networks," which can span computer security (COMPUSEC), DCO, and DCO-RA. The second is "developing cyber weapons as weapons of war, doing the intelligence preparation of the battlefield for their employment, and planning for their employment," or OCO. The third is "protecting the nation at large from cyber-attack," again implying COMPUSEC, DCO, and DCO-RA measures, but taking into consideration whole-of-government and interagency coordination (Carter 2012).

Brown and Tullos (2012) propose dividing cyber operations into three categories that fall along a spectrum of stealth: cyber access (most stealthy), cyber disruption, and cyber-attack (least stealthy). *Cyber access* refers to the ability to retrieve information from a target network without altering the basic functionality of that system. *Cyber disruption* refers to operations that prevent the target network from maintaining full functionality, but do not have any effects outside of the system. *Cyber-attack* refers to operations that result in physical or "real-world" effects outside of the target network.

The growing prospect of these capabilities over the past decade has led to an increased emphasis on *resilience*, or "the ability to provide acceptable operations despite disruption." DODIN resilience relies on a convergence of NETOPS, IA, and DODIN operations (Defense Science Board 2013).

Due to the fast-paced emergence of cyberspace and cybersecurity operations, the definitions and descriptions currently in place most likely will evolve significantly over the next few years. As discussed in the rest of this chapter, the DoD continues to explore the organization and implementation of its cyber efforts, and its associated formal doctrine will transform as necessary.

Cyber Warfare

Unlike the terms in the previous section, there is currently no doctrinal or legal definition for the term *cyber warfare* (Gervais 2012). However, the term is used frequently and informally in scholarly writing, international engagement, media coverage, and DoD discussions. In general, cyber warfare refers to warfare that takes place within cyberspace, regardless of the physical effects it may or may not cause outside the networks in question. Although almost all policymakers agree that cybersecurity is an important issue to address, there are two primary schools of thought regarding how high the threat of cyber warfare is to the United States. The first school of thought is that the threat of cyber-attack against the U.S. homeland is imminent, ongoing, and/or destructive, and needs to be addressed accordingly. The second is that the threat of cyber-attack has been overly emphasized and/or inflated, and needs further study before more resources are committed.

Advocates for increased funding and focus on military cyber operations are referred to as cyber hawks. They cite the growing frequency of state-on-state attacks, economic espionage, cybercrime, cyber terrorism, and hacktivism as evidence of the need for increasing funding (Senate Committee on Armed Services 2013). After the August 2012 cyber-attacks against Saudi Aramco, the Secretary of Defense warned that a similar attack against the United States "could be as destructive as the terrorist attack of 9/11. Such a destructive cyber-terrorist attack could virtually paralyze the nation" (Panetta 2012). Due to the U.S. dependence on IT, both for economic and defensive purposes, the country has a large attack surface for adversary cyber operations. This attack surface includes the utilization of vulnerable home networks for personal computing and mobile device usage, workplace networks that frequently fall prey to social engineering, and combat networks that sometimes choose convenience over security. Cyber hawks encourage "establishing a sense of urgency" and fear that relentless media coverage of cybersecurity issues is creating public desensitization and complacency (Brickey et al. 2012). Secretary of Defense Hagel (2013b) states, "Malicious cyber-attacks, which hardly registered as a threat a decade ago, are quickly becoming a defining security challenge for our time, for all our institutions. They are putting America's economic and technological advantages and our industrial base at risk. And they threaten our critical infrastructure." Overall, the argument for focusing on the threat of cyber warfare centers on the U.S. susceptibility to these kinds of attacks and the need to intensify preparations to defend and respond.

On the other hand, advocates for de-escalating cyber tensions are referred to as cyber doves; they believe the cyber hawks are exaggerating doomsday scenarios and creating an alarmist atmosphere. Many suspect a flourishing cyber-industrial complex is purposely using intimidating rhetoric to induce fear to increase federal, and subsequently defense contractor, engagement in cybersecurity. For example, the Commission on Cybersecurity for the 44th Presidency states "inadequate cybersecurity and loss of information has inflicted unacceptable damage to U.S. national and economic security" and makes several resource-intensive recommendations based on that assumption, but does not cite evidence of these threats (Langevin et al. 2008). Brito and Watkins (2011) compare current cyber rhetoric to the faulty reasoning used before the U.S. invasion of Iraq, suggesting that the administration and the media have over-hyped the threat in order to support related governmental goals. Other cyber doves propose that overemphasis of cyber threats leads to poor decision-making processes in business and government, such as preemptively investing in inefficient protection measures or reducing privacy and freedom of information. Misattribution of criminal activity to nation-states also can result in flawed foreign policy strategy (Filshtinskiy 2013). Those who advocate for calmer rhetoric do not necessarily disagree with the need to improve the cybersecurity of the United States, but instead encourage doing so in a more measured manner than is currently being practiced. This careful thought will foster less extreme reactions when making decisions regarding prioritization of government resources, foreign policy, and legislative agendas as they apply to the cyberspace domain.

These differences of opinion draw attention to the ambiguity of the term *cyber warfare* and exactly what it means. Due to the newness and uniqueness of the cyberspace domain, doctrine analysts and policymakers often rely on analogies from the physical domains of land, sea, air, and space to make decisions (Butler 2013). These parallels are not always accurate, and lead to pronounced debate over what constitutes cyber warfare and how the United States should prepare and respond.

DoD Preparation for Cyber Warfare

Regardless of which viewpoint is more accurate, the DoD has focused on preparing for cyber warfare. The 2011 National Defense Authorization Act called for a report from the DoD regarding "missions and activities that the Department may choose to conduct in cyberspace." In response, the DoD outlined its deterrence posture for cyberspace, which includes planning to maintain U.S. cyberspace superiority while being prepared to impose costs on adversarial use of the Internet (Department of Defense 2011a). In support of these goals, the DoD continues to grow its capacity for security-centered NETOPS and DODIN operations, IA awareness, cyber counterintelligence, and OCO, DCO, and DCO-RA capabilities.

One of the results of the increased focus on cyber warfare has been the establishment of U.S. Cyber Command (USCYBERCOM) as of May 21, 2010. USCYBERCOM's mission is to "plan, coordinate, integrate, synchronize, and conduct activities to: direct the operations and defense of specified Department of Defense information networks and; prepare to, and when directed, conduct full-spectrum military cyberspace operations in order to enable actions in all domains, ensure US/Allied freedom of action in cyberspace and deny the same to our adversaries." The commander of USCYBERCOM reports to U.S. Strategic Command, and is made up of four service elements: Army Cyber Command, 24th Air Force, Fleet Cyber Command, and Marine Forces Cyber Command (USCYBERCOM 2010). As of March 2013, USCYBERCOM consisted of more than nine hundred personnel, supported by a $182 million budget (Senate Committee on Armed Services 2013). Despite current fiscal limitations, those numbers will continue to grow quickly. In early 2013 *The Washington Post* reported that USCYBERCOM would be hiring approximately four thousand personnel, both military and civilian. This influx of manpower will be used to stand up "national mission forces," "combat mission forces," and "cyber protection forces" (Nakashima 2013b).

DoD's increased focus on cyber warfare and cyber operations has resulted in extremely high demand for a capable cyberspace workforce. The perception of a high-threat environment, whether justified or not, has increased the resources made available for hiring skilled personnel to meet this need. However, as discussed here, the DoD will continue to struggle to find enough people with the right qualifications to meet this demand for many years to come.

Laws and Policies

There are many laws and policies that govern the DoD's cyberspace operations. Due to the newness of the domain and the speed with which technology changes, these documents remain in a constant state of change and many are in the process of being redrafted. However, there are a few foundational concepts and documents that will have long-term significance to the military cyberspace workforce.

Title 10 and Title 50

Members of the DoD are able to operate under authorities granted in Titles 10 and 50 of the U.S. Code. The term *Title 10* is informally used to refer to military operations, whereas *Title 50* generally refers to intelligence collection. Because the cyberspace domain lends itself to both intelligence collection and military operations (or one in support of the other), the distinction between which authority is in use often is critical to determining the committee or subcommittee responsible for congressional oversight of a function (Wall 2011). The commander of USCYBERCOM simultaneously functions as the director of the National Security Agency. This can make drawing the line between intelligence activities in cyberspace and military operations in cyberspace a complex task. One method used to determine under which authority an activity falls is to specify whether the task originated from the director of National Intelligence (Title 50) or the Secretary of Defense (Title 10).

The *Title 50* definition of intelligence activities includes covert action, which is defined as "an activity . . . to influence political, economic, or military conditions abroad, where it is intended that the role of the United States Government will not be apparent or acknowledged publicly." Traditional military activities do not fall under the definition of covert action. This raises the question of whether a military cyberspace operation is regarded as covert due to its secretive nature, or as traditional military activity, due to direction and control by a military commander.

Currently, when directed by the President and Secretary of Defense, cyberspace operations are considered a traditional military activity with no reference to whether the activity will be acknowledged by the United States. Therefore, cyberspace operations fall under Title 10 unless they are specifically for intelligence collection purposes (Wall 2011).

DoD Policy and Directives

The following policies and directives provide direction for DoD operations in the cyberspace domain. Each policy chronologically builds on the last, but new policy is constantly being drafted and rewritten.

President George W. Bush established the Comprehensive National Cybersecurity Initiative (CNCI) under *National Security Presidential Directive 54/Homeland Security Presidential Directive 23* in 2008. The CNCI contains twelve initiatives:

1. Manage the Federal Enterprise Network as a single network enterprise with Trusted Internet Connections.

2. Deploy an intrusion detection system of sensors across the federal enterprise.

3. Pursue deployment of intrusion prevention systems across the federal enterprise.

4. Coordinate and redirect research and development (R&D) efforts.

5. Connect current cyber ops centers to enhance situational awareness.

6. Develop and implement a government-wide cyber counterintelligence (CI) plan.

7. Increase the security of our classified networks.

8. Expand cyber education.

9. Define and develop enduring "leap-ahead" technology, strategies, and programs.

10. Define and develop enduring deterrence strategies and programs.

11. Develop a multipronged approach for global supply chain risk management.

12. Define the federal role for extending cybersecurity into critical infrastructure domains.

Each of these initiatives, including the DoD, applies to the federal government as a whole (Bush 2008).

In 2009, President Barack Obama directed a "clean-slate" review of U.S. policy regarding cybersecurity. The resulting Cyberspace Policy Review recommended establishing clear leadership at the "highest levels of government," prioritizing cybersecurity and technology education among the U.S. population, collaborating with the private sector to increase cybersecurity, building incident-response capabilities, strengthening infrastructure defenses, and encouraging innovation. The report provides a clear set of action plans and framework for execution (White House 2009).

In 2011, the DoD published its *Strategy for Operating in Cyberspace* (DSOC), which outlines the DoD responsibilities in fulfilling existing federal cybersecurity policies. The strategy directs five initiatives:

1. Treat cyberspace as an operational domain to organize, train, and equip so that DoD can take full advantage of cyberspace's potential.

2. Employ new defense operating concepts to protect DoD networks and systems.

3. Partner with other U.S. government departments and agencies and the private sector to enable a whole-of-government cybersecurity strategy.

4. Build robust relationships with U.S. allies and international partners to strengthen collective cybersecurity.

5. Leverage the nation's ingenuity through an exceptional cyber workforce and rapid technological innovation.

Strategic Initiatives 1 and 3 address the development of the military cybersecurity workforce and direct the DoD to ensure proper manpower resources, training, and expertise are available to fulfill its missions in cyberspace (Department of Defense 2011b).

In 2013, the White House published an executive order titled "Improving Critical Infrastructure Cybersecurity" charging the U.S. to identify and protect CIKR in cyberspace. Because the DoD is responsible for defending the United States, the mandates included in the executive order directly apply to the military workforce (Obama 2013).

Within the DoD, Department of Defense Directive 8570.01 has provided direction for IA training, certification, and workforce management since 2004 (Department of Defense 2007). However, the DoD has recognized that cyber operations require many more skillsets than IA, and is currently drafting a directive that will nullify DoDD 8570.01 and address the entire cyberspace workforce.

These are the foundational policies and directives that guide the DoD's actions in the cyberspace domain, but the fast-paced development of technology and norms will require continuous updates. When planning how to manage the military cyberspace workforce, it is important to stay up to date on new policy expansions.

International Law

The CNCI and DSOC mention engagement with international partners and allies; the *International Strategy for Cyberspace*, published in 2011, provides executive branch guidance for that engagement. The section dedicated to military policy directs the DoD to defend national assets against international threats and develop military alliances to encourage bilateral and multilateral situational awareness and defense capabilities (White House 2011). Therefore, the cyberspace workforce must be prepared to work with international allies and partners.

However, agreements on international laws in cyberspace are tenuous. Articles 2(4) and 51 of the UN Charter refer to the prohibition of use of force and right to self-defense in the case of an armed attack, respectively (United Nations 1945). The effects of cyber operations vary on a more uniform continuum than combat in the traditional domains of land, sea, air, and space. Therefore, it is not often clear which article in the UN Charter regulates a particular cyber operation. This is an ongoing legal discussion with no internationally agreed-upon answer. To read more on this open-ended debate, refer to Gervais (2012), Hathaway et al. (2012), Kesan and Hayes (2012), and Lin (2010).

The Stuxnet virus is an example of how a lack of clear international cyberspace law can cause uncertainty. In 2010, an Iranian nuclear facility was infected with a virus, dubbed "Stuxnet," that used four zero-day capabilities to disrupt the power to centrifuges and frequency-converter drives in the facility, potentially delaying Iranian nuclear development by years. The off-the-shelf nature of the tactics and tradecraft of the virus made technical attribution essentially impossible, although later media reports implied U.S. or Israeli involvement (Farwell and Rohozinski 2011). Regardless, it was clear that Iran had suffered a cyber-attack from an outside source, and Stuxnet has since been used as an example for the application of international law. *The Tallinn Manual on the International Law Applicable to Cyber Warfare* commissioned by the North Atlantic Treaty Organization does not conclusively classify Stuxnet as a use of force or self-defense, and states that "significant legal and practical challenges stand in the way of definitively concluding that a cyber operation has initiated an international armed conflict" (Schmitt 2013). For more information on the *Tallinn Manual* and international law, see chapter 8.

Due to the lack of clarity in international law, the DoD cyberspace workforce must be knowledgeable about the issues and ready to adapt to changes in international policy and what types of operations fall within the boundaries of acceptable actions. Policymakers also will have to be prepared for extensive discussion of when and how the military is justified to initiate OCO or DCO-RA against another nation.

Fundamental Issues Unique to the DoD

Despite the authorization and resources now available to the DoD to build a cyber operations capability, there are aspects of working in a military cyberspace environment that will produce unique challenges in recruiting skilled personnel. These challenges will require members of the DoD cyberspace workforce to be knowledgeable about the ever-evolving threats and issues, be flexible enough to adapt to a changing environment, and be creative enough to develop solutions.

Military versus Civilian Career Development

In the private sector, employees usually are hired based on educational background and prior work experience. Members of the military, on the other hand, often are trained from the ground up. The DoD prides itself on developing its own professionals from scratch instead of hiring personnel who have already been fully trained in a particular field. Many enlisted recruits enter the service with only a high school diploma or a couple semesters of college. Many officers commission into the service with a degree that is mostly unrelated to their intended career field. Although entry tests such as the Armed Services Vocational Aptitude Battery may help determine the career field of military members, the branch they join takes on the responsibility of their career development. For the military cyberspace workforce, this means the DoD will have to maintain a robust training and development system for its operators and technicians.

Clearance Requirements

Most military cyberspace operations require a top-secret clearance, and the remainder requires at least a secret clearance. Some positions may even require a polygraph examination before an individual is allowed access to the facility. This means that any potential applicant for the cyberspace workforce must be able to obtain and keep a security clearance for the duration of employment. The security clearance requirement creates two primary challenges for developing the cyberspace workforce. First, there may be a pool of individuals who have the necessary aptitude to become skilled cyberspace operators, but whose activities prior to enlisting or commissioning will prevent them from obtaining the necessary clearance. Second, the procedure for obtaining the clearance can be very lengthy and can delay the hiring process enough to make the position less appealing for the applicant. The DoD must acknowledge and address the challenges that the security clearance requirements create during the recruitment and hiring process.

Cybersecurity and Civil Liberties

In 2009, the White House commissioned a review of cyberspace policy as it related to its effect on civil liberties. The report states protection of civil liberties and privacy for American citizens remains a priority as the nation explores methods of improving cybersecurity. Because cybersecurity incident reporting by the private sector may need to be transmitted to military or intelligence agencies, use of such information requires "rules and oversight, particularly for the protection of privacy rights" (White House 2009). This has proven to be a recurring legal and policy challenge.

Greer (2010) recommends three avenues for protecting privacy and civil liberties while expanding cyberspace capabilities: transparency, oversight, and clarity of roles and missions. Transparency refers to discussing operations "as openly and as candidly as possible," when classification restrictions allow. This will allow the American public to participate in decision making regarding the balance between privacy and security. Oversight means having the proper mechanisms in place to review all activities for compliance with U.S. laws and policies, and if possible, making the results of reviews publicly available. The DoD must also maintain clarity of roles and missions to ensure that intelligence and military authorities are used appropriately. This chapter discusses authorities in more depth in the Laws and Policies section.

In June 2013, the privacy and security discussion came to the forefront of media coverage when Edward Snowden, a former defense contractor, leaked top secret documents about a program called PRISM and claimed the National Security Agency collects data on U.S. citizens. In response, the director of National Intelligence released a fact sheet stating that all PRISM collection is authorized under Section 702 of the Foreign Intelligence Surveillance Act (FISA). The fact sheet also detailed oversight of this collection by the FISA Court,

Congress, and the Executive Branch to ensure civil liberties remain protected (Director of National Intelligence 2013). Although many members of Congress defend the utility and legality of such collection, others believe that "Americans would be stunned if they learned how the government had interpreted Section 215 of the Patriot Act" (Barnes, Lee, and Nakashima 2013).

This debate over how to protect civil liberties and the privacy of the American people while improving cybersecurity will continue as technology continues to improve. Military cyberspace capabilities will advance over time and remain a popular topic in these discussions. Therefore, the military cyberspace workforce must remain aware of the issues, develop creative solutions that satisfy military objectives while protecting constitutional rights, and work with the various oversight authorities to ensure that operations stay within the limits of law and policy.

Attribution and Risk to International Relations

Unlike the other military domains, attribution to attacks in cyberspace is extremely difficult. There are three points at which attribution can be established. In order of increasing complexity they are the geographic location of the host from which the attack originated (usually established via the Internet protocol address, which can be spoofed or hidden), the owner of the host machine, and the person or organization that authorized the attack (Mudrinich 2012). It is challenging to determine attribution at any one of these three points, much less ascertain the intent of an attack or plan an appropriate response.

For example, consider the Chinese cyber espionage referenced in the introduction, referred to as Advanced Persistent Threat 1 (APT1). Mandiant's attribution of these intrusions is based on evidence that is convincing, but not irrefutable. The cyber activity originates out of the same city as Unit 61398. Unit 61398 requires specialized computer operations training, and Mandiant observed consistent use of common screen names throughout PLA and malware development forums and websites. Although complicated, it would be possible to falsify this evidence. Mandiant addresses the unlikely possibility of misattribution in the report:

> The sheer scale and duration of sustained attacks against such a wide set of industries from a singularly identified group based in China leaves little doubt about the organization behind APT1. We believe the totality of the evidence we provide in this document bolsters the claim that APT1 is Unit 61398. However, we admit there is one other unlikely possibility:
>
> A secret, resourced organization full of mainland Chinese speakers with direct access to Shanghai-based telecommunications infrastructure is engaged in a multi-year, enterprise scale computer espionage campaign right outside of Unit 61398's gates, performing tasks similar to Unit 61398's known mission. (Mandiant 2013)

Even a miniscule amount of doubt in attribution is worth addressing because the results may have broad-reaching international repercussions. Erroneous attribution of cyber aggression to a state actor could lead to a misinformed U.S. response. Similarly, the inability to attribute cyber aggression definitively to a specific state actor could leave the United States unable to respond, demonstrating to would-be attackers that they are unlikely to experience consequences for their actions (Filshtinskiy 2013).

The anonymous nature of cyberspace will continue to challenge U.S. military response options. The military cyberspace workforce will need to stay informed about technological solutions that can assist with attribution and improve the information on which decision makers rely. As Secretary of Defense Hagel (2013b) states, "Attribution is not impossible, but it is not as simple as identifying a navy sailing across the ocean or an army crossing a border to attack you. This is a fundamentally different, more insidious kind of threat than we've ever seen. One that carries with it a great risk of miscalculation and mistake."

Interagency Coordination

Because cyberspace encompasses a wide variety of U.S. government objectives, the DoD regularly coordinates with multiple interagency organizations. The Department of Homeland Security (DHS), the Department of Justice (DOJ), the Department of State, and the Intelligence Community are the DoD's primary partners on cybersecurity issues, but other agencies such as the Department of Energy, the Department of Commerce, and the Department of the Treasury often are important contributors when malicious activity in cyberspace threatens their security. One of USCYBERCOM's top five priorities is to encourage partnership with each of these government agencies and departments to enable a whole-of-government perspective on cybersecurity issues (Alexander 2011).

To properly achieve this coordination, leaders at all levels of the DoD's cyberspace workforce will need to have a complete understanding of each of these organization's roles and responsibilities. The ability to communicate with, and understand the priorities of, each government agency will allow for a holistic perspective when prioritizing and conducting operations.

Threats

The DoD's mission is to "provide the military forces needed to deter war and protect the security of our country" (Department of Defense 2013a). To accomplish this mission, the military forces must maintain situational awareness of the threats that threaten U.S. security. The cyber domain accommodates a host of malicious actors, all with different motives and tactics.

Foreign Threats

The United States faces multiple threats from state-sanctioned cyber actors of foreign countries that possess varying degrees of capability and intent. China, Russia, and Iran have been recognized as the primary threats in the past, but North Korea is now showing increased capability and intent.

China presents the greatest quantity of malicious cyber activity, to the extent that they have been characterized as a "strategic threat to the U.S. national interest" (U.S. House of Representatives 2013a). However, the challenge of attribution as referenced earlier in this chapter makes it difficult to prove that the malicious cyber activity originating in China is state-sanctioned.

Russia, on the other hand, presents the greatest superiority of malicious cyber activity, and has shown sophisticated capability regarding the use of the cyberspace domain for more traditional military operations. In 2008, Russia enhanced its destructive attacks on Georgia through the use of offensive cyber operations. Additionally, the intelligence-dependent culture generated by the Cold War-era KGB contributes to Russia's intent to gain information about other nation-states through exploitation of computer networks.

Although Iran's cyber resources may not be as prolific or advanced as China's and Russia's, attacks like those against Saudi Aramco as mentioned in the introduction show the fruits of Iran's heavy investment in cyber capabilities. Additionally, organizations such as the Izz ad-Din al-Qassam Cyber Fighters have claimed credit for cyber-attacks against U.S. financial institutions (Gorman and Yadron 2013; U.S. House of Representatives 2013a).

Each of these countries has been recognized in the media for conducting cyber operations against U.S. interests, and other foreign countries may soon join their numbers. Aside from foreign nation-states, the DoD also must recognize the threat of foreign cyber terrorism, which could cause destructive effects on its own or increase the chaos caused by a physical or kinetic attack. For example, an April 2013 breach of the Associated Press Twitter account resulted in the Dow dropping 150 points. The Syrian Electronic Army eventually claimed the tweet that stated "Breaking: Two Explosions in the White House and Barack Obama is injured" (Fisher 2013). If a similar false report were combined with real-world attacks, the effect would be compounded. Terrorist organizations also may use cyberspace to coordinate operations (Cassim 2012), which directly challenges the U.S. cyberspace superiority.

The DoD must be knowledgeable and prepared for the possibility of increased frequency and complexity of foreign cyber threats. The cyberspace workforce will depend heavily on intelligence gathered about these threats in order to develop cyber options for national leaders.

Insider Threats

The insider threat, both intentional and unintentional, also poses a great risk to the DoD. No matter how well built the cyber defenses of the DoD, one individual with the access and ability to circumvent safety measures can put the security of cyber assets at risk.

Sometimes this risk can be created unintentionally through lack of training, indifference, or the desire to make systems more convenient and accessible. For example, in 2011, the DoD discovered the Agent.btz malware in classified systems. Because classified networks are physically separated, only a USB device could have transferred the malware. Although the origin of the first infection is unknown, it is very possible that an inexperienced or thoughtless user connected an unauthorized USB drive that had been infected via an unclassified system (Nakashima 2011). The DoD can best address the unintentional insider threat through extensive IA training for all network users and careful management of user access.

Intentional insider threats, on the other hand, are more challenging to address. In 2010, Private First Class Bradley E. Manning was charged with "communicating, transmitting, and delivering national defense information to an unauthorized source," "disclosing classified information concerning the national defense with reason to believe that the information could cause injury to the United States," and "exceeding authorized computer access to obtain classified information from a United States department" for releasing a series of classified cables to the website WikiLeaks (U.S. Divison Center 2010). In 2013, the DoD experienced an echo of Manning's leaks when Edward

Snowden disclosed the PRISM program to *The Guardian* (Greenwald, MacAskill, and Poitras 2013). Regardless of either Manning's or Snowden's intentions, they both presented an intentional insider threat through the deliberate transfer of sensitive and classified information to networks on which it was not authorized to reside. The DoD will have to consider what measures will be taken with the cyberspace workforce to prevent similar occurrences in the future, such as re-examining the clearance process or building more restrictive access rules. As of June 2013, members of Congress and military leadership discussed the risks of extensive contractor hiring in relation to the insider threat and the need to review clearance-granting procedures (O'Harrow, Priest, and Censer 2013).

Both intentional and unintentional insider threats have the potential to disrupt DoD cyberspace operations and reduce IA. Because both of these threats originate from within the cyberspace workforce, selection and training of personnel will depend heavily on security requirements.

Criminal Threats

Cybercrime is typically handled within law enforcement channels, as cybercrime laws originate in Title 18 of the United States Code (18 U.S.C.), the Criminal and Penal Code. This code directs law enforcement of identity theft, hacking, intrusion into computer systems, and child pornography (Levin, Goodrich, and Ilkina 2013). Although cybercrime has the potential to disrupt DoD operations, the responsibility to investigate and prevent this threat falls with the DOJ and the DHS.

Hacktivist Threats

Hacktivism is the use of hacker techniques in the cyberspace domain to advocate a political position. The intelligence community regards hacktivists as a relatively minor threat in general because most use fairly unsophisticated techniques and tend to cause disruption of networks rather than destructive effects (U.S. House of Representatives

2013b). However, the DoD should continue to maintain awareness of hacktivist tactics to prepare response options in case of an extremist attack that threatens U.S. or international security.

Status of the Workforce

This chapter has addressed DoD terminology and policy for cybersecurity, general concepts behind cyber warfare, unique challenges to the military cyberspace workforce, and potential cyber threats to U.S. security. The question remains, how do we protect our future through education of a military cyberspace workforce? Because the military's role in cyberspace is still being defined, the roles of its cyberspace workforce are continuously in flux. A developing draft of the Department of Defense Cyberspace Workforce Strategy classifies the workforce into four categories: cyberspace operations, cybersecurity, cyberspace IT, and intelligence (Department of Defense 2013b). These categories are loosely based on the National Initiative for Cybersecurity Education's National Cybersecurity Workforce Framework, which provides "a common understanding of and lexicon for cybersecurity work" for federal agencies, experts in the field, and industry partners (National Initiative for Cybersecurity Education 2013).

The cyberspace operations workforce, at a minimum, requires the knowledge, skills, and abilities (KSAs) to conduct OCO, DCO, and DCO-RA. The cybersecurity workforce also requires KSAs related to DCO. The cyberspace IT workforce is oriented to conduct NETOPS and DODIN operations. Finally, the cyberspace-focused intelligence workforce acts in support of OCO, DCO, and DCO-RA, as well as conducting cyber counterintelligence. In addition to these specifically outlined roles, the entire DoD workforce is responsible for IA and must be trained accordingly.

In 2009, the Partnership for Public Service and Booz Allen Hamilton conducted a study of the state of the federal cybersecurity workforce, including the DoD. The study revealed a significant shortage of cybersecurity expertise and emphasized the weaknesses in recruiting and retaining programs. Talent gaps are currently filled with an overabundance of contractors, which cost taxpayers more than military or government civilian personnel and do not provide a long-term solution or knowledge base (Partnership for Public Service 2009).

The DoD is quickly realizing the need to improve its cyberspace workforce. A Defense Science Board task force report emphasized the need to understand cyber threats, maintain deterrence, develop defensive and offensive capabilities, and change the culture of the DoD to take cybersecurity more seriously. The primary means to achieve this is through "a DoD-wide cyber technical workforce . . . developed to support the build-out of the cyber critical survivable mission capability" in order to maintain cyberspace superiority (Defense Science Board 2013).

Recommendations for Best Practices

The necessity of a skilled cyberspace workforce is clear, but the means for fostering this workforce are still maturing. The next decade will see many changes in how the DoD recruits, develops, and retains its cyberspace workforce, and there are several best practices that may assist in these efforts.

Developing a Professional Community and Culture

Hacker culture began to develop as far back as 1961 with the Massachusetts Institute of Technology's computing clubs, and gradually progressed into an ethos of experimentation, creative thought, critical thinking, and open information sharing (Raymond 2000). Over time, the term *hacker* became increasingly used to describe malicious activities online, or the disruptive tactics used by some vigilante or *hacktivist* actors (Juliano 2012). Regardless of intent, much of this loose-knit community maintains a cultural philosophy that takes pride in technical ability, imagination, and practical application.

The DoD does not have the resources to compete with financial incentives of the private sector, so recruiting an accomplished cyberspace workforce will depend heavily on the appeal of the culture available to employees. Each of the other war-fighting domains (land, sea, air, and space) inspires a particular mindset among those who use them for their primary operations, and the cyberspace domain will be no different. The cyberspace workforce should be taught about its history, from the first cyber combat unit (the 609th Information Warfare Squadron), to the first strategic uses of cyberspace operations. Integrating cyber heritage into professional military education will help establish a sense of community, pride, and importance in history (Healy 2012).

In addition to official measures, a professional association that unites the broad variety of DoD cyber professionals could create an even stronger sense of camaraderie, opportunities for networking, and avenues for collaborative problem solving. The Military Cyber Professionals Association, established in 2013, aims to "develop the American military cyber profession" through online interactions, publications, and educational opportunities (Billingsley 2013). Although the organization is still very young, its founder envisions a group similar to the Association of Old Crows or the Air Defense Artillery Association, both of which provide a robust professional forum for members (Stewart 2013).

Both official DoD functions and outside organizations have the potential to help build a community and culture that would attract curious, energetic, and engaged cyberspace professionals, and these opportunities should be pursued.

Improved Training for the Cyberspace Workforce

The cyberspace workforce must have extensive knowledge of adversary capabilities, hands-on evaluation beyond the traditional certification tests, a thorough understanding of risk management, the ability prevent intrusions instead of reacting to intrusions after they occur, prioritization of the integration between security and providing network services, and the opportunity to exercise in simulated networks. To provide the training necessary for these capabilities, the DoD should increase the availability of realistic hands-on training platforms, link network accesses until specific training or certification milestones have been met, and provide thorough education on ethical standards (Reid 2012).

Expand Cybersecurity Awareness within DoD

Although the majority of this chapter has specifically addressed the DoD cyberspace workforce, it is important to note that all DoD personnel interact constantly with and depend heavily on the DODIN. As already mentioned, the insider threat can be unintentional, and all personnel must be educated in how to reduce the threat. The Defense Information Systems Agency developed a "Cyber Awareness Challenge" in October 2012 that provides a game-like interface in which the participant must complete several IA tasks and study best practices. Along with the usage of tools such as this challenge, maintaining cybersecurity awareness should be a regular topic of conversation in day-to-day military operations.

Future Trends

As emphasized in the previous section, training is a critical part of developing the DoD's cyberspace workforce. Therefore, the DoD has begun to develop strong ties with academia and university research centers. This will help grow educational resources for the cyberspace workforce of the future, which will be crucial to the expansion of the DoD cyberspace workforce as outlined in the CNCI and DSOC. Due to the current limited pipeline to bring cyberspace professionals into the military workforce, the DoD will also have to look for creative solutions to maximize the resources available (Kay, Pudas, and Young 2012; Kallberg and Thuraisingham 2013).

Cross-Flow between Active Duty, Reserves/Guard, Civilian, and Contractor

The DoD will most likely invest large amounts of time, money, and manpower to grow the cybersecurity workforce. One potential drawback to this approach may be that military personnel capitalize on DoD-provided education by obtaining jobs in the commercial sector after their service commitment is complete. Although this benefits the nation as a whole by dispersing cybersecurity awareness throughout the population, it would be prudent for the DoD to encourage these personnel to remain connected to the defense community as reservists or guardsmen. This tactic would allow personnel to gain a perspective of alternative cybersecurity practices while still contributing to the defense of the nation.

Additionally, members transitioning out of the military should be encouraged to consider applying to government civilian positions in the cyberspace workforce. These positions increase continuity within the cyberspace workforce and may help secure a solid foundation of institutional knowledge within the community.

Finally, former military cyberspace experts may choose to work within the defense industrial base (DIB) and provide contractor services to the DoD. Although this would at least help retain experience and knowledge within the workforce, it might not provide the long-term continuity or cost-effectiveness that the DoD needs. However, this cross-flow would contribute to securing the DIB resources on which the military relies.

Engagement with the Defense Industrial Base

The DoD will continue to engage increasingly with the DIB to secure resources outside the DODIN. As part of these efforts, the U.S. government has established channels to "furnish classified threat and technical information to voluntarily participating DIB Companies or their Commercial Service Providers" through the DIB Enhanced Cybersecurity Services, and assisted with improvement of DIB network defenses under the DIB Cyber Security/Information Assurance Program. Additionally, many DIB organizations now see the benefit of hiring personnel "who have walked the halls of government and industry" and have a thorough understanding of the threats to the DIB (Defense Industrial Base 2012; Vautrinot et al. 2013). The next few years will most likely see strengthened ties between the DoD and the DIB as these objectives are pursued through U.S. government programs.

Cybersecurity Job Market for Veterans

One more potential trend for the DoD cybersecurity workforce will be an increase in opportunities available to veterans. Programs like the 9/11 GI Bill and the Veterans Retraining Assistance Program offer educational resources for veterans who want to become part of the nation's cybersecurity workforce (Department of Homeland Security 2013). Additionally, academic efforts to provide educational resources to veterans contribute to the availability of cybersecurity workforce personnel. Mississippi State University, for example, provides no-cost training in digital forensics to wounded warriors (Vautrinot et al. 2013). As the United States withdraws from Afghanistan, there may be a large pool of veterans who will be interested in joining the DoD cyberspace workforce, especially with the incentive of specialized training.

Conclusion

This chapter has provided an overview of cybersecurity issues in the context of the DoD and some of the processes that are in place to provide a cyberspace workforce capable of addressing these issues. The cyberspace domain is complex and is not yet completely defined or understood from a DoD perspective, so many of these issues will morph or be interpreted differently over the next decade. Regardless, it is clear that the DoD and U.S. government consider the nation's cybersecurity to be a top priority, and extensive resources will be committed to building the DoD's cyberspace workforce. This chapter has provided some insight into how those resources might best be focused to create an exceptionally skilled and capable cyberspace workforce.

Sources of Further Information

• Department of Defense on Cybersecurity. http://www.defense.gov/home/features/2010/0410_cybersec/

- Department of Defense Issuances. http://www.dtic.mil/whs/directives/index.html

- Department of Homeland Security on Cybersecurity. http://www.dhs.gov/topic/cybersecurity

- National Initiative for Cybersecurity Education. http://csrc.nist.gov/nice/index.htm

- National Security Agency Information Assurance Resources. http://www.nsa.gov/ia/index.shtml

- National Security Council on Cybersecurity. http://www.whitehouse.gov/cybersecurity

- U.S. Cyber Command Fact Sheet. http://www.stratcom.mil/factsheets/Cyber_Command/

References

Alexander, Keith B. 2011. "Building a New Command in Cyberspace." *Strategic Studies Quarterly* 5: 3–12. Accessed June 3, 2013. http://www.au.af.mil/au/ssq/2011/summer/summer11.pdf.

Barnes, Robert, Timothy B. Lee, and Ellen Nakashima. 2013. "Government Surveillance Programs Renew Debate about Oversight." *Washington Post*, June 8.

Billingsley, Joe. 2013. *Military Cyber Professionals Association*. Accessed July 1, 2013. https://milcyber.org/.

Brickey, Jon, Jacob Cox, John Nelson, and Gregory Conti. 2012. "The Case for Cyber." *Small Wars Journal* 8. Accessed June 2, 2013. http://smallwarsjournal.com/jrnl/art/the-case-for-cyber.

Brito, Jerry, and Tate Watkins. 2011. "Loving the Cyber Bomb? The Dangers of Threat Inflation in Cybersecurity Policy." *Harvard National Security Journal* 3:39–84.

Brown, Gary D., and Owen W. Tullos. 2012. "On the Spectrum of Cyberspace Operations." *Small Wars Journal* 8 Accessed June 2, 2013. http://smallwarsjournal.com/jrnl/art/on-the-spectrum-of-cyberspace-operations.

Bush, George W. 2008. *National Security Presidential Directive 54/Homeland Security Presidential Directive 23* (NSPD-54/HSPD-23).

Butler, Sean C. 2013. "Refocusing Cyber Warfare Thought." *Air & Space Power Journal* 27:44–57.

Carter, Ashton B. 2012. "Remarks by Deputy Secretary of Defense Ashton B. Carter." *Annual Air & Space Conference and Technology Exposition*, September 19.

Cassim, F. 2012. "Addressing the Spectre of Cyber Terrorism: A Comparative Perspective." *Potchefstroom Electronic Law Journal* 15:380–415.

Defense Industrial Base. "Cybersecurity Activities." Accessed June 3, 2013. http://dibnet.dod.mil.

Defense Science Board. 2013. *Task Force Report: Resilient Military Systems and the Advanced Cyber Threat.* Washington, DC: Department of Defense.

Department of Defense. 2007. *Department of Defense Directive* 8570.01.

———. 2011a. *Department of Defense Cyberspace Policy Report: A Report to Congress Pursuant to the National Defense Authorization Act for Fiscal Year 2011, Section 934.* http://www.defense.gov/home/features/2011/0411_cyberstrategy/docs/NDAA%20Section%20934%20Report_For%20webpage.pdf.

———. 2011b. *Department of Defense Strategy for Operating in Cyberspace.*

———. 2013a. *About the Department of Defense.* Accessed June 17, 2013a. http://www.defense.gov/about/#mission.

———. 2013b. *Draft: Department of Defense Cyberspace Workforce Strategy.*

———. 2013c. *Joint Publication 1-02: Department of Defense Dictionary of Military and Associated Terms.*

Department of Homeland Security. 2013. *Opportunities for Veterans in Cybersecurity.* Accessed July 1, 2013. http://www.dhs.gov/join-dhs-cybersecurity.

Director of National Intelligence. 2013. *Facts on the Collection of Intelligence Pursuant to Section 702 of the Foreign Intelligence Surveillance Act.*

Donilon, Thomas E. 2013. "The United States and the Asia-Pacific in 2013." Lecture given at Asia Society New York, March 11.

Farwell, James P., and Rafal Rohozinski. 2011. "Stuxnet and the Future of Cyber War." *Survival* 53:23–40. doi: 10.1080/00396338.2011.555586.

Filshtinskiy, Stas. 2013. "Cybercrime, Cyberweapons, Cyber Wars: Is There Too Much of It in the Air?" *Communications of the ACM* 56:28–30. doi: 10.1145/2461256.2461266.

Fisher, Max. 2013. "Syrian Hackers Claim AP Hack that Tipped Stock Market by $136 Billion. Is it Terrorism?" *Washington Post*, April 23.

Gervais, Michael. 2012. "Cyber Attacks and the Laws of War." *Berkeley Journal of International Law* 30:525–79.

Gorman, Siobhan, and Danny Yadron. 2013. "Banks Seek U.S. Help on Iran Cyberattacks." *Wall Street Journal*, January 15.

Greenwald, Glenn, Ewen MacAskill, and Laura Poitras. 2013. "Edward Snowden: The Whistleblower Behind the NSA Surveillance Revelations." *The Guardian*, June 9. http://www.guardian.co.uk/world/2013/jun/09/edward-snowden-nsa-whistleblower-surveillance.

Greer, John N. 2010. "Square Legal Pegs in Round Cyber Holes: The NSA, Lawfulness, and the Protection of Privacy Rights and Civil Liberties in Cyberspace." *Journal of National Security Law & Policy* 4.

Hagel, Chuck. 2013a. Speech delivered at National Defense University. *National Defense University*, April 3. http://www.defense.gov/speeches/speech.aspx?speechid=1764.

———. 2013b. Speech delivered at University of Nebraska-Omaha. *University of Nebraska-Omaha*, June 19.

Hathaway, Oona A., Rebecca Crootof, Philip Levitz, Haley Nix, Aileen Nowlan, William Perdue, and Julia Spiegel. 2012. "The Law of Cyber-Attack." *California Law Review* 100:817–85.

Healy, Jason. 2012. "Claiming the Lost Cyber Heritage." *Strategic Studies Quarterly* 6:11–19. http://www.au.af.mil/au/ssq/2012/fall/fall12.pdf.

Juliano, Stephanie. 2012. "Superheroes, Bandits, and Cyber-Nerds: Exploring the History and Contemporary Development of the Vigilante." *Journal of International Commercial Law & Technology* 7: 44–64.

Kallberg, Jan, and Bhavani Thuraisingham. 2013. "Cyber Operations Bridging from Concept to Cyber Superiority." *Joint Forces Quarterly* 1Q 2013:53–58.

Kay, David J., Terry J. Pudas, and Brett Young. 2012. "Preparing the Pipeline: The U.S. Cyber Workforce for the Future." *Defense Horizons* 1–15.

Kesan, Jay P., and Carol M. Hayes. 2012. "Mitigative Counterstriking: Self-Defense and Deterrence in Cyberspace." *Harvard Journal of Law & Technology* 25:415–529.

Langevin, James R., Michael T. McCaul, Scott Charney, and Harry Raduege. 2008. *Securing Cyberspace for the 44th Presidency*. Edited by James A. Lewis. Washington, D.C.: Center for Strategic and International Studies.

Levin, Avner, Paul Goodrich, and Daria Ilkina. 2013. "International Comparison of Cyber Crime." *Privacy and Cyber Crime Institute, Ted Rogers School of Management, Ryerson University.*

Lin, Herbert S. 2010. "Offensive Cyber Operations and the Use of Force." *Journal of National Security Law & Policy* 4:63–86.

Mandiant. *APT1: Exposing One of China's Cyber Espionage Units.* Accessed http://intelreport.mandiant.com/Mandiant_APT1_Report.pdf.

Mudrinich, Erik M. 2012. "Cyber 3.0: The Department of Defense Strategy for Operating in Cyberspace and the Attribution Problem." *Air Force Law Review* 68:167–206.

Nakashima, Ellen. 2011. "Cyber-Intruder Sparks Massive Federal Response—and Debate Over Dealing with Threats." *Washington Post*, December 19.

———. 2013a. "Confidential Report Lists U.S. Weapons System Designs Compromised by Chinese Cyberspies." *Washington Post*, May 27.

————. 2013b. "Pentagon to Boost Cybersecurity Force." *Washington Post*, January 27.

National Initiative for Cybersecurity Education. *The National Cybersecurity Workforce Framework*. Accessed http://csrc.nist.gov/nice/framework/.

Obama, Barack. 2013. *Executive Order—Improving Critical Infrastructure Cybersecurity*.

Office of the Secretary of Defense. 2013. *Annual Report to Congress: Military and Security Developments Involving the People's Republic of China*.

O'Harrow, Robert Jr., Dana Priest, and Marjorie Censer. 2013. "Amid Rise of Outsourcing, Shakier Vetting." *Washington Post*, June 11, 1.

Panetta, Leon E. 2012. "Remarks by Secretary Panetta on Cybersecurity to the Business Executives for National Security, New York City." U.S. Department of Defense. October 11.

Partnership for Public Service. 2009. *Cyber In-Security: Strengthening the Federal Cybersecurity Workforce*.

Raymond, Eric S. 2000. *A Brief History of Hackerdom*. Thyrsus Enterprises. http://www.immagic.com/eLibrary/ARCHIVES/GENERAL/AUTHOR_P/R000825P.pdf.

Reid, Desmond A. 2012. *Cyber Sentries: Preparing Defenders to Win in a Contested Domain*. Carlisle, PA: Department of Military Strategy, Planning, and Operations, U.S. Army War College.

Schmitt, Michael N., ed. 2013. *Tallinn Manual on the International Law Applicable to Cyber Warfare*. New York, NY: Cambridge University Press.

Senate Committee on Armed Services. 2013. *Statement of General Keith B. Alexander, Commander United States Cyber Command*. U.S. Senate. March 27.

Stewart, Kenneth A. 2013. "Cyber Warriors Professional Association Another Sign of Evolving Battlefield." *Naval Postgraduate School*. Accessed August 8, 2013. http://www.nps.edu/About/News/Cyber-Warriors-Professional-Association-Another-Sign-of-Evolving-Battlefield.html.

U.S. Cyber Command. 2010. "Cyber Command Fact Sheet." Department of Defense. http://www.defense.gov/cyber.

U.S. Division Center. 2010. "Soldier Faces Criminal Charges." U.S. Department of Defense. http://www.defense.gov/News/NewsArticle.aspx?ID=59918

U.S. House of Representatives. 2012. *The Iranian Cyber Threat to the United States*. Committee on Homeland Security, Subcommittee on Counterterrorism and Intelligence, and Subcommittee on Cybersecurity, Infrastructure Protection and Security Technologies.

————. 2013a. *Cyber Threats from China, Russia and Iran: Protecting American Critical Infrastructure*. Subcommittee on Cybersecurity, Infrastructure Protection, and Security Technologies. March 20.

————. 2013b. *Worldwide Threat Assessment of the US Intelligence Community*. House Permanent Select Committee on Intelligence.

United Nations. 1945. Charter of the United Nations.

Vautrinot, Suzanne, Charles Beard, Jeffrey A. Martinez, and Matthew R. Kayser. "Cyber Professionals in the Military and Industry—Partnering in Defense of the Nation." *Air & Space Power Journal* 27 (2013): 4–21.

Wall, Andrew E. 2011. "Demystifying the Title 10–Title 50 Debate: Distinguishing Military Operations, Intelligence Activities & Covert Action." *Harvard National Security Journal* 3: 85–142.

White House. 2009. *Cyberspace Policy Review: Assuring a Trusted and Resilient Information and Communications Infrastructure.*

———. 2011. *International Strategy for Cyberspace: Prosperity, Security, and Openness in a Networked World.*

Chapter 3

_____

Cybersecurity and Health Care

Sean Murphy

What I may see or hear in the course of the treatment or even outside of the treatment in regard to the life of men, which on no account one must spread abroad, I will keep to myself holding such things shameful to be spoken about.

—Hippocratic Oath

Fundamental Issues that are Unique to Cybersecurity in Health Care

Cybersecurity has been defined as the ability to protect or defend the use of cyberspace from cyber-attacks (Kissel 2013). In simpler terms, this refers to the use of information technology (IT) to exploit IT. The effect of cyberspace and cyber-attacks on health care is a relatively recent phenomenon, but it must be noted that information privacy and security has been a key concern in health care for almost as long as health care providers have treated patients. The advent of electronic health care records, digital payment systems, and interconnected health IT systems has begun to force the health care industry to become aware of cybersecurity as well (see Figure 3.1).

Although there are many cybersecurity issues in health care that are shared with other industries, these issues have a unique effect

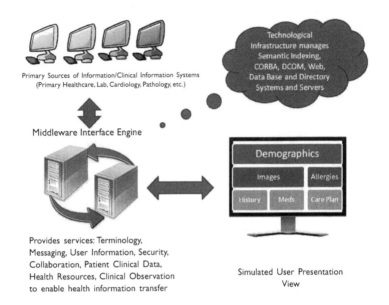

Figure 3.1. The electronic health record (EHR): The cornerstone of health care information.

on health care. For instance, malicious code attacks or hacking into health care networks can cause bodily harm or be life threatening to patients. On the other hand, preventing or responding to cyber-attacks presents distinct challenges for the health care sector. The cybersecurity best practices put in place in banking, retail, industrial control, and education, if indiscriminately applied to the health care setting, can actually lead to patient safety issues, including death (Bolte 2005).

The electronic health record (EHR) is a longitudinal collection of patient-centric health care information available across providers, care settings, and time (Katehakis et al. 2001). It is a central component of an integrated health information system. Because of its importance to the business of health care, the EHR is the cornerstone of any discussion about cybersecurity and health care. The unique challenges the EHR provides stem from the fact that it is typically decentralized across multiple entities that may or may not have a relationship (let alone a connection) with each other; not all of the sensitive information is digital.

ιe that is unique to the health
curity is implemented is in the
organization is regulated more
devices, clinical practices, and
to oversight from regulators at
and in industry-specific regulation is the Joint Commission.
ent, not-for-profit organization
twenty thousand health care
ed States. Health care organiza-
oint Commission, which seems
ommission started in 1951 and
cation has become recognized
reflects an organization's com-
mitment to meeting certain performance standards (Joint Commission 2013). In terms of patient safety, one of the initiatives the Joint
Commission oversees is the reporting of sentinel events. These are
unexpected occurrences involving death or serious physical or psychological injury, or the risk thereof. The loss of limb or function qualifies as a serious injury. The phrase "or the risk thereof" includes any
near-miss event where a process or procedure done incorrectly could
result in serious adverse outcome, even if it did not this time. Such
events are called *sentinel* because they signal the need for immediate
investigation and response (Joint Commission 2011). The point here
is that the health care industry, as an industry that at its core does no
harm, put patient safety squarely in the cost–benefit analysis of any
cybersecurity consideration.

Related to the patient safety issue is the concept of *e-iatrogenesis*.
Merriam-Webster online (2013) defines the term *iatrogenesis* as the
"inadvertent and preventable induction of disease or complications
by the medical treatment or procedures of a physician or surgeon."
E-iatrogenesis is "patient harm caused at least in part by the application of health information technology" (Weiner et al. 2007). Borrowing from the spirit of the term, health care cybersecurity practitioners
can certainly contribute to the induction of complications very easily.
They can cause patient harm by the application of offensive or defensive cybersecurity measures. As stated earlier, even the best practices

can be detrimental if introduced without an understanding of the clinical context. Think of the harm caused by using a vulnerability patch management program and applying patches to the enterprise at a non-peak time. As the software updates the clients on the local area network with the latest antivirus and operating system (OS) updates, it also is affecting networked medical devices. Medical devices like physiological monitors, imaging systems, and infusion technologies are FDA-regulated special purpose computing platforms. To the casual observer, the systems look like standard office automation with client-server architecture and Windows OS. But they are not treated like office automation systems; medical devices support direct patient care. If these medical devices are not specifically excluded from the automated update process, there is a great risk for complications. One hypothetical scenario is of a forced reboot of a telemetry system monitoring patients in the intensive care unit at three o'clock on Sunday morning; this could be life threatening. Another possible unintended consequence might be an antivirus quarantine of all files with .dcm file extension (this signifies a Digital Imaging and Communications in Medicine file type, or DICOM). If not specifically excluded from the antivirus scan, all images found within the Picture Archiving and Communications System (PACS) or digital radiology system will be unavailable to the radiologist or emergency room physician during the update. These examples are not as hypothetical as one might imagine. E-iatrogenesis is a challenge that requires health care cybersecurity professionals to tailor their strategies using the same *do no harm* focus as the providers they support.

Another issue unique to health care is the fact that patients may delay care or not seek it at all due to fear of the health care organization losing their information. It is rare in other industries that customers will refuse to patronize an organization that loses their data, especially at the risk of their health and well-being. In fact, "abnormal churn" (Ponemon Institute 2013) or unnatural turnover of customers is highest, and more expensive, in health care. Most people do not change banks when their bank account number is compromised. The majority of credit card users do not close their accounts and open new accounts with another company after a credit card breach. There is not the same fear of embarrassment if financial information is lost or stolen as when health care information is exposed. It has become almost acceptable to receive a notice in the mail that some sensitive financial or personal piece of information has been lost by a company. The typical consumer is accustomed to an offer of credit monitoring for a year (Experian 2012). But beyond that, there is an arguable effect on the company at fault, both in reputation and bottom line. In health care, the effect of data loss has very different, dramatic effects, very few of which can be addressed with credit monitoring.

The greatest fear patients have associated with the loss of their sensitive health data is embarrassment of public exposure. Coupled with this risk and associated stigma, groups like the RAND Corporation estimate that roughly half of the 620,000 returning service members from Iraq and Afghanistan who meet criteria for post-traumatic stress disorder or traumatic brain injury actually seek care. Of those who delay or do not seek care, most cite privacy concerns. Although some of these may be related to disclosure relating to a military commander's need-to-know, many are simply linked to the risk of not receiving confidential services without fear of adverse consequences (Tanielian and Jaycox 2008). The real impact of that fear is that patients delay or do not seek care. In the treatment of illnesses like sexually transmitted diseases, behavioral health, and other sensitive conditions, this delay or denial can cause others to get sick or hurt, or cause the patients themselves to suffer needlessly. The fear of unauthorized disclosure can even sabotage a patient's health care, as behavioral health patients mask their identity, change providers regularly, and impede providers by lying about their history (Felt-Lisk and Humensky 2003).

Laws and Policies Relevant to Cybersecurity in Health Care

The health care environment is heavily regulated. Entire academic courses are available to enumerate and explore the most relevant regulations. This chapter concentrates on the primary federal regulations shaping the health care environment, namely the Health Insurance

Portability and Accountability Act (HIPAA), found at 45 Code of Federal Regulations (CFR) 160, 162, and 164. For purposes of illustration only, a small sample list of additional federal regulations is provided in Table 3.1.

HIPAA was enacted in 1996 and has evolved through amendments over the years (see Figure 3.2): the Privacy Rule, the Security Rule, the Health Information Technology for Economic and Clinical Health (HITECH) Act, and in 2013, the Omnibus HIPAA Rule. Each of these must be discussed in its own right. HIPAA defines a sensi-

Table 3.1. Select Federal Regulations Governing Health Care Privacy and Security

Federal Health Care Guidance
Federal Policy for the Protection of Human Subjects ("Common Rule"); 45 CFR 46.101
The Federal Drug and Alcohol Confidentiality Law; 42 U.S.C. § 290dd-2 and 42 CFR Part 2
Sarbanes-Oxley Act (SOX); 2002
Payment Card Industry (PCI) Data Security Standard (DSS); (PCI DSS)
Federal Trade Commission (FTC), Identity Theft Red Flags and Address Discrepancies Under the Fair and Accurate Credit Transactions Act of 2003; Final Rule
Family Educational Rights and Privacy Act; 20 U.S.C. § 1232g; 34 CFR Part 99
Guidance for Industry: Cybersecurity for Networked Medical Devices Containing Off-the-Shelf (OTS) Software; with supplement, Content of Premarket Submissions for Management of Cybersecurity in Medical Devices: Draft (as of June 14, 2013). Guidance for Industry and Food and Drug Administration Staff.

HIPAA and as amended

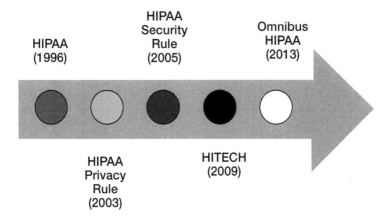

Figure 3.2. Timeline of HIPAA and as amended.

tive type of data known as Protected Health Information (PHI). PHI is individually identifiable health information that is transmitted or maintained electronically or by any other medium by an organization subject to HIPAA law. Organizations subject to HIPAA are categorized as covered entities or business associates. A covered entity is an entity that must comply with any or all of the HIPAA rules; that means certain providers (hospitals/doctors' offices), health plans, and health care clearinghouses that are regulated by the HIPAA Security Rule and/or the HIPAA Privacy Rule. A business associate is an entity independent of a HIPAA-covered entity that handles PHI received from or provided to the covered entity (Scholl et al. 2008).

HIPAA was put into place for reasons far beyond privacy and security. After almost twenty years and four amendments, HIPAA is now basically synonymous with health care information privacy and security. It is the framework for compliance for health care organizations related to cybersecurity. HIPAA standards are principally drawn from several industry-agnostic standards such as the best practices

established by the National Institute of Standards and Technology
(NIST), Federal Information Security Management Act, and the Privacy Act.

The 1996 HIPAA ruling required the Department of Health
and Human Services (HHS) to enact a separate Privacy Rule and a
Security Rule. HHS did so in 2003 by publishing the Privacy Rule.
For organizations subject to HIPAA, the Privacy Rule established the
first national standards to protect a patient's PHI. These standards
limit the use and disclosure of PHI, require health care organizations
to provide patients an account of each entity to which they disclose
PHI for billing and administrative purposes, and give patients the right
to access their own medical records. At the same time, constraints on
use and disclosure are not meant to restrict the availability of PHI
for legitimate health care operations. The Privacy Rule also clarified
the requirement for a covered entity to establish a Business Associate Agreement, a type of contract that imposes HIPAA safeguards
on organizations providing PHI-handling services or functions that
are covered by HIPAA (Department of Health and Human Services
2013). The Privacy Rule also creates the promise of a penalty fine
for organizations found to be the source of a health care data breach
or that fail to give patients access to their medical records. At this
point, cybersecurity in health care was truly in its infancy due to the
relative absence of health care–specific IT, in contrast to industries
like banking, industrial control, or telecommunications.

That began to change in 2005, when HHS published the Security Rule. This law covered a growing concern in health care, the
digitizing of the EHR. The HIPAA Security Rule applies standards
governing the use and disclosure of electronic PHI; it does not apply
to PHI found in oral and paper form. The Security Rule specifically
comes into play for most medical practices regarding remote access
to health care systems. The cybersecurity professional is constantly
vigilant against the vulnerabilities that are introduced when data is
accessed and transferred from outside the organization's firewall or
across the Internet. An organization is equally vulnerable when providing outside access without proper safeguards in place. The Security

Rule acknowledges these concerns and establishes some framework for keeping digital PHI more secure.

At this point in the history of HIPAA, covered entities were certainly required to safeguard PHI, both under the Privacy Rule and electronic PHI under the Security Rule, but they were not required to give notice to the individuals whose information was inappropriately disclosed through a data breach. The next evolution in HIPAA amendments began to address this in the Health Information Technology for Economic and Clinical Health (HITECH) Act (Department of Health and Human Services 2009). It was a part of the American Recovery and Reinvestment Act of 2009, commonly referred to as the Stimulus, or Recovery Act. HITECH makes significant changes to HIPAA, including notifying individuals, and in some instances, media outlets when there has been a data breach. In general, HITECH privacy and security provisions also include expanding the definition of a business associate and requiring compliance with the same privacy and security rules as providers and health insurers. HITECH also strengthened enforcement of federal privacy and security laws by increasing penalties for violations and providing greater resources for enforcement and oversight activities through HHS and the state attorneys general.

Finally, the most recent amendment to HIPAA is the Omnibus HIPAA Rule (Federal Register 2013). Chief among its effects on the health care industry has been even more clarification of the term *business associate* than was provided in HITECH. A specific illustration of how the law has expanded the universe of newly defined business associates is those who consider themselves "data cloud providers" or subcontractors. Previously, it was unclear if they had direct liability under HIPAA as business associates providing a HIPAA-covered service. The Omnibus HIPAA rule clarified the definition of business associate to include *anyone* who handles PHI for any reason. Only a subcontractor who merely acts as a conduit of the information and who never stores or sees the data can sidestep the business associate requirements. An Internet service provider fits this definition, but not many other types of IT providers for health care organizations do. It does not matter if business associates actually sign an agreement; they are still directly liable under the law according to HHS (D'Emanuele, Smith, and Martyn 2013). Another major impact of the Omnibus HIPAA rule is the change in breach notification. Previously, HITECH established the "harm threshold" that defined a breach as an event that "compromises the security or privacy of the protected health information" and "poses a significant risk of financial, reputational, or other harm to the individual." Under the new rules, health care organizations must notify patients if there is a breach of their PHI using a risk assessment that has clarified what constitutes unauthorized disclosure. The assessment expands their obligation by changing the litmus test to risk for compromise. Frankly, breaches are now presumed reportable unless a documented risk assessment demonstrates that there is a "low probability of PHI compromise."

Although HIPAA makes up just a portion of the federal regulations governing cybersecurity in health care, it becomes clear that cybersecurity in health care presents unique and dynamic considerations. The regulatory environment in health care cybersecurity and information protection is a topic for much more study and analysis. See the Sources of Further Information section of this chapter for more resources on this subject area.

Standards Applicable to Cybersecurity in Health Care

As the examination of HIPAA law and its amendments demonstrates, health care cybersecurity is based on standards. Most of these standards are common across all industries, but many are unique to the health care environment. In fact, health care cybersecurity can draw on international standards. For instance, medical devices like computed tomography or linear accelerators are secured using international standards as well as frameworks established in the United States because the same medical devices used in the United States also are used worldwide. It would severely affect medical device manufacturers to respond to just U.S. standards and ignore international cybersecurity concerns.

The Health Level 7 (HL7) group has built a very important technical standard in the health care cybersecurity area. HL7 "Level Seven" refers to the seventh level of the International Organization for Standardization seven-layer communications model for Open Systems Interconnection—the application level (Health Level Seven International 2013). This nonprofit, international body is comprised of experts in data interchange and health care operations. They develop comprehensive frameworks and related standards for the exchange, integration, sharing, and retrieval of electronic health information that supports clinical practice and the management, delivery, and evaluation of health service using American National Standards Institute-accredited standards. The mission of HL7 is to support the interfacing of health care systems, many of which are disparate and proprietary. Without a common set of standards, these systems would not be able to interconnect. Imagine a pharmacy system that could not exchange prescription information with the EHR; all data would have to be manually input. HL7 standards have reduced this problem. Specific to cybersecurity, HL7 has published several privacy and security standards. The key standard for the HL7 is the Clinical Document Architecture (CDA), which outlines the data elements, message headers, and document standards for representing medical and legal health care encounters. The standard includes transactional-based security approaches, like the Secure Sockets Layer. Confidentiality provisions are then able to rely on the application platforms of the legacy systems. HL7 CDA Version 3 contains the necessary data objects, attributes, and transaction contents to support these confidentiality controls (Shoniregun, Mtenzi, and Dube 2010). Table 3.2 contains additional examples of other standards applicable to health care cybersecurity.

In the health care setting, the same traditional security triad applies: confidentiality, integrity, and availability (CIA; Harris 2012). In the health care environment, the CIA triad enables two very important considerations: *reliability* and *privacy* of health information.

The first step in assuring CIA in health care is to conduct a risk assessment. See Figure 3.3 for an illustration of a risk assessment framework found in health care. Although an assessment of risk is not unique to health care, what is special is the HIPAA regulatory

Table 3.2. Select Standards Specific to Cybersecurity in Health Care Protecting Information: Confidentiality, Integrity, and Availability

NIST Special Publication (SP) 800-66, Rev 1, Oct 2008: An Introductory Resource Guide for Implementing the Health Insurance Portability and Accountability Act (HIPAA) Security Rule
ISO 27799:2008: Health Informatics—Information Security Management in Health Using ISO/IEC 27002 Information Technology—Security Techniques—Code of Practice for Information Security Management
European Union (EU) Data Protection Directive, Article 29 Working Party: Working Document on the Processing of Personal Data Relating to Health in Electronic Health Records (EHR)
HITRUST Alliance Common Security Framework (CSF)
NIST 2014 Edition Meaningful Use Test Tools
Healthcare Information Technology Standards Panel (HITSP) Security and Privacy Technical Note, (TN) 900, (2009)

ISO, International Organization for Standardization; NIST, National Institute of Standards and Technology

requirement tied to government fines and penalties for health care organizations and business associates who do not conduct at least one risk assessment annually.

From the risk assessment comes a level of assurance for information protection that yields reliability. On the CIA triad, reliability is related to the availability and integrity of data; it is particularly applicable in health care because the health care provider has a compelling need to have the right information at the right time. It is a need that requires more than just information availability. One of the considerations in health care that troubles information security providers for health care data (e.g., cloud providers) is in the area of downtime. The requirement for continuity of operations and disaster recovery (DR) can seem like health care is on par with critical infrastructure

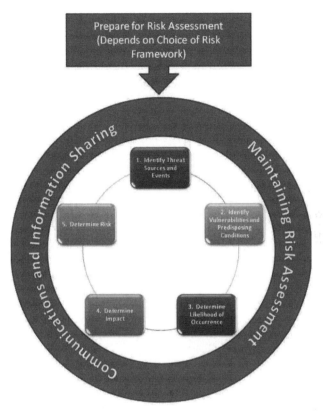

Figure 3.3. Risk assessment framework (adapted from National Institute of Standards and Technology 2012).

organizations. If a cloud provider (as a business associate) does not understand this requirement, and is reluctant to agree to provide that level of uptime, the lack of information reliability can be disastrous.

Within the construct of reliability is the imperative of data integrity. Using the same example of the cloud provider, a health care organization subject to HIPAA must be able to produce a copy of all medical records it has created, collected, maintained, and disclosed for purposes of treatment, payments, and operations. In some cases, such as a data breach investigation, the health care organization can be under a tightly controlled timeline to produce a complete record. In cases where the cloud provider co-mingles multiple customers' data (including non–health care customers), it has proven difficult to make the data available and certify its completeness (Greene 2012).

Privacy also takes on special considerations within the health care setting. Privacy, as it is generally defined, is the protection of information in terms of confidentiality and the need to know. It is recognized as a human right in many countries and is the cornerstone of the patient–physician relationship. In terms of the CIA triad, it is a blending of confidentiality and integrity. It can take the CIA triad that is typically illustrated as an equilateral triangle and stretch it into some very atypical shapes.

A good way to explain the effect health care operations have on the historical provision of CIA is to introduce the increasingly integrated nature of health care information privacy and security. Privacy is sometimes described as "what" information needs to be protected. Security, in turn, is described as "how" you protect the "what" (Herold 2002). In health care, the concerns of privacy have moved into situations that involve more IT-based solutions. In the past, medical records were primarily paper-based, and physical security was the biggest consideration. But now that more records are digitized, network architecture, intrusion detection systems, and malware protection are more important than cipher locks and locked file cabinets (although they still have a place of prominence). In the end, because of the unique blending of privacy and security and the CIA triad in health care, the cybersecurity professional in a health care setting will need to be alert to the reliability and privacy issues.

Cybersecurity Threats in Health Care

Because of the regulatory environment, health care organizations must carefully track and control how health care information is used. Whether a threat is internal or external in nature, the risk for unauthorized disclosure must be measured and controlled. It is not to be understated; reliability of accurate data in health care can be a matter of life or death. Network downtime due to a malicious code infiltration or a denial of service attack can wreak havoc in a health care organization, especially in one that lacks a proper (and tested) DR and contingency plan.

Like any digital organization with sensitive information, cybersecurity threats that challenge health care come from internal sources such as the workforce, and external sources such as an adversary. Health care, however, has some threats that differ in terms of purpose and effect. The first comes from within the organization. Inappropriate access of patient data can be a result of credentialed users abusing their privileges. In the case of a health care system, this does not mean the user has elevated privileges, such as system administrator rights. It means they access information that they do not have a need to know at a given point in time. This is called snooping. A prime example is a current case where Kim Kardashian and seventeen other patients had their medical records breached. Six medical workers were fired from Cedars-Sinai Medical Center in Los Angeles for allegedly trying to access Kardashian's medical records along with other celebrity patients (Stebner 2013). It does not matter that the same provider may have delivered care to the patient sometime in the past, or even that it has dozens of patients with the same condition. Snooping is highly prevalent with VIP patients. Snooping is compounded by the growing underground cyber economy where these individuals access the records with the intent to acquire data and then sell it to the highest bidder (Symantec Corporation 2008).

The cybersecurity response to snooping has been an increasing use of tools that provide a type of alert, similar to what the banking or retail industries use for fraud alert. A health care organization can monitor use and disclosure of health information by authorized users based on preset rules of behavior. In other words, personnel who have a user account with a profile that is grouped to "Pediatrics" may be able to access medical records on patients ages eighteen and younger, depending on the other preset rules. This access would not result in a flag or alert. The challenge in health care when combating snooping occurs when that same preset rule is in place, and now a member of the health care organization profiled to a group titled "Health Information Management" accesses a record of a child under the age of eighteen. That access could be snooping by a friend of a parent, or an element of cybercrime. It also might be a records management analyst accessing the record for a medical coding audit. The key to successful fraud alerts is setting the rules for access appropriately. In health care, those rules tend to be highly complex and variable.

An example of the adversary, or threat from outside the health care organization, is the exploitation of medical devices. For fans of the television drama *Homeland*, a particularly scary episode featured a scenario that may be worth referencing. A terrorist succeeds in remotely hacking into the pacemaker of the vice president of the United States using the device's serial number. By hacking into the device, the terrorist is able to cause the device to malfunction and induce a heart attack. Although that might seem far-fetched (*Homeland* is a *fictional* drama), the concept of hacking medical devices has been successfully demonstrated. In 2008, a team of researchers from the University of Washington, Harvard Medical School, and the University of Massachusetts at Amherst published research that stated they were able to access a common cardiac defibrillator remotely (Feder 2008) by using off-the-shelf radio and computer equipment. Although this was done in a lab, some suggest real-life conditions would make the experiment unlikely, as access would require unnaturally close proximity for an extended period of time, which would draw attention. However, the researchers were able to steal personal information from the device and to induce fatal heart rhythms. They were able to reprogram it to shut down and to deliver jolts of electricity that would potentially be fatal, if the device had been on a person.

To counter these threats, the FDA continues to provide guidance to manufacturers of medical devices to build in controls in order to effectively reduce the chance of a cybersecurity breach to the device. The FDA has a lead role in pushing quality initiatives for medical devices containing software or programmable logic that can be vulnerable to cybersecurity incidents (Klein and Kagan 2013). Because of the patient safety risks, it is imperative that health care information security professionals are constantly diligent against malware and computer viruses that can contaminate medical devices.

Status of the Cybersecurity Workforce within Health Care

Within the information security profession, workforce shortages are well documented. In the 2013 International Information Systems Security Certification Consortium (ISC²) Global Information Security Workforce Study, 56 percent of respondents said that their organization had "too few" information security workers. The ISC² survey canvassed the opinions of a cross section of professionals from C-level officers to security analysts to managers. Respondents came from several different industries, including 4 percent from health care (Suby 2013). In this constituency, 52 percent believed that security breaches are one of the major effects of not having enough qualified information security professionals.

To address health care workforce competency, the nation's Healthcare and Public Health Information Sharing and Analysis Center (NH-ISAC) is working on a framework to help prepare future health care cybersecurity professionals. The framework is based on the NIST's National Initiative for Cybersecurity Education. The goal of the NH-ISAC is to identify and foster health care cybersecurity education, training, and certification programs related to health sector-specific "role-based" cybersecurity functions, responsibilities, tasks, competencies, and job descriptions (National Health Information Sharing and Analysis Center 2012).

As the education level of cybersecurity in health care is addressed, the ability to measure and assure competency is needed. Of the various ways to do that, an objective, third-party assessment is becoming commonplace in health care. For instance, the American Health Information Management Association has instituted the Certified in Healthcare Privacy and Security (CHPS) credential. This credential indicates personnel who have competence in designing, implementing, and administering comprehensive privacy and security protection programs in all types of health care organizations. The CHPS credential is special because it originates from a leading health care information management organization that has recognized the digitizing of the medical record.

Cybersecurity professional associations are beginning to recognize the unique nature of the health care environment. Although long-standing benchmark credentials exist in cybersecurity (e.g., CISSP, GISP, Security+), few cybersecurity professional organizations have created health care-specific concentrations. However, with the number and severity of PHI data breaches that have occurred over the past three to five years, the need to measure competency for cybersecurity awareness and capability in the health care setting is growing. Leading organizations like ISC² are either developing a credential, or at a minimum, sponsoring continuing education programs for health care cybersecurity practitioners.

In summary, the multidirectional approach of focusing on cybersecurity in health care, from health care organizations developing cybersecurity credentials and cybersecurity professional associations growing a health care practice, is encouraging. Both show a commitment to advancing privacy and security management practices, lifelong learning, and professional development. The talent shortage and continued health care data breaches signify the need for more training and more competency measures. The number of task forces and workgroups teaming together from cybersecurity and health care results in a positive outlook for some time to come. Having an educated workforce that is aware of cybersecurity risks is critical to mitigating these risks.

Recommendations for Cybersecurity
Best Practices in Health Care

The best action a health care organization can take to protect itself is to create and maintain an organization with a high level of cybersecurity awareness. This is no small task when one considers the challenges. The EHR is decentralized, with multiple access points, has many different legacy systems feeding data into it, and is used by numerous personnel with all of their different roles and profiles. Managing this process is not only the responsibility of the health care cybersecurity professionals in the organization. Such a small and often understaffed group simply could not perform it. Therefore, one of the most effective best practices is to provide continuous communication and awareness to all health care employees on the importance of cybersecurity. To be clear, this is actually a requirement under HIPAA, but the need and impact go far beyond HIPAA.

Secondary in importance only to awareness, health care cybersecurity must be built into all projects and products that involve PHI. In the cybersecurity world, this is called defense in depth. It is important to recognize that the layered approach to securing information has to be applied to the entire information life cycle. Taking the implementation of an EHR system as an example, health care cybersecurity is best applied first during selection and procurement of the EHR software and processing product. Consideration should be made for things like the Certification Commission for Health Information Technology (CCHIT) certification of the product. CCHIT is recognized as an HHS Authorized Certification Body (ONC-ACB) for certifying EHRs to support meaningful use. With this certification, a health care organization can be assured that the software meets established cybersecurity thresholds. Once the EHR is procured, the organization should look at challenges to implementation including perimeter security, the legacy network architecture, medical devices, and any legacy clinical information systems that will interconnect with the EHR system. Assessing the security of these transactions is critical. A backdoor opening, or a nonsecure connection, can lead to data loss or a data breach. Moving to the go-live stage, there are a few more important considerations. Having users who are properly trained on the system, including their roles in protecting the PHI, is often overlooked. Additionally, having users appropriately profiled in the system can prevent users gaining higher levels of access than needed, or an inability to properly audit access. There are many more cybersecurity controls that need to be layered in. The key point is that the best practice is to assess the need for the controls as the project is executed. Too often, the project is completed, only to find out that no one ever thought of the security implications. For instance, if an EHR project did not account for the requirement to have a

DR plan and backup storage, the additional costs for that project to add on these deliverables might be staggering post-implementation. Because these requirements are mandated by HIPAA, they must be factored into the project for all the new secure, digitized information systems that the organization did not have previously, both on and off premises.

One of the most compelling arguments for the special considerations within health care cybersecurity is the use and securing of medical devices. A best practice in health care has been the segmentation of all medical devices from the environment of regular office automation, other clinical systems, and financial applications. The U.S. Department of Veterans Affairs pioneered the concept in its *Medical Device Isolation Architecture Guide* published in 2004. This guide has been refined over the years and modeled in other federal systems. The goal of the architecture is a five-step approach for moving networked medical devices from the more common open or flat Local Area Network (LAN) to a more protected Virtual Local Area Network or VLAN structure. In computer networking, a VLAN is created by using a router or switch to partition one or more distinct broadcast domains. These are mutually isolated so that data can only pass between them via one or more routers. Medical devices can be segmented in this way due to their nature and purpose. Unlike normal computing patterns that must use ports and protocols typically targeted by the adversary, medical devices typically use ports and protocols *only* used for their communication. A good example is DICOM. In a PACS, imaging modalities will transmit images using the DICOM protocol over TCP/IP using proprietary ports. The traffic is highly predictable and is perfect for using intrusion detection systems to monitor; the traffic is typically point-to-point so any deviations, highjacked or spoofed, can be quickly caught and severed.

This architecture is important for two reasons. First, vulnerabilities faced by the LAN relating to attacks on medical devices that can cause patient safety issues are mitigated. Second, the medical devices themselves do not present a vulnerability to the LAN in times when the patch management of the medical devices is not at the same standard as the LAN. As mentioned previously, an antivirus update or an OS vulnerability patch may have to be tested and evaluated by a medical device manufacturer before it is approved for loading on their medical device, even in organizations where the hospital owns the device. This delay may cause the patch management cycle to be out of sync. A virus introduced to the medical device isolation architecture, although a problem, is limited to the medical device enclave.

A very complex issue in health care is the growing reliance on mobile devices. More health care practitioners are using tablets and handheld devices as inputs into the system and for viewing results. The additional wrinkle in this scenario is that the trend is for these mobile devices to be personal, not owned or maintained by the health care organization. When it comes to PHI, the use of these devices, which may have any number of non–health care applications with vulnerabilities, becomes a concern when complying with HIPAA. The health care cybersecurity analyst really has little assurance that the devices are on a secure platform with up-to-date antivirus signatures. The scenario described here is commonly referred to as bring your own device (BYOD). Clinical practitioners and IT leadership alike are embracing BYOD. From the IT perspective, BYOD reduces the need to budget for technology refresh, maintenance costs, and inventory control. However, protecting sensitive information from cyber-attacks and other risks is a huge challenge. This is where the concept of virtual desktop interfacing (VDI) becomes a best practice as it integrates with BYOD. VDI is a service where remote servers host the actual desktop environment for a user. The user accesses this service over a network using a secure remote display protocol or VPN. To the user, their access has the look and feel of their desktop system with access to shared resources, while all the computing goes on in the data center, not on their particular device. Because data is not transmitted across the network and is not saved to the user's local device, concerns for securing PHI in transit and at rest are mitigated. A lost tablet that is used to access a hospital's EHR is no longer the cause of a data breach because there is no PHI persistent on the device. Some case studies are available that document how VDI and BYOD improve data protection and lower health care costs (Horowitz 2010; ProActive Solutions, Inc. 2013).

Future Trends in Cybersecurity within Health Care

It is always exciting to forecast the future of cybersecurity within health care. There have been many predictions, not all of which have come true. For instance, Bill Gates famously said, "Two years from now, spam will be solved" at the 2004 World Economic Forum (Fogarty 2012). Yet, today spam still contributes between 70 percent and 90 percent of Internet mail. The use of cybersecurity has helped reduce that number, but much email is still generated and replicated by non-human spam. No one can accuse Gates of not having a clear vision of the future, but the truth remains, predicting the future, particularly in a field as dynamic as cybersecurity in health care, is not a perfect science.

To begin with, the increasing use of mobile devices and BYOD initiatives will continue to be embraced as cybersecurity protections and strategies evolve. Specifically in health care, mobile technologies will improve health care monitoring, delivery, and reporting. A very interesting subspecialty within health care where this has potential is in home health care delivery. Devices ranging from physiological monitors to environmental testers located in a patient's home and connect to a health care provider's EHR will proliferate. Additionally, physicians are like any other mobile device users these days; they want to use their own personal mobile devices (BYOD) for personal and work tasks. In some cases, the financial benefits are clear. Instead of purchasing the best available ultrasound machine for as much as $100,000, the physician can plug in an attachment to a mobile phone that provides much of the same functionality for just $7,495 (Kharif 2011). However, not being able to provide information assurance for the physician's or patient's personal smartphone may result in data integrity issues due to malware, for instance.

The cybersecurity concerns for these devices will be important with reference to privacy and reliability. The privacy of the PHI as it is stored in small, mobile devices and transmitted across the public Internet will drive identity management solutions and encryption technologies. From a reliability perspective, mobile devices used in the home health setting will be a challenge. It would not be feasible to expect a patient's home network and Internet service provider to provide a service level that meets or exceeds what the health care organization and its third-party vendors may provide. The use of network monitoring alerts that include informing caregivers that a device on the network has stopped communicating is helpful. The fear is that these alerts, combined with the clinical alerts like elevated blood pressure, increased heart rate, or rapid weight gain, both of which are suggestive of congestive heart failure, could lead to similar alert fatigue that is already a challenge within the EHR environment with drug interaction alerts and contraindication warnings (Brown 2013).

Another prediction for the future of cybersecurity in health care is the big data aspect of cybersecurity. Big data is the ability to gather and analyze huge sets of data that are so complex that normal database management tools or traditional data-processing applications cannot handle them. As a result, new tools and processes are being implemented. In health care, big data allows a new perspective of the population's health as well as on longitudinal personal health. In the end, it promises to customize health care down to a genetic level, creating a truly personalized health plan specific to the patient, the condition, and the expected outcomes.

Defense in depth is a flat model of integrated information security processes. Big data in cybersecurity terms can truly integrate the collection of incidents, alerts, and patches for the individual computer system, where issues like special purpose and proprietary configuration of medical devices can be managed at the speed necessary when a new antivirus is introduced every few minutes of each day. Many experts note that as many as two hundred thousand new malicious applications are introduced daily. The ability to monitor, remedy, and notify the manufacturers, providers, and end users in health care settings is virtually impossible without the analytical tools and processing power big data promises (Woodie 2013).

The future of cybersecurity in health care will see organizations change their spending patterns away from the primary focus of securing the perimeter. As hackers and cybercriminals have improved their attacks, firewalls, intrusion detection systems, and router configurations have been losing their effectiveness. Big data drives systems that have intelligence in their core, and health care organizations will move to implement them. The perimeter defenses will not disappear, but the integration of central management systems that provide more dynamic and agile controls will be engineered. Key to their success is the ability to process and make sense of huge data streams from all the sources that are collecting cybersecurity data and analyze it rapidly to make decisions. These central management systems also have another big data feature, the ability to analyze data whether it is structured or unstructured. In essence, the complete three-dimensional picture of an organization will be possible to visualize, including internal and external threats, vulnerabilities, assets, and infrastructures. What is more, the big data analytics will also tie into the organizational information governance processes so that policy and compliance activities can predict, not just respond to, an adversary's actions. One of the most compelling promises of big data is the idea that the overall cybersecurity capability can be self-learning. Everything from abnormal activity in identity management or behavior between medical devices can be ever changing; the devices must be able to learn from past experiences. New rules of behavior and actionable guidance will be implemented based on lessons learned and applied automatically. In the health care environment, rules of behavior can be extremely complex. Automatically quarantining machines or blocking user access can lead to patient harm. Having an intelligent, self-learning capacity that evolves health care cybersecurity and is smart enough to understand health care holds great potential (Curry et al. 2013).

Sources of Further Information

This chapter does not attempt to cover the overall curriculum that is cybersecurity. As it applies to all industries, including government and military, cybersecurity has common principles, impacts, and challenges. This chapter concentrates on these in health care specifically. For comprehensive resources related to cybersecurity in general, the following sources are recommended:

Harris, Shon. 2012. *CISSP All-in-One Exam Guide*, 6th ed. New York: McGraw-Hill.

Panko, Raymond. 2009. *Corporate Computer and Network Security*, 2nd ed. Upper Saddle River, NJ: Prentice Hall.

Tipton, Harold F. and Micki Krause. 2007. *Information Security Management Handbook*, 6th ed. Boca Raton, FL: CRC Press.

To explore the use and importance of the EHR and digital information in health care:

Gartee, Richard. 2013. *Electronic Health Records: Understanding and Using Computerized Medical Records*, 2nd ed. Upper Saddle River, NJ: Prentice Hall.

Miller, Joe. 2005. *Implementing the Electronic Health Record: Case Studies and Strategies for Success*. Boca Raton, FL: Productivity Press.

Stein, Todd, ed. 2005. *The Electronic Physician: Guidelines for Implementing a Paperless Practice*. Chicago: Allscripts.

Cybersecurity in health care is a topic that is generating more research and additional interest. The following professional organizations and resources are just a couple that are leading the way in developing and sharing information:

American Health Information Management Association (AHIMA), at http://www.ahima.org.

Health Information Management and Systems Society (HIMSS), at www.himss.org.

A few additional resources that do not fit nicely into any certain category but are useful for a better understanding of cybersecurity in health care are:

ACS Communications. *Becker's Hospital Review* at http://www.beckershospitalreview.com.

ECRI Institute. 2009. *Medical Technology for the IT Professional: An Essential Guide for Working in Today's Healthcare Setting*.

Plymouth Meeting, PA: ECRI Institute. This guide is essential in providing context for information technology professionals working in the healthcare environment.

Trotter, Fred and David Uhlman. 2011. *Hacking Healthcare: A Guide to Standards, Workflows, and Meaningful Use*. Cambridge, MA: O'Reilly Media.

References

American Medical Association. 1920. *AMA Principles of Medical Ethics*.

Bolte, Scott. 2005. "Cybersecurity for Medical Devices: Three Threads Intertwined." PowerPoint Presentation to *Cybersecurity of Medical Devices Conference*. April 12. www.fda.gov/downloads/MedicalDevices/Safety/MedSunMedicalProductSafetyNetwork/ucm127923.ppt.

Brown, Troy. 2013. "Repeated EHR Alerts Desensitize Clinicians." *Medscape Medical News*, May 28. Accessed July 15, 2013. http://www.medscape.com/viewarticle/804829.

Curry, Sam, Engin Kirda, Eddie Schwartz, William H. Stewart, and Amit Yoran. 2013. "Big Data Fuels Intelligence-Driven Security." *RSA and EMC²*. Accessed July 7, 2013. http://www.emc.com/collateral/industry-overview/big-data-fuels-intelligence-driven-security-io.pdf

D'Emanuele, Ross C., Alissa Smith, and Nadia Martyn. 2013. "Final HIPAA Rule Will Regulate Business Associates, Change HIPAA Breach Notification Obligation." *Dorsey & Whitney LLP*. January 25. Accessed July 4, 2013. http://www.dorsey.com/eu_htr_hipaa_rule_012513.

Department of Health and Human Services. 2009. "Health Information Technology for Economic and Clinical Health Act." February 17. Accessed July 20, 2013. http://www.hhs.gov/ocr/privacy/hipaa/understanding/coveredentities/hitechact.pdf.

———. 2013. "Sample Business Associate Agreement Provisions." In *Business Associate Contracts*. January 25. Accessed July 7, 2013. http://www.hhs.gov/ocr/privacy/hipaa/understanding/coveredentities/contractprov.html. Department of Veterans Affairs. 2004. *Medical Device Isolation Architecture Guide*. St Louis: Center for Engineering & Occupational Safety and Health (CEOSH). Accessed July 11, 2013. http://www.nwfusion.com/news/2004/VA_VLAN_Guide_040430.pdf. Experian. 2012. "Data Breach Response Guide." Accessed July 7, 2013. http://www.experian.com/assets/data-breach/brochures/response-guide.pdf.

Feder, Barnaby J. 2008. "A Heart Device Is Found Vulnerable to Hacker Attacks." *New York Times*, March 12. Accessed July 9, 2013. http://www.nytimes.com/2008/03/12/business/12heart-web.html?_r=0.

Felt-Lisk, Suzanne, and Jennifer Humensky. 2003. "Privacy Issues in Mental Health and Substance Abuse Treatment: Information Sharing Between Providers and Managed Care Organizations: Final Report." *Department of Health and Human Services*. January 17. Accessed June 23, 2013. http://aspe.hhs.gov/datacncl/reports/MHPrivacy/MHPrivacy.pdf.

Fogarty, Kevin. 2012. "Tech Predictions Gone Wrong." *Computerworld*, October 22. Accessed June 24, 2013. http://www.computerworld.com/s/article/9232610/Tech_predictions_gone_wrong.

Greene, Adam H. (2012). "Navigating HIPAA While Moving to the Cloud." *Healthcare Information and Management Systems Society*. Accessed July 10, 2013. http://www.himss.org/files/HIMSSorg/content/files/CS07NavigatingHIPAAWhileMovingtotheCloud.pdf.

Harris, Shon. 2012. *CISSP All-in-One Exam Guide*, 6th ed. New York: McGraw-Hill.

Health Level Seven International. 2013. "About HL7." Accessed July 8, 2013. http://www.hl7.org/about/index.cfm?ref=nav.

Herold, Rebecca. 2002. "What Is The Difference Between Security and Privacy?" *CSI Alert*, July. Accessed July 2, 2013. http://www.privacyguidance.com/downloads/privacyandsecurity.pdf.

Horowitz, Brian T. 2010. "EMC, VMWare Deploy VDI Cloud at North Carolina Hospital." *eWeek*, December 9. Accessed July 20, 2013. http://www.eweek.com/c/a/Health-Care-IT/EMC-VMware-Deploy-VDI-Cloud-at-North-Carolina-Hospital-783508.

The Joint Commission. 2011. *Comprehensive Accreditation Manual for Hospitals: The Official Handbook*. Accessed July 20, 2013. http://www.jointcommission.org/assets/1/6/2011_CAMH_SE.pdf.

———. 2013. "About the Joint Commission." http://www.jointcommission.org/about_us/about_the_joint_commission_main.aspx.

Katehakis, Dimitrios G., Stelios Sfakianakis, Manolis Tsiknakis, and Stelios C. Orphanoudakis. 2001. "An Infrastructure for Integrated Electronic Health Record Services: The Role of XML (Extensible Markup Language)." *Journal of Medical Internet Research*, 3(1). doi:10.2196/jmir.3.1.e7.

Kharif, Olga. 2011. "GE-Philips Health Equipment Market Opens as Smartphones Win FDA Nod: Tech." *Bloomberg*, September 29. Accessed July 2, 2013. http://www.bloomberg.com/news/2011-09-29/ge-philips-health-equipment-market-opens-as-smartphones-win-fda-nod-tech.html.

Kissel, Richard, ed. 2013. *NIST IR 7298 Revision 2: Glossary of Key Information Security Terms*. National Institute of Standards and Technology. May. Accessed July 7, 2013. http://nvlpubs.nist.gov/nistpubs/ir/2013/NIST.IR.7298r2.pdf.

Klein, Sharon, and Odia Kagan. 2013. "Unhack My Heart: FDA Issues Guidance To Mitigate Cybersecurity Threats In Medical Devices." *Pepper Hamilton LLP*. Last modified July 4. Accessed July 21, 2013. http://www.

mondaq.com/unitedstates/x/248634/Data+Protection+Privacy/Unhack+
    My+Heart+FDA+Issues+Guidance+To+Mitigate+Cybersecurity+Threa
    ts+In+Medical+Devices.
Merriam-Webster. 2013. "Definition of iatrogenesis." Accessed August 12,
    2013. http://www.merriam-webster.com/medical/iatrogenesis
"Modifications to the HIPAA Privacy, Security, Enforcement, and Breach
    Notification Rules Under the Health Information Technology for Eco-
    nomic and Clinical Health Act and the Genetic Information Non-
    discrimination Act; Other Modifications to the HIPAA Rules." 2013.
    Federal Register 78(17). January 25. Accessed June 30, 2013. http://www.
    gpo.gov/fdsys/pkg/FR-2013-01-25/pdf/2013-01073.pdf.
National Health Information Sharing and Analysis Center. 2012. "National
    Healthcare Cybersecurity Protection & Education." http://www.nhisac.
    org/wp-content/uploads/National-Healthcare-Cybersecurity-Protection-
    Framework_NH-ISAC.pdf.
National Institute for Standards and Technology. 2012. NIST SP 800-30 Revi-
    sion 1: Guide for Conducting Risk Assessments. Accessed July 5, 2013.
    http://csrc.nist.gov/publications/nistpubs/800-30-rev1/sp800_30_r1.pdf.
Ponemon Institute. 2013. "2013 Cost of Data Breach Study: Global Analysis."
    Symantec Corporation. May. https://www4.symantec.com/mktginfo/white-
    paper/053013_GL_NA_WP_Ponemon-2013-Cost-of-a-Data-Breach-
    Report_daiNA_cta72382.pdf.
ProActive Solutions, Inc. 2013. "Healthcare VDI Implementation." Accessed
    July 20, 2013. http://www.proactivesolutions.com/wps/wcm/connect/
    b1c59f80486d65428ca6ed083cdfab32/VDI_CaseStudy_9.11_Final.pdf?
    MOD=AJPERES&CACHEID=b1c59f80486d65428ca6ed083cdfab32.
Scholl, Matthew, Kevin Stine, Joan Hash, Pauline Bowen, Arnold Johnson,
    Carla Dancy Smith, and Daniel I. Steinberg. 2008. NIST Special
    Publication 800-66 Revision 1: An Introductory Resource Guide for
    Implementing the Health Insurance Portability and Accountability Act
    (HIPAA) Security Rule. National Institute of Standards and Technol-
    ogy. October. Accessed July 20, 2013. http://csrc.nist.gov/publications/
    nistpubs/800-66-Rev1/SP-800-66-Revision1.pdf.
Shoniregun, Charles A., Fredrick Mtenzi, and Kudakwashe Dube. 2010. Elec-
    tronic Healthcare Information Security. New York: Springer.
Stebner, Beth. 2013. "Kim Kardashian Baby: Six People Fired for 'Improperly
    Accessing' Medical Records at L.A. Hospital where Reality Star gave
    Birth." New York Daily News, July 13. Accessed July 11, 2013. http://
    www.nydailynews.com/entertainment/gossip/hospital-workers-fired-
    accessing-kim-kardashians-medical-records-report-article-1.1398107#
    ixzz2Z27pNtrl.

Suby, Michael. 2013. "2013 (ISC)² Global Information Security Work-force Study." (ISC)². Accessed July 2, 2013. https://www.isc2.org/uploadedFiles/%28ISC%292_Public_Content/2013%20Global%20Information%20Security%20Workforce%20Study%20Feb%202013.pdf.

Symantec Corporation. 2008. *Symantec Global Internet Security Threat Report, Trends for July-December 07.* Vol 13. http://eval.symantec.com/mktginfo/enterprise/white_papers/b-whitepaper_internet_security_threat_report_xiii_04-2008.en-us.pdf.

Tanielian, Terri, and Lisa H. Jaycox, eds. 2008. *Invisible Wounds of War: Psychological and Cognitive Injuries, Their Consequences, and Services to Assist Recovery.* Santa Monica, CA: Rand Publishing.

Weiner, Jonathan. P., Toni Kfuri, Kitty Chan, and Jinnet B. Fowles. 2007. " 'e-Iatrogenesis': The Most Critical Unintended Consequence of CPOE and Other HIT." *Journal of the American Medical Informatics Association* 14(3):387–8. doi: 10.1197/jamia.M2338.

Woodie, Alex. 2013. "Big Data at the Heart of a New Cyber Security Model." *datanami,* July 3. Accessed July 20, 2013. http://www.datanami.com/datanami/2013-07-03/big_data_at_the_heart_of_a_new_cyber_security_model.html.

Chapter 4

Cybersecurity and Telecommunications

K. Maman and Tom Connors

Introduction

The Vulnerable State of Cybersecurity in a Hyperconnected World

Each day, the world becomes more dependent on telecommunications. In the last decade alone, the dramatic growth in broadband connectivity, spearheaded by the mobile revolution and the explosion of social media, has forced disruptive changes on numerous industries. As difficult as it may be to comprehend, this is just the early stage of a major revolution that will affect the world as profoundly as the agricultural and industrial revolutions before it. Portio Research estimates that the worldwide mobile subscriber base reached over 6.5 billion in 2012. Portio further estimates that 655 million smartphone handsets were shipped during 2012, representing 39 percent of handset shipments. It forecasts that by 2016, the worldwide mobile subscriber base will increase to 8.5 billion and smartphones will comprise over 50 percent of the handset shipments. The dramatic increase in the use of smartphones represents a virtual tsunami of mobile device adoption that is gathering momentum, particularly in developing economies, where, according to a recent *Time* article, a UN study noted that more people have access to mobile phones than have access to toilets. For many, the smartphone will be the primary computing device compared with tablets or personal computers. The mobile revolution, combined with the social media phenomenon, will drive additional applications and capabilities far beyond what we see today. However, this dramatic revolution will be accompanied with a similar dramatic increase in potential vulnerability to cyber threats unless there is a fundamental shift in the cybersecurity capabilities of our public and private institutions. Telecommunications carriers and equipment companies will play a vital role in the global cybersecurity ecosystem of the future.

It is worth considering how vital mobility and connectivity have become to the U.S. economy and everyday life. For instance, CTIA (originally known as the Cellular Telecommunications and Internet Association, now called simply The Wireless Association) has noted that wireless adds something on the order of $150 billion to the U.S. gross domestic product each year and contributes to the employment of nearly four million people (Altschul and Marinho 2013). Between 2009 and 2012, mobile traffic grew more than 1,200 percent, doubling each year for the past four years. A recent Mobile Work Exchange study of U.S. federal employees conducted by CTIA found that employees had increased their productivity by the equivalent of nine hours per week thanks to the adoption of mobile devices. That alone yielded gains totaling some $28 billion. Interestingly, these gains were accomplished with nearly half of federal employees using their own devices under a bring-your-own-device (BYOD) policy.

Although people are generally familiar with the expanding capabilities of smartphones and their ability to render clear images and video (and the disruptive effect these devices have had on consumer electronics including digital cameras, camcorders, and MP3 players), the true potential of the mobile platform is really just starting to be realized, thanks to the hundreds of thousands of applications available to users. The continuing and rapidly accelerating advancements in processing speed, storage, graphics, and power combined with the continued, dramatic increases in the availability of high-speed wireless bandwidth will enable innovations far beyond what is contemplated in our current environment. Add to that the growth of smart grids, wearable technology, and machine-to-machine (M2M) technology and the nature of the hyperconnected world of the near future becomes clearer.

In fact, M2M technology is an element of what is being called the *Internet of Things*, a term coined in 1999 by Kevin Ashton, cofounder of the Auto-Id center at the Massachusetts Institute of Technology (MIT) that refers to the trend of connecting a wide variety of devices or objects to ubiquitous broadband. The accelerating pace at which a wide variety of hyperconnected devices (e.g., medical monitoring, home appliances and security, autos/telematics, to name a few) are just as, if not more so, revolutionary than the explosion of mobile technology. The Internet of Things implicitly invites the application of big data to the ocean of information it will help create. Although the technological limitations of the past continue to recede exponentially, the security implications and potential vulnerabilities accelerate at a similarly dramatic rate.

As with mobile technology (and it is worth noting that much of the Internet of Things will likely be mobile, too), there are many contributing parties and technologies at the hardware and application levels and in the ownership and transmission of data. As the Internet of Things evolves, it will likely come to dwarf the existing scale of connectivity. For instance, according to David Evans, chief futurist for the Cisco Internet Business Solutions Group (IBSG), the number of Internet connections globally exceeded the world's population in 1998. A substantial portion of this growth is "non-human" and the proportion is set to grow rapidly. An ABI Research report (2013) projects that there will be more than thirty billion wirelessly connected devices in service by 2020!

Because this number encompasses such a tremendous range of technologies and use cases, developing and implementing security practices for the future will require a flexible and widely encompassing approach that is technology-neutral and delivers the kind of security and privacy that users will want and need, without excessive complexity or rigidity that could discourage or disrupt innovation or carry significant overhead.

As convergence among technologies becomes a reality, and as wireless connectivity becomes ubiquitous and accepted, security measures will need to evolve with respect to the requirements of users, and the capabilities and purposes of that which is connected. Security (and privacy) may need to become more content sensitive: Rather than "locking down" the devices, it will be important to have a contextual view of information and help ensure that information that is sensitive and important is appropriately protected and respected.

Because the Internet of Things is a global phenomenon, it is also critical that future cybersecurity practices address emerging challenges on a global basis. As shown by recent tensions between the United States and China relating to allegations of widespread, state-sponsored cyber intrusions originating from China into both public and private institutions or the tension between the United States and Russia relating to the Edward Snowden incident, the management of cybersecurity will continue to be heavily affected by geopolitical considerations and challenges as well as global regulations.

The dramatic increase in the volume and complexity of cyber-attacks on public and private institutions, especially those sponsored by nation-states, is especially ominous when one considers that the dependence on the Internet of Things will only increase to serve our potential vulnerability to cyber-attacks unless dramatic improvements are made to "harden" our cyber defenses and improve our resiliency.

State of the Cybersecurity Telecommunications Workforce

Putting People in a New Context

The ceaseless advances in processing power and software, married with sensors, data, and other factors, have continued to advance automation and lead it in new directions. Indeed, even defining this new frontier is difficult. However, where traditional automation, now a familiar story around the world, focused mostly on repetitive tasks with only a modest need for built-in intelligence, the new wave of automation has a far greater reach. For instance, manufacturing automation often involved moving and placing materials and performing specific, repetitive activities such as drilling a hole or milling a certain segment of metal. Over time, these processes became more qualitative and less reliant on human operators, leading to the "lights-out" factory, where machines operated autonomously for relatively long periods.

What is different now is that the technology is affecting a huge new swath of employment. Machines automated by computers can begin to understand and respond to voice commands and other inputs that are not narrowly predefined. The instructions can now be unstructured rather than rigid and procedural (consider the intelligence of Google's self-driving car for example). This opens huge opportunities to employ computers to drive new kinds of automation. In fact, computers can search for relevant information and make decisions about it, as is the case in the automated discovery processes used increasingly in legal disputes, with minimal human oversight. Again, this implies a new mastery over unstructured data, until recently a domain for human intelligence alone.

It is highly unlikely that humans will be removed completely from these processes in the near future. Humans can discern subtleties of meaning and relevance that, at least today, still escape machine intelligence. Yet, the ability of machinery to sort through essentially unlimited amounts of data without ever tiring makes this new capability extremely powerful wherever it is applied. Because machine intelligence also includes the ability to learn from experience, much as humans do, using algorithms to detect patterns that might not even be clear to people, it is likely that these capabilities will continue to improve rapidly.

As noted by Erik Brynjofsson and Andrew McAfee in *Race Against The Machine*, "We are in the throes of a Great Restructuring. Our technologies are racing ahead but many of our skills and organizations are lagging behind. So it's urgent that we understand these phenomena, discuss their implications, and come up with strategies that allow human workers to race ahead with machines instead of racing with them."

Cybersecurity is one area where there is a severe shortage of qualified job applicants, and employers from both the public and private sectors are actively competing for a limited pool of qualified talent. Both the Department of Homeland Security (DHS) and the National Security Agency (NSA) have publicly stated their plans to dramatically increase their hiring of cybersecurity specialists, whereas private industry will need to accelerate hiring to address the growing need. In addition to aggressively hiring computer security professionals

to support and maintain their back office infrastructure, several tele-
coms are focusing on cybersecurity services as ripe opportunities for
revenue growth from commercial clients.

Current Issues in Telecom Cybersecurity

Long-Range Forecast: Cloudy and Unsettled with
High Risk of Disruption

Then, there is the cloud. A catchphrase that gained currency in the
wake of the dot-com bubble, cloud computing has gone from leading
edge to mainstream in a wide range of use cases. The telecommunications sector, obviously, is a critical enabler of the cloud because
physical disaggregation and seamless communication linkages are its
essence. Larger telecom providers are increasingly leveraging their network capabilities to provide cloud-based services to enterprise clients,
with a focus on particular industries where highly reliable and secure
communications are especially critical such as in health care.

The reasons for the rise of cloud computing are both technical
and financial. On the technology side, available bandwidth has grown
dramatically. Businesses and even individuals have access to substantial
data-movement capabilities, meaning that many kinds of activities,
except perhaps those requiring real-time and high-speed transaction
processing, can now be processed or stored remotely, echoing in some
ways the old era of "dumb" terminals connected to a powerful but
relatively distant mainframe. The difference now is that there is a
seamless availability of processing power and data storage that allows
tasks to be handed off easily from one layer to another.

On the business side, cloud computing has the potential to
broadly rationalize costs and investments. Instead of a patchwork of
solutions and investments in information technology (IT) made by
each organization in response to ever-changing requirements, the cloud
represents the potential for leveraging scale, leveraging leading practices, and hiring for the capabilities an organization needs when and
only when it needs them. Rather than capital-intensive investments
in projects that often have associated risk, companies can now look

toward a future where defining requirements is tantamount to fulfilling those requirements, solutions can be commoditized, and choices are a matter of selecting those with preferred price-performance options. The bottom line is that cloud computing should be less expensive than traditional alternatives, which could in itself have a profound effect on an organization's cost structure.

In fact, cloud computing is well on its way to fulfilling the hopes of its proponents. As a critical element in a connected, global infrastructure, cloud computing supports or enables many other types of technology and innovation, particularly mobile Internet. Applications depend on external resources and the cloud is generally where those resources exist. McKinsey (2013) expects the "total economic impact of cloud technology" to range from $1.7 trillion to $6.2 trillion annually by 2025, thanks in part to delivery of cloud-based services, but also from potential improvements in enterprise productivity.

Exactly how this transformation may unfold is not so clear. For example, the market, which is potentially vast, remains in its infancy. McKinsey authors speculate that large enterprise customers of current cloud providers could even decide to leverage their own assets and knowledge base and become providers in their own right. Competition could grow internationally if regulatory barriers are lowered, and numerous startups or existing companies could continue to reshape the market as providers or customers. For the customers, whether they are in business, government, or academia, the ability to rapidly acquire, use, and dispose of computing power could produce a flurry of entrepreneurial activity as the cloud pushes aside many traditional barriers to entry for startups.

Then, there are the unknowns and potential risks. For instance, many businesses and individuals remain uncomfortable with the security of the cloud, despite its generally strong record so far. But were major security glitches to appear, confidence could erode. Furthermore, virtualization, a technology that is central to the cloud, also provides wide benefits to businesses, allowing them to gain higher utilization and reliability from their existing assets. With virtualization growing in parallel with the cloud, it remains a potential alternative for those not susceptible to the lure of outside IT services. Additionally, wholesale adoption of the cloud by larger enterprises remains largely unexplored from a migration and operational perspective. Still, although the exact scale and timeline of cloud adoption may remain in question, it is likely to be a game changer for many organizations while potentially disrupting some of the traditional players in the software and hardware industry.

The Security Side of Technological Change

Meanwhile, security efforts have barely kept up with the emerging challenges, and doomsayers warn of a cyber 9/11 on the horizon. Fortunately, governments and the telecommunication and IT industry are increasingly working together to begin to address the numerous challenges.

It is worth considering what is meant by cybersecurity. The International Telecommunications Union (2013) has defined cybersecurity as follows:

> Cybersecurity is the collection of tools, policies, security concepts, security safeguards, guidelines, risk management approaches, actions, training, leading practices, assurance and technologies that can be used to protect the cyber environment and organization and user's assets. Organization and user's assets include connected computing devices, personnel, infrastructure, applications, services, telecommunications systems, and the totality of transmitted and/or stored information in the cyber environment. Cybersecurity strives to help ensure the attainment and maintenance of the security properties of the organization and user's assets against relevant security risks in the cyber environment. The general security objectives comprise the following:
>
> • Confidentiality: protecting information from unauthorized disclosure
>
> • Integrity: protecting information from authorized modification
>
> • Availability: ensuring information is accessible when needed

That clarity is good to keep in mind in thinking about the challenges ahead and how to balance responses with business priorities.

Deloitte Touche Tohmatsu Limited's (DTTL) "2013 Global Security Study for the Technology, Media & Telecommunications (TMT) Industry: Raising the Bar" conveys the cybersecurity challenges. A key finding is a delineation of the top five security threats. In 2012, according to the Deloitte survey, these threats were:

1. Mobile devices (34 percent)

2. Security breaches involving third parties (25 percent)

3. Employee errors and omissions (20 percent)

4. Faster adoption of emerging technologies (18 percent)

5. Employee abuse of IT systems and information (17 percent)

Cybersecurity threats continue to increase on multiple fronts, including "hacktivists," cybercriminals, and state-sponsored actors intent on targeting intellectual property and customer information, and increasing business disruption. The TMT survey noted that the increased adoption of emerging technologies, such as the cloud, helped fuel the level of security breaches; 75 percent of the 138 global organizations surveyed were reported to have suffered a breach. The overarching message of the survey is clear: TMT companies need to significantly increase their investments in information security to better manage the real risks to the business while also meeting the public expectation of improved information security.

Deloitte's survey shows that more than half of the respondents report spending between just 1 percent and 6 percent of their IT budget on information security. Moreover, 52 percent of respondents indicated that their expenditures on security are falling behind or just starting to catch up to previous years' investment levels.

Irfan Saif, who leads Deloitte's security and privacy services to the TMT industry, noted: "The threats to information have never been at a higher level and in today's hyper connected world there is no such thing as an isolated threat" (Deloitte 2011). Unfortunately, he adds, many TMT organizations are investing a smaller portion of their IT budget than in previous years on information security. "This level of investment and attention is insufficient to effectively address a corporate responsibility to manage risk and the public imperative of improved information security."

A further finding of the survey is that chief information security officers (CISOs), who are primarily responsible for information security at many organizations, are stretched far beyond a reasonable capacity. For instance, many CISOs, including 51 percent of survey participants, also handle business continuity management, disaster recovery planning, physical security, and risk management. According to Saif, information security should not be viewed as just a CISO activity. There needs to be more C-level attention to security and a corporate climate that fosters proactive management of growing security risks. Cross-functional collaboration and ownership are integral to an effective enterprise information security program. Additionally, CISOs also must manage the growing number of threats introduced by employees themselves via increased use of social media and use of personal mobile devices in the workplace.

Mobile devices, which are discussed later, were identified as the top security threat for 2012, according to almost 40 percent of respondents. Specifically, although the concept of BYOD as opposed to providing corporate-owned mobile devices to employees offers many potential benefits, it also presents many challenges and potential issues in a variety of areas including data confidentiality, employee privacy, application development and distribution, and mobile device support.

Not lost in the survey is the increased scrutiny focused on information security and corresponding increased regulatory efforts by governments around the world to protect the public. As a result, compliance with information security regulations and legislation is rated the top security initiative for TMT companies.

Likewise, the National Cyber Security Alliance (NCSA) and security vendor McAfee have released an online safety survey showing a gap between good practices and the real world (JZ Analytics

2012). For instance, 64 percent of users polled said they believed their smartphones were safe from hackers. However, 64 percent have never installed security software or applications to protect against viruses or malware, and 58 percent have never backed up their devices. Likewise, according to the survey, some 48 percent of working Americans say they are allowed to use a personal tablet, smartphone, or laptop to perform job functions, and 31 percent of those surveyed say they can connect to their work network using these devices. Yet, a full 44 percent say their employers do not have formal policies regulating device usage, indicating huge security vulnerability.

More vulnerabilities emerge every day and are exploited by those with malicious intent. Although there is certainly ongoing progress, over all, the cybersecurity picture is grim.

Similarly, CompTIA, the IT industry association, recently completed its Tenth Annual Information Security Trends survey, which highlighted three major trends. One of those trends is the growing acceptance of, and dependence on, the cloud, where vulnerabilities in transit remain an important cause for concern. Another is mobility, which has skyrocketed in importance. In contrast with cloud security, where much of the underlying technology is familiar and closely related to what has been used in-house for years, mobility and especially the BYOD trend are based on less-mature technology that often is inherently less secure, yet more and more personal and corporate data transits or resides in the mobile environment. Indeed, the rush to innovate, adding features and getting to the consumer market first has, in some cases, resulted in creating new vulnerabilities that have been exploited. With so much vulnerable personal and corporate information, some observers see this as the new frontier for hackers. Finally, the CTIA study noted the dangers associated with unprecedented rank-and-file access to technology, which the cases of Bradley Manning and Edward Snowden illustrate. In government and the private sector, relatively low-level individuals may possess access to information and the means to steal or disburse information that can be extremely damaging to the organizations for which they work. In the past, the limits of technology made similar escapades far more difficult, but often security practices have not kept up with this new threat.

Similar to previous years, 2013 has been pockmarked with devastating and embarrassing security failures that have added cost and risk for individuals, enterprises, and governments. New headlines also point to the widespread and growing practice of government hacking and spying on other governments and entities. In other words, the threat is no longer simply from clever and sometimes well-organized criminal elements, but from deep-pocketed entities with nearly unlimited resources. And there is no indication that attackers have done more than whet their appetites.

Current Threats in Telecom Cybersecurity

Threat Technology

As attacks are multiplying in number, their sophistication is growing as well. For instance, distributed denial of service (DDoS) attacks are no longer just standalone events. Increasingly DDoS attacks are being used to mask other kinds of targeted attacks, simultaneously overwhelming institutional defenses. Botnets, which occur when a computer is affected by malware and are used to perform automated tasks of which the user is unaware, are readily available for use by bad actors and have increased in sophistication to the point where they can acquire identities and appear to be legitimate users. Malware remains a potent threat vector that can affect individuals and institutions, costing organizations millions of dollars just to try to keep up.

The Verizon 2013 Data Breach Investigations Report, spanning more than 47,000 reported security incidents, 8,621 confirmed data disclosures, and at least 44 million compromised records, quantified many aspects of the current threat environment. For instance, 37 percent of breaches affected financial organizations; 24 percent occurred in retail environments and restaurants; 20 percent of network intrusions involved manufacturing, transportation, and utilities; 20 percent hit information and professional services firms; and 38 percent of breaches affected larger organizations. Furthermore, although acknowledging anecdotal evidence of the substantial threat from insiders, Verizon researchers found overwhelming evidence of the large outsider threat: 92 percent of reported incidents were perpetrated by outsiders, whereas just 14 percent were committed by insiders and a mere 1 percent implicated a company's business partners.

The authors of the Verizon report pointed out the vital and dangerous role played by malware in mounting attacks. Indeed, although the percentage of data breaches involving malware was lower in 2012, that is only a relative number; in fact the absolute number of malware attacks continues to grow and puts the method in the top two threats. At present, attackers who already have gained access to a system are the most frequent users of malware. Distribution of malware by email also is an important threat. And, the authors note, "malware seeks to . . . 1) grant or prolong access and control, 2) capture data, or 3) weaken the system in some way." Achieving those goals together often is the ultimate aim.

Of the many different types of malware, spyware, including key loggers and form-grabbers, saw the largest increase, according to Verizon researchers. However, they warn, the "individual pieces of malware used in such attacks are often multifunctional." Furthermore, financially oriented breaches tend to depend on spyware to perform functions such as capturing payment card data at point-of-sale terminals. Other forms of spyware include screenshot grabbers, RAM scrapers, and utilities.

Not far out on the horizon are other as-yet underexploited vulnerabilities, including highly virtualized environments, where virtual-machine-to-virtual-machine communication is rarely monitored, or at least not monitored effectively. Similarly, a transition to Internet Protocol version 6 (IPv6) may leave some organizations vulnerable, because security systems and processes often remain focused on IPv4.

In other words, cybersecurity capabilities are being challenged on many fronts. In little more than a generation, the threat picture has evolved from the occasional rogue hacker, such as the teenager portrayed in the 1980s movie *WarGames*, to highly sophisticated, often secretive, and frequently state-supported threats, and the aforementioned organized criminals and hacktivists. This new environment produces more threats, and threats that continually change; there is no time for organizations to catch their breath. The threat just grows more dangerous.

Even brief and relatively unsophisticated events can be consequential. For instance, an April 2013 attack on the Associated Press's Twitter account falsely reported a bomb attack at the White House, briefly causing a full percentage point drop in financial markets (including a reduction of $136.5 billion in the S&P 500 Index). Also in the first quarter of 2013, a successful global effort to steal from ATMs was revealed. It is believed that hackers broke into the network of payment card-processing companies, allowing them to transfer huge positive balances to large numbers of prepaid Visa and MasterCard debit cards. Account numbers were then sent to local criminals who then loaded them onto fake cards. In a matter of hours, nearly $45 million was stolen.

DDoS attacks have grown in ferocity and intensity, too. Starting in fall 2012, for example, U.S. banks endured a withering series of attacks. Then in March 2013, a DDoS attack in Europe, known as Operation Stophaus, targeted The Spamhaus Project, a Geneva-based not-for-profit organization that has focused on fighting Internet spam operations. Spamhaus faced traffic levels of 300 gigabytes per second, resulting in problems not only for Spamhaus, but also in delays and disruptions across many parts of the Internet.

Even when organizations do invest in advanced security technologies, there remains the traditional vulnerability of human beings. Many kinds of attacks exploit human gullibility and good will. Attacks often are so well disguised that even sophisticated users can get taken in. Advanced persistent threats and other kinds of attacks often include "phishing" attacks and similar scams that encourage individuals to accept malware files, provide corporate or personal information, or visit dangerous websites. Many organizations have tried to combat these threats with education and stricter policies, but success has been elusive. Scammers are continuously adapting and evolving their specific approaches.

To be successful, education must be ongoing and consistent so that issues remain top of mind and so that users are kept up to date about emerging threats. Threat actors recognize that insiders have knowledge and access, so engaging individuals to participate inadvertently in an attack can be very worthwhile from an attacker's perspective and will thus remain vulnerable over the long term. In addition to active attacks, it also is important that users are consistently educated about the acceptable use of mobile devices, USB drives, and other good data-handling practices. Beyond education, there also are good housekeeping practices that often are inconsistently applied. Companies, for example, sometimes fail to handle the security issues related to employee termination, which can leave former employees with extensive access to sensitive data. And, of course, insiders who might be tempted to breach trust need to be clearly informed of potential consequences so they will have a strong incentive to avoid such behavior.

The infamous Nosal case, from several years ago, in which a trusted employee departed with sensitive information, should have put organizations on notice to be particularly aware of those with access to sensitive data. In that instance, resulting in a court case, the *United States v. Nosal*, a ruling from the U.S. Court of Appeals for the Ninth Circuit, held that employees could not be criminally prosecuted under the Computer Fraud and Abuse Act (CFAA) if they violated an employer's computer-use policies (although Nosal was not able to escape other charges, such as theft of trade secrets). The ruling called into question the meaning of the crucial phrase, "exceeded authorization" from within the CFAA statute, in a case where employees are authorized to access the computer and do not actually circumvent existing protection mechanisms.

More recently, of course, theft of secrets and exceeding authority have become the stuff of headlines around the world with the previously mentioned actions of self-proclaimed whistleblower Edward Snowden, who was last employed through a consulting services provider for the federal government, Booz Allen Hamilton, as a system administrator at an NSA facility in Hawaii. Snowden had held previous positions under a high-level security clearance at both the NSA and CIA. By his own admission, he used his knowledge of the agencies and their secret programs to access classified documents that he arranged to provide to the press, specifically *The Guardian* newspaper, based in the United Kingdom.

In fact, it is crucial that individuals like Snowden, such as database administrators or firewall administrators with additional levels of access and the ability to access many kinds of sensitive data, not to mention the capacity to "cover their tracks," be clearly informed about potential enforcement actions should they ever breach institutional trust. And, of course, they need to be monitored themselves to ensure that they are not lax in their practices, or, indeed, engaging in prohibited activities. A recent article in the *New York Times* pointed out that Snowden, publicly described by the federal government as a system administrator, actually appears to have had a role with much higher access to systems and inside information, making the lack of oversight under which he operated even more surprising (Shane and Sanger 2013).

Even the *Nosal and Snowden* cases are only two extreme examples from among many. Another recent article in the *New York Times* highlighted two other representative major insider actions that were simply the result of employee discontent (Drew and Sengupta 2013). The first example cited was of a network administrator in the municipal government of San Francisco who changed many of the passwords across the network when he learned that he was going to be laid off. For twelve days, he held the city government hostage until he finally revealed the passwords that he held, in the meantime causing widespread disruption of government activities. More recently, a New Jersey pharmaceutical company suffered nearly $1 million in damages when an irate former IT administrator succeeded in deleting critical files, disrupting company operations for days.

But there are glimmers of hope and change. Although the historical response to cyber threats seems inadequate by many measures, there are grounds for optimism, particularly in the form of government initiatives and public–private initiatives.

Telecommunications Sector Impact

Of course, for the telecommunications (telecom) sector, cybersecurity brings a specific set of challenges, especially given the central role it plays as the conduit for sensitive traffic and data, as well as a potential attack vector.

The DHS National Infrastructure Protection Plan puts particular emphasis on the importance of the telecom sector (U.S. 2009). The DHS notes that the nation's communications infrastructure is a complex system of systems that incorporates multiple technologies and services with diverse ownership. Specifically, that infrastructure includes wireline, wireless, satellite, cable, and broadcasting capabilities, and includes the transport networks that support the Internet and other critical information systems. The communications companies that own, operate, and supply the infrastructure have usually considered potential natural disasters and accidental disruptions in crafting resilience architecture, business continuity plans, and disaster recovery strategies. The interconnected and interdependent nature of these service provider networks has fostered crucial information-sharing and cooperative response and recovery relationships for decades. "Even in today's highly competitive business environment, the community has a long standing tradition of cooperation and trust because problems with one service provider's network nearly always impact networks owned and operated by other network providers," the study notes.

Although carriers have the capacity to monitor traffic, they typically do so inconsistently and often only in a minimal way, in support of general performance goals. In fact, to date, carriers have been reluctant to take on the cost and responsibility associated with greater monitoring of either metadata or actual content. However, the potential benefits of higher levels of monitoring may eventually force a change. The recent disclosures of monitoring performed by the National Security Agency (known as PRISM and disclosed publicly by the Snowden incident) of meta phone records and social media traffic has triggered significant debate on the delicate balance between protecting national security interest against preserving an individual's constitutional right to privacy. In defense of the existing monitoring procedures, the director of the FBI recently cited twelve potential terrorist threats that were averted because of the intelligence collected from the PRISM program. Additionally, in the aftermath of terrorist incidents like the Boston Marathon bombing, some have noted that there were clear signals (including social media activity) that could have potentially averted the incident if there were stronger monitoring capabilities and better ability to connect the dots in cyberspace that become clear indicators of a looming threat after the fact.

Mobile: The Weakest Link

Technologically, one of the most worrisome aspects on the horizon for cybersecurity is the dramatic, rapid growth of mobile device adoption. Portio Research estimates that the worldwide mobile subscriber base reached over 6.5 billion in 2012. Portio further estimates that 655 million smartphone handsets were shipped during 2012, representing 39 percent of handset shipments. It forecasts that by 2016, the worldwide mobile subscriber base will increase to 8.5 billion and smartphones will comprise over 50 percent of the handset shipments. Over the next several years, as the majority of cellphone users convert to smartphones, there will be a vast increase in the scale of mobile computing. When combined with the projected exponential increase in M2M communications (e.g., vehicle telematics, industrial, and medical applications), it becomes apparent why many believe we are only in the early stages what some refer to as the Mobile Revolution.

By some estimates, more than half of all mobile applications have significant security vulnerabilities such as corrupt code. These issues, among others, could delay the full maturation of the era of hyperconnectedness and perhaps even limit the ability of mobile technology to achieve its full potential. Security for mobile devices is an inherently complex subject. Malware, for instance, which is a familiar challenge in the desktop environment, is hardly recognized as a concern by device users, and anti-malware is almost unknown. Similarly, current overreliance on single-factor authentication is too risky. Devices will need to move toward multifactor authentication, which will need to become the rule rather than the exception. Mobile personal identifiers may make devices more powerful and part of the solution rather than part of the problem. The dimensions of this approach could include locational information, biometrics, and alerts.

Beyond the device itself, organizations are looking at technologies such as VPN-less access that can eliminate the need to open ports in the firewall. Similarly, creation of an on-device "sandbox" to isolate applications and data from each other may help provide more resilience and protection across the system. Greater use of encryption can also help with these issues. To aid in implementing and managing these policies and technologies, many organizations are setting up specific BYOD policies and both mobile device management and mobile application management solutions.

Securing the Telecom Equipment Supply Chain

A related, but less visible issue is telecom supply chain security. Telecom providers depend on equipment, software, and services from many sources, and the rising trend toward embedding intelligence into hardware proportionately increases the potential vulnerability of the hardware to cyber threats. Instances of counterfeit equipment inadvertently placed in service have been occurring with increasing frequency. As more functionality becomes embedded in software, the potential for misdeeds grows. Indeed, these issues have been at the heart of recent controversies in the United States and Europe over potential purchases from Huawei Technologies, a Chinese company banned from doing business by some countries.

These supply chain security issues are particularly important to the telecommunications industry. However, answers are not simple. In May 2013, Congress took a look at the issue through the House Subcommittee on Communications and Technology, which held a hearing on how to address supply chain security challenges. A stated goal was, essentially, how to avoid killing the goose that has laid the golden egg, namely the invaluable connectivity to which business, government, and consumers have grown accustomed.

Although a range of views came from the hearing, a common theme focused on the need to avoid knee-jerk, simplistic overreactions that might dampen technological evolution and reduce the effectiveness of existing technology. On the other hand, technological Balkanization needs to be avoided. The hearing included testimony about the range of initiatives being considered or implemented within government, such as the Department of Defense–proposed supply chain regulations built on the implementation of Section 818 of the 2012

National Defense Authorization Act (NDAA) and Section 833 of the 2013 NDAA, which would demand that suppliers implement systems to detect counterfeit electronic components. Meanwhile, a report from the House Permanent Select Committee on Intelligence also urged avoidance of equipment made by Huawei and ZTE, due to concerns about the relationship of those suppliers to the Chinese government (Rogers and Ruppersberger 2012).

Cybersecurity Laws and Policies

As in much of the rest of the world, in the United States there have been many efforts to strengthen cybersecurity through legislation and regulation. For instance, there have been more than fifteen bills proposed across twenty committees in Congress. The reluctance to legislate and the risks for depending on voluntary action were on display in 2012, when Sen. Jay Rockefeller wrote to the CEO of every company in the Fortune 500, seeking information on what steps they had taken or planned to take to address the security of their IT systems. This effort, for the most part, yielded little, as companies were wary of sharing information or opening their practices to further scrutiny, although this does not necessarily mean that companies are not focusing on the issues.

From a regulatory standpoint, the U.S. approach to cybersecurity is highly fragmented, with agencies and departments, including the FBI, Department of Justice, and DHS, among others, each taking different paths. The problem is also far beyond the scope of what one nation can address by itself since the Mobile Wave is a global phenomenon. For instance, Romania is reputed to have more hackers per capita than any other nation, and some nations, particularly in Asia, have not only done little to crack down on cyber villains but are actively supporting and encouraging cyber-attacks.

Furthermore, as noted previously, state-sponsored or state-tolerated activities, such as industrial espionage, notably by countries such as China and Iran, represent an ongoing challenge. And by the same token, the deployment of the Stuxnet virus against Iran, presumably by Western interests, shows just how dangerous and uncontrollable this form of cyber-attack can be because of the exposure to potential further modification/mutation that can cause the virus to infect far more that the originally intended victims, including the original authors. Cyber-war activities will play an increasingly critical role in modern warfare including activities such as shutting down an enemy's defense system, disrupting critical infrastructure, and so on.

President Obama's Cybersecurity Order

In response to the need to do more and the apparent inertia of legislators, regulators, and the private sector, in February 2013, President Obama issued a Cybersecurity Executive Order (White House 2013) that outlined policies intended as an alternative to the much criticized Cyber Intelligence Sharing and Protection Act (CISPA) that failed in the U.S. Senate in 2012. The key points of Obama's executive order included recognition that information warfare among nation-states is a reality and that, as a first step, the U.S. government will coordinate the development of a cybersecurity framework in concert with the private sector to reduce cyber risk to critical infrastructure firms including selected utilities, financial services, government agencies, and telecommunications firms. The aim of the framework is to expand current government programs and engage private-sector subject-matter specialists. The National Institute of Standards and Technology was assigned primary responsibility for developing the framework and at the time of this publication, had released discussion drafts. Consistent with feedback received from the business community, the framework is not intended to be prescriptive but focuses on the cyber capabilities that critical infrastructure firms should have. For better or worse, the executive order is largely voluntary and, without incentives, may have limited effect. However, there is a risk that blatant disregard of the framework could expose a company to litigation should an incident occur. At a minimum, the Cybersecurity Framework will help to continue the dialogue and raise awareness among executives regarding the role of cybersecurity in U.S. national security.

Recommendations and Best Practices for the Future

Looking ahead, there needs to be increased investment and focus on secure software development. One approach to application security is to find vulnerabilities and fix them before they are deployed. Organizations frequently have dedicated teams to do just that. Research vice president and Gartner Fellow, Joseph Feiman, has defined three technology approaches to vulnerability testing and monitoring: Static Application Security Testing; Dynamic Application Security Testing, which takes a run-time approach to testing; and Interactive Application Security Testing, which combines the first two approaches (SC Magazine 2012). However, these approaches are quite costly. Alternatives are emerging but are not yet in the mainstream. For instance, some advocate for creation of more secure code, perhaps through standard security mechanisms built into libraries and frameworks.

Big Data

Although the PRISM program may have generated a great deal of negative press when Snowden revealed it, one of the keys to improved security is the increased leveraging of big data for monitoring. At present, current monitoring is relatively limited, and focuses primarily on metadata. Furthermore, data analysis often occurs with too much lag time. There is some evidence, for example, that more rapid analysis of information associated with the alleged Boston Marathon bombers could have prevented the attack. Another fact, implicit in the Snowden revelations, is the size and scope of one nation's cyber efforts, not previously well documented anywhere. Presumably, many other nations have efforts of a similar scale, as yet only revealed indirectly through analysis of cyber-attacks. That means any given organization, and particularly organizations in the telecom industry, can expect to be faced with a growing spectrum of potentially hostile players, in addition to whatever demands their own national governments make on them. To be sure, improving these areas will require directly addressing privacy issues. However, if the public and government officials and legislators truly understand not only the day-to-day costs of fighting cyber-attacks but also the extent of potential damage that could stem from a true cyber 9/11, they may be more inclined to support these measures. Very likely, mobile platforms, heretofore a problem area in security, will come to play a major role in providing a solution, particularly through implementation of multifactor authorization.

In these challenges and transitions, telecom companies will play a major role, but many areas need to be addressed. For instance, tier 1 Internet providers may be required to provide more detailed information and analysis of the traffic they carry. Or, they may collaborate and work more closely with government agencies in analyzing traffic. Because cybersecurity is a global issue, there will be a need for global coordination.

Securing the telecom supply chain also will be critical. Again, a combination of private and government initiatives may be needed. A 2011 MIT study, "The Future of the Electric Grid," on which telecommunication operations depend, included a focus on growing cyber threats, noting, "Data communications will increasingly link the various components of the grid, from generator to transmission line to substation to distribution network to consumer meter, and to equipment and appliances within homes and businesses." Therefore, the MIT report explains, the much more interconnected grid of the future will likely have vulnerabilities that are not present in today's grid. The huge increase in electronic devices such as automated meters will introduce means of access that attackers can use to penetrate computer systems or other communicating equipment, increasing the risk for both intentional and accidental communications disruptions. According to the MIT report, the North American Electric Reliability Corporation predicts that these disruptions "can result in a range of failures, including loss of control over grid devices, loss of communications between grid entities or control centers, or blackouts."

An issue that will be most difficult to resolve is who will pay for cybersecurity activities and, when it comes to nations that are resistant to enforcement efforts, who can take on the global coordination and diplomacy that will be needed. One possible solution could be the development of nongovernmental organizations on a national or international level, similar to the U.S.-based Underwriters Laboratory (UL), which can help provide validation and structure for cooperation.

There has been a trend for years toward consensus-based approaches to standards in many fields, as exemplified by the role of ASTM International, formerly known as the American Society for Testing and Materials, which has been a recognized leader in the development and delivery of international voluntary consensus standards. Currently, about twelve thousand ASTM standards are used around the world. Its standards development effort is driven by the contributions of its members, which includes more than thirty thousand technical specialists and business professionals.

Getting to a better and more secure future will not be easy. There is a need for more education and awareness among executives, leaders, governments, and the public globally. In the telecom sector, the nature of work has changed from analogue-based technology to an all-digital, IP-based technology that results in a significant change in training a suitable workforce to address the cybersecurity vulnerabilities associated with the new technology. The 2013 (ISC)² Global Information Security Workforce Study, prepared by Booz Allen Hamilton with the assistance of Frost & Sullivan, noted the importance of IT security professionals as "critical guardians in the protection of networked operations and informational assets" (Suby 2013). However, they noted, because of new developments such as BYOD, cloud computing, and social media, information security professionals "must be highly adaptable in learning and applying new skills, technologies, and procedures in order to manage a dynamic range of risks."

Even with past annual growth in the double digits, workforce shortages persist. Fifty-six percent of respondents believe there is a workforce shortage, compared with only 2 percent who believe there is a surplus. The effect of this shortage is greatest on the existing workforce. Knowledge and certification of knowledge weigh heavily in job placement and advancement. A broad understanding of the security field was the top factor in contributing to career success, followed by communication skills. Nearly 70 percent of those surveyed view certification as a reliable indicator of competency.

According to the study, slightly more than 46 percent of all respondents indicated that their organizations require certification, and among those respondents, 50 percent of (ISC)² members and 39 percent of non-members indicate certification is a requirement. Those in the government-defense sector are the most emphatic on this point; 84 percent state certification is required, "and a distant, but still high, second is info tech at 47 percent." Although regulations are a primary driver for certification in government defense, in the private sector 74 percent of respondents view certification as a primary indicator of competency.

How to Train and What to Train

Enhancing cyber-threat education will require responses at many levels. Certainly, training, certification, and degree programs have fallen far behind the requirements of today. To be sure, technology helps with response strategy, but skilled specialists can help ensure that the response is as effective as possible. There is a need for a more standardized curriculum across learning institutions, and increased collaboration with relevant government institutions (e.g., the National Initiative for Cybersecurity Education [NICE]) as well as telecom equipment vendors.

One example of a leading program initiative is NSA's new program to prepare college students for careers in cybersecurity. Specifically, in 2012 the NSA launched a National Centers of Academic Excellence in Cyber Operations Program to expand the pool of professionals with skills in this area, as an outgrowth of NICE. The program is designed to identify institutions that offer a deeply technical, interdisciplinary curriculum centered on fields such as computer science, computer engineering, and electrical engineering. It will provide select participants with the chance to participate in cutting-edge summer seminars at NSA. According to the agency, although many of the nation's colleges and universities offer courses or promote projects in cybersecurity, the new program integrates academic disciplines, "with a focus on technology and the techniques associated with specialized cyber operations," namely collection, exploitation, and response. For example, each new center is also required to include an academic unit covering the related legal and ethical issues.

For the 2012–2013 academic year, schools selected for participation were Dakota State University, South Dakota; the Naval Postgraduate School, California; Northeastern University, Massachusetts; and the University of Tulsa in Oklahoma. The NSA program is, in addition to 145 existing centers of academic excellence in research and information assurance education, jointly overseen by the NSA and the DHS. According to NSA, the primary goal of the program is to expose students to the scientific and intellectual foundation of cyber operations, and to demonstrate how such knowledge could be applied in cyber careers with the government.

End-User Training

Because attackers so frequently exploit insiders through a variety of subterfuges, training insiders, which often has been neglected in the past, needs to improve substantially. It is not enough to simply prepare policies and then allow them to languish in training or human resources manuals. Rather, training must be continually and regularly reinforced. This can be accomplished through a spectrum of approaches. Some organizations have chosen a simple and "fun" approach, mixing educational posters with participatory games and online quizzes to reinforce learning and keep it top of mind.

Traditional lectures and classroom settings can have value, of course, especially at an introductory level, but more creative efforts will likely be needed over the longer term to make sure employees do not let down their guard. Having security teams keep end-users apprised of threats is also helpful; then they are armed with knowledge that is truly relevant. Just as with advertising, repetition is the key. There is no substitute for refreshing learning, at least quarterly but perhaps more often.

One technique that has significant potential involves launching fake attacks, typically phishing-style scams, to see if users are alert enough to spot problems. However, practitioners caution against using employee failures against them. The emphasis should be on learning and practice, not on determining whether an individual passed or failed. Indeed, organizations need to guard against the risk that their training activities become so heavy-handed they discourage employees from the normal conduct of business. While 100-percent compliance with cybersecurity policies and procedures may not be realistic, greatly improved performance is an achievable goal.

Collaboration on the Cutting Edge

Collaboration between the private sector and educational institutions may include setting up training labs. Because the cost for setting up a lab is relatively high, such training labs can be configured in several ways, and to spread the cost, can be made remotely accessible by various educational institutions with some of the cost covered through sponsorship from telecom vendors and telecom companies.

Similarly, there is a need for broader collaboration between public and private sectors. President Obama's executive order is one attempt, but it is still dependent on voluntary action. Without regulatory strictures and financial incentives, players may continue to be unwilling to make the significant investments required. If voluntary approaches fail, regulation is probably inevitable. US Telecom, the broadband association, has expressed support for CISPA, legislation that is one example. But the measure remains controversial and failed in the Senate again this year. However, CISPA may continue to be one of the better options for moving forward. CISPA (H.R. 3523 in the 112th Congress and H.R. 624 in the 113th Congress) is a proposed law that would permit sharing of Internet traffic information between the U.S. government and various technology and manufacturing companies. The primary point of the bill is to help the federal government investigate cyber threats and improve the security of networks. CISPA has reportedly been criticized by advocates of Internet privacy and civil liberties, including the Electronic Frontier Foundation, the American Civil Liberties Union, Free Press, Fight for the Future, and Avaaz. org, as well as various conservative groups, because it includes too few limits on how and when the government may monitor a private individual's Internet browsing information. However, in addition to US Telecom, CISPA had garnered support from leading technology companies such as Microsoft, Facebook, AT&T, IBM, and Apple Inc., as well as the influential U.S. Chamber of Commerce.

As an amendment to the National Security Act of 1947, which does not currently contain provisions pertaining to cybercrime, CISPA adds provisions that describe cyber-threat intelligence as "information in the possession of an element of the intelligence community directly pertaining to a vulnerability of, or threat to, a system or network of a government or private entity, including information pertaining to the protection of a system or network from either 'efforts to degrade, disrupt, or destroy such system or network.'" CISPA would also require the director of National Intelligence to set up means to permit the intelligence community to share information with the private sector.

In the nearer term, there is a crucial need for appropriate investments in innovation and solutions, as well as in education. There is a crying need for new approaches such as a UL-like organization, as suggested earlier, or perhaps a universal service fund to help pay for security. At the college and university level, there needs to be immediate action to work with industry and government to better define career paths and to craft appropriate educational opportunities.

At a recent cybersecurity event in Florida, Lt. Gen. Harry Raduege Jr., USAF (Ret.), chairman, Deloitte Center for Cyber Innovation, Deloitte Services LP, noted that, "Cyber is a phenomena that . . . has changed the world. Now, cyber security, cyber threats, cyber-attacks have entered into all of our lives, whether it's into our business lives or personal lives" (Deloitte 2013). That reality must permeate industry, especially the telecom sector, if the cyber threats of the present and future are to be successfully met and mastered.

References

ABI Research, Inc. 2013. "Research News: More Than 30 Billion Devices Will Wirelessly Connect to the Internet of Everything in 2020." Accessed May 9, 2013. http://www.abiresearch.com/press/more-than-30-billion-devices-will-wirelessly-conne.

Altschul, Michael F., and John. A. Marinho. 2013. "COMMENTS OF CTIA—The Wireless Association In the Matter of Joint Working Group on Improving Cybersecurity and Resilience Through Acquisition." *Notice OERR-2013-01; Docket No. 2013-0002; Sequence 10.* Accessed June 7, 2013. http://files.ctia.org/pdf/GSA_CTIA_Comments_June7th_2013.pdf.

CompTia. 2013. "Tenth Annual Information Security Trends Study." Accessed July 28, 2013. http://www.comptia.org/research/security.aspx.

Deloitte. 2011. "Broader Security Threat Landscape, Increased Use of Emerging Technologies Require More Information Security Investment by TMT Companies: Deloitte Survey." Dec. 29. http://www.prnewswire.com/news-releases/broader-security-threat-landscape-increased-use-of-emerging-technologies-require-more-information-security-investment-by-tmt-companies-deloitte-survey-135441403.html.

Deloitte. 2013. "Blurring the Lines: 2013 Global Security Study" Accessed July 28, 2013. http://www.deloitte.com/tmtsecuritystudy.

Deloitte. 2013. "Cyber Security Forum." June 6. Accessed July 28, 2013. http://www.wctv.tv/news/headlines/Cyber-Security-Forum-210488431.html.

Drew, Christopher, and Somini Sengupta. *New York Times.* June 23, 2013. "N.S.A. Leak Puts Focus on System Administrators." Accessed July 28, 2013. http://www.nytimes.com/2013/06/24/technology/nsa-leak-puts-focus-on-system-administrators.html?pagewanted=2&_r=0&emc=eta1&pagewanted=print.

International Telecommunications Union. 2013. s.v. "cybersecurity." Accessed August 7, 2013. http://www.itu.int/ITU-R/asp/terminology-definition.asp?lang=en&rlink={4B499A4A-3E11-4AE6-9B03-46FB1A662507}.

JZ Analytics. 2012. "2012 NCSA / McAfee Online Safety Survey." *National Cyber Security Alliance and McAfee.*

Massachusetts Institute of Technology. 2011. "The Future of the Electric Grid." December 5. http://mitei.mit.edu/publications/reports-studies/future-electric-grid.

McKinsey Global Institute. 2013. "Disruptive Technologies: Advances that will Transform Life, Business, and the Global Economy." Accessed July 28, 2013. http://www.mckinsey.com/~/media/McKinsey/dotcom/Insights percent20and percent20pubs/MGI/Research/Technology percent20and percent20Innovation/Disruptive percent20technologies/MGI_Disruptive_technologies_Full_report_May2013.ashx.

Portio Research Limited. 2013. "Portio Mobile Factbook 2013" Accessed September 6, 2013. http://www.portioresearch.com/media/3986/Portio%20Research%20Mobile%20Factbook%202013.pdf.

Rogers, Mike, and Dutch Ruppersberger. 2012."Investigative Report on the U.S. National Security Issues Posed by Chinese Telecommunications Companies Huawei and ZTE." *U.S. House of Representatives.* http://

intelligence.house.gov/sites/intelligence.house.gov/files/Huawei-ZTE Investigative Report (FINAL).pdf.

SC Magazine. 2012. "Application Security." Accessed September 11, 2013. https://www.aspectsecurity.com/uploads/2013/02/SC-Magazine_AppSecurity_ebook.pdf.

Shane, Scott, and David E. Sanger. *New York Times*. June 30, 2013. "Job Title Key to Inner Access Held by Snowden." Accessed July 20, 2013. http://www.nytimes.com/2013/07/01/us/job-title-key-to-inner-access-held-by-snowden.html?hpw.

Suby, Michael. 2013. "2013 (ISC)² Global Information Security Workforce Study." *(ISC)²*. https://www.isc2.org/uploadedFiles/percent28ISC percent 292_Public_Content/2013 percent20Global percent20Information percent 20Securitypercent20Workforcepercent20Studypercent20Feb percent20 2013.pdf.

Time. March 25, 2013. "More People Have Cell Phones Than Toilets, U.N. Study Shows." Accessed July 28, 2013. http://newsfeed.time.com/2013/03/25/more-people-have-cell-phones-than-toilets-u-n-study-shows/.

U.S. Department of Homeland Security. 2009. "National Infrastructure Protection Plan." https://www.dhs.gov/sites/default/files/publications/NIPP_Plan.pdf.

Verizon. 2013. "The 2013 Data Breach Investigations Report." http://www.verizonenterprise.com/resources/reports/rp_data-breach-investigations-report-2013_en_xg.pdf

White House. 2013. "Executive Order—Improving Critical Infrastructure Cybersecurity." Accessed February 13, 2013. http://www.whitehouse.gov/the-press-office/2013/02/12/executive-order-improving-critical-infrastructure-cybersecurity.

Chapter 5

Cybersecurity and Finance

Anthony M. Bargar

Introduction

Although to date there have been few catastrophic attacks to the global financial industry, a systematic attack is a near certainty. We need only look to the cyber-attack made against South Korea in 2013 that prevented private citizens from withdrawing money from ATMs and resulted in a 1 percent loss to the local equity market. That attack demonstrates the critical need for heightened cybersecurity in the financial industry, and offers just one example of the effect this type of attack can have on an economy.

The global financial services sector is comprised of highly complex and interconnected information and communication technologies, their associated processes, and the people who operate and use them. This creates difficulties in risk management and increases the need for security controls.

The banking and finance sector is comprised of a multitude of mostly private entities that work in concert to form the backbone of the world economy. There are more than twenty-nine thousand financial firms that provide a variety of services and products to their customers. In addition to the banks, credit unions, and thrifts that are familiar to most people, the sector also includes insurance companies, security brokers, investment companies, and financial institutions. This abundance of companies working worldwide has tremendous influence, and watching the stock market is as important for individuals as it is for nations. These companies allow customers to deposit funds, make payments to other parties, provide credit and liquidity, invest funds for both the long and short term, and transfer financial risks (Department of Homeland Security 2013).

Cybersecurity Threats, Security Breach Risks, and Trends in the Financial Sector

The financial system is vulnerable to attack because it is diverse, interdependent, ambiguous, and highly regulated (Bris 2007). Diversity enables resiliency; it often is thought of in physical security terms, where multiple physical pathways enable access. If one network node should suddenly go down, another node is able to pick up the slack and allow continued access. This application of diversity protects only against unsophisticated attacks, such as a physical attack or a distributed denial of service (DDoS). When confronted with a more sophisticated, advanced persistent threat, the same diversity actually provides a larger attack surface. This increases the chances of an adversary gaining access because of the multiple entry points.

Interdependence is the idea that all parties share a responsibility to contribute to and protect a system. Since the financial information technology (IT) enterprise is dependent on shared critical infrastructures and complex networks, it is vulnerable to attack and exploitation. Both the public and private sectors share a common infrastructure that they do not control. Often, the boundaries for these networks are not clearly defined, and in some cases, such as Europe, these networks can span countries. International law is not clear regarding these undefined boundaries, which make the protection and defense of the networks more complicated. When confronted with a cross-border cyber-attack, it is not often known which nation or entity is responsible for bringing the adversary to justice, or whether the victim can be pursued across international borders. Will local investigators respond quickly on a positive attribution? Although the financial industry is not unique in confronting these challenges, they are of greater concern due to the financial sector's global footprint, which amplifies these concerns due to the rapid, transnational nature of business.

An ambiguous system is one that is open to more than one interpretation; in order for security to work on a network as large as the global financial network, there must be well-planned enterprise architectures. There is little in the way of industry standards when it comes to security configurations in the financial industry, and system administrators have too much autonomy in designing their own. This lack of industry standards is compounded because system security often is an afterthought, rather than a planned part of the greater enterprise architecture design. More often than not, this leads to point-solution technologies added on afterward to reduce risk. The builders of the space shuttle were well aware that they needed to plan for every contingency in case of a system failure, or else they would face the possibility of another disaster like Apollo 13. Those designing the enterprise architecture must be similarly diligent in planning for failure, as sophisticated cyber adversaries often understand the targeted system design better than those who designed it. Cyber adversaries are meticulous in their probing and evaluation of data flows and system connectivity and are able to exploit any feature, including trust relationships, which often provide a pathway into systems.

The financial industry is highly regulated. This is a double-edged sword, however; the regulations prevent certain features from becoming ambiguous but they can cause additional worries. Organizations often are forced to justify costly investments in information security and never really commit fully to security measures, opting instead to simply "check the box."

Security monitoring of financial industries is constant, operating around the clock. In order to fulfill this obligation, many organizations use a third-party management security service provider (MSSP).

These providers meet the monitoring requirements, but often do not offer enough protection. The problem for these MSSPs is that they work in quantity, and not necessarily quality. They use a multitenant organization, in which a group of security analysts observes the security of ten to twelve companies each. The small number of analysts, coupled with the large number of companies under observation, makes the MSSPs a less than ideal method of monitoring security.

Cybersecurity Standards and Laws in the Financial Sector

The difficulties in addressing the standards and laws of the financial sector stem from its multinational character. Each nation sets different regulations for the industry, making "standards" something of a misnomer. The goal of the financial industry is primarily to produce dividends for its stockholders, although different governments and ideologies have divergent perspectives on this matter. In order to address the issues of cybersecurity, Congress continues to consider proposals defining the federal government's responsibility in regulating cyberspace. These proposals have recently met with resistance from privacy groups, and as recently as April 2013, the Senate defeated passage of the Cyber Intelligence Sharing and Protection Act (CISPA; Library of Congress 2012). Despite CISPA's failure, Congress will continue to make proposals to address the complex and ever-evolving mandate of our cybersecurity.

One important piece of legislation that affects cybersecurity is the Gramm-Leach-Bliley Act, or the Financial Services Modernization Act of 1999. Under this legislation, financial institutions must protect information gathered about individuals (Bureau of Consumer Protection Business Center 2002). Financial institutions also must have methods in place to protect against anticipated threats and unauthorized access of such records (Sourcefire 2013).

Furthermore, as part of the Fair and Accurate Credit Transactions Act of 2003, companies must put into place measures to protect that data and provide for appropriate disposal of consumer information. A company has flexibility in determining the best way to meet that requirement, but each company is under the jurisdiction of the appropriate agency. To aid that endeavor, "the Federal Financial Institutions Examination Council (FFIEC), already have issued guidance regarding their expectations concerning the proper disposal of all of an institution's paper and electronic records" (Federal Register 2004).

One important provision under the USA Patriot Act affects financial institutions as well. Under the Patriot Act, financial institutions must make provisions for enhanced scrutiny of any account filed by a "non-United States person" in order to prevent the possibility of money laundering (Federal Financial Institutions Examination Council 2006). Banks must have methods of verifying a customer's identity and must crosscheck individuals against lists of terrorists and terrorist organizations. The success of a bank in preventing money laundering may prove important to future mergers, as the primary federal regulator must take into consideration the company's effectiveness before allowing a merger to take place (Federal Reserve Bank of St. Louis 2002).

Risks to the Financial Industry as a Result of Extensive Automation

All IT industries are haunted by the specter of cyber risks, but there are some risks that are unique to the financial industry.

First and foremost, financial institutions must sell their product to their clients by offering confidence and stability. Shareholders, clients, and the general public will simply take their business to a competitor if it appears the institution lacks stability. In order to project this confidence, the institution must have a reliable reputation, and any attack on the brand itself may have significant repercussions. If the company website is hacked, how can it say that it is capable of protecting other sensitive material? It suggests that the company is not doing enough to protect its own IT systems. Companies often attempt to keep attacks made against them private for fear it will affect brand reputation. Baroness Pauline Neville-Jones, the Minister of State for Security and Counter Terrorism at the Home Office in the United Kingdom said that "It's clear that criminals get away with quite considerable sums, but companies are not talking about it because of reputation . . . shared situational awareness is absolutely vital to construct cybercapacity and defences" (Espiner 2010).

Competitors offer significant security problems as well because company-on-company crime is a serious and real threat. Often the information is shared inadvertently, but sometimes these are targeted attacks used to gain competitive intelligence. Some of the tactics employed by agents of corporate espionage include social engineering and deliberate entry through a company's wireless network.

One of the most blatant displays of one company stealing from another involves China and CyberSitter, a filtering program created in the United States to prevent minors from accessing inappropriate material. Code from the CyberSitter program appears to have been taken and used in Green Dam, a filter placed on all computers sold in China (Gross 2010).

A powerful agent that can prevent this from happening is data leak or data loss protection technology. Comprehensive training for employees also can address this challenge. Giving them the tools and training to ensure encryption, authentication, and identity is challenging but rewarding. This ensures employees are involved in the security of data through its entire life cycle, from creation, to usage, to destruction. Employees are taught how to create data, label existing data, and understand the protection mechanisms. This type of involvement is challenging, however, and requires a complete enterprise solution that encompasses how data is used throughout the company. A company's sensitive information also must be shared with suppliers and be accessible to third parties, as well as over mobile devices. Moreover, the company itself must work to create a system of checks and balances, which will involve both the legal department and contracts and procurement.

Another serious challenge in managing the security of financial sector companies comes in the form of a myriad of insider threats (Moore et al. 2005). Often, by the very nature of their business, insiders at financial sector firms have access to sensitive information that can be used for individual gain through the use or sale of information. This is the basis of insider trading, where an individual has prior knowledge of an event and the direct or indirect understanding of how an individual or individuals might gain.

Whistleblowers pose a threat when they feel personally slighted by their corporation or morally obligated to report a crime should it occur. Their role in society is important, and often lauded by the public after they have exposed malfeasance. In fact, July 30, 2013 was declared National Whistleblower Appreciation Day in recognition for all they had done for democracy (National Whistleblowers Center 2013). Nonetheless, their actions can cause tremendous harm to the company who employs them. Knowing that they will be required to prove the wrongdoing, the whistleblower may collect evidence to be turned over to an attorney. They are protected under Section 1057 of the Dodd-Frank Wall Street Reform and Consumer Protection Act of 2010 to hold that information, but once the sensitive material is obtained, the whistleblower is not likely to protect the information, as it is stored outside the corporation's security enclave (United States Department of Labor 2010).

Disgruntled employees pose a threat for any number of reasons. An employee who feels slighted may not attempt to collect and disseminate information, as in the case of the whistleblower, but he or she still may cause a security risk by making inappropriate comments in social media. An angry tweet might alert adversaries of a potential entry point for exploitation, even if the individual did not intend anything insidious.

Thoroughly disgruntled employees will likely leave for another corporation, and when they do, they will take all their secrets and contacts with them. Not all employees will feel morally responsible for their previous employer's secure information, leading to potential breaches, or they might seek to damage the company directly. For instance, in 2002 a logic bomb deleted ten billion files at one financial institution, resulting in approximately $3 million in losses. The perpetrator turned out to be a disgruntled employee upset over a bonus (Moore et al. 2005).

In order to combat these numerous insider leaks, a corporation may attempt any number of the following strategies: monitoring outbound Internet traffic, controlling removable media, strong host-based protection (e.g., locking out USB devices), strong mobile device security, background checks and proper lockups with other legal mechanisms like Non-Disclosure Agreements, enforcement of laws and company regulations, and a global identity and access management solution, which ensures that double-checks are in place for the most important employees and those in a position of trust.

Advanced supply chain attacks are gaining in frequency and sophistication. Although governments worldwide are preparing themselves for just such an attack and there are numerous efforts to mitigate these risks, the private sector has traditionally lagged in providing adequate protections against these sophisticated threats.

There is a serious danger that any organization's supply chain for electronic components, including microchips, could be compromised at some stage by hostile agents. These agents could directly alter the circuitry of the electronic components or substitute counterfeit components with altered circuitry. The altered circuitry could contain malicious firmware that would function in much the same way as malicious software, although such firmware can prove both much harder to detect and to resolve if identified. For example, if the electronic components were connected to a network that enemy attackers could access, the malicious firmware could give them control of connected information systems. Scott Borg, director of the U.S. Cyber Consequences Unit cautioned that "microscopically small and enormously complex circuits inserted surreptitiously into military or security hardware could potentially turn U.S. weapons against their users" (Magnuson 2010). Even if the malicious firmware was not connected to any network accessible to information systems the attackers could access, it might still contain logic bombs that could cause terrible harm. A logic bomb in a securities trading system, for example, could lie dormant until the system engaged in certain activities indicating a high degree of mobilization. These triggers might then lead to the execution of the logic bomb. A logic bomb could then shut down core information systems, creating a denial of service and introducing difficult-to-replicate random errors in transactions processed or worse, and actively turn the equipment controlled by the information system against those operating it. Fannie Mae, the government-sponsored mortgage lender, narrowly avoided being the victim of a logic bomb that was set to wipe out servers and cost the company millions of dollars (Claburn 2009).

The four types of cyber-attacks against each stage of the supply chain and precautions against each are as follows:

1. Cyber-attackers interrupt the operation
    -   Mandatory continuous sharing of production across the supply chain
    -   Maintenance of alternate sources

2. Cyber-attackers corrupt the operation (such as by inserting malware)
    -   Strict control of environments where key intellectual property is being applied
    -   Logical tamper-proof seals
    -   Physical tamper-proof seals
    -   Effective sealing and tracking of containers
    -   Obfuscation in the ordering/distribution process (e.g., blind ship, using data masking)

3. Cyber-attackers discredit the operation (undermining trust, damaging brand value)
    -   Logging of every operation and who is responsible

4. Cyber-attackers undermine the basis for the operation (loss of control, loss of competitively important information)
    -   Versioning as a tool for protecting intellectual properties

Challenges to Security in the Financial Sector

One of the greatest threats to the financial industry involves matters of national security. We have entered a new kind of cold war in which the adversaries pursue us across the web and into cyberspace.

Today, we are less worried about a nuclear threat than we are about the potential for damage to our critical infrastructure through cyber-attack. The good news is that in our global economy, all countries are somewhat dependent on one another; after all, if one nation's financial system is attacked or disrupted, it affects the economies of all nations. That does not, however, prevent a country with a competing economy from demonstrating its national power or strategic deterrence tactics of access and tradecraft. Neither does it take into consideration a terrorist threat because their ultimate goals are to cause destruction without regard to collateral damage. That makes the need to protect our financial interests even more important. A victory by the enemy is not in just the damage it does to a single enemy, but to the entire nation-state. Although a damaging attack against a bank may wipe out money, it also demonstrates that the targeted country could be vulnerable to similar attacks, raising the stature of the adversary while harming the reputation of the attacked.

Most of these attacks are singular, targeting a single adversary at a specific time, and require years of work to gain access to the closed systems. These also result in quick discovery and mitigation, although the time it takes to be reconstituted depends on the destructive nature of the attack. In 2010, a computer worm, whose target was an Iranian nuclear plant the West suspected was being used to create weapons-grade materials, was discovered. The worm, using a unique combination of characteristics, demonstrated the ability to potentially control a physical system (O'Murchu 2010). Stuxnet is a chilling success that demonstrates the potential for these kinds of attacks; a virus like it could be turned against the financial services industry.

It is becoming increasingly important for global companies to form alliances with the governments in which they are regulated. The host nation's defense and intelligence communities will have the access to sensitive information needed to stop an advanced nation-state attack that can also help global companies. A key challenge will be the need for security clearances as well as foundational trust among public and private sectors so that information can be shared.

A growing threat to financial industries is cyber hacktivism. With a growing number of people dissatisfied with the wealthy one percent of the United States, some of the more radical elements of the population are taking reactionary approaches to what they view as their oppressors. Hollywood has helped foster an image of the financial industry as one that is rife with greed, corruption, and disdain for those beneath them with such films as *The Firm*, *Boiler Room*, and *Wall Street*. Hacktivism is possible due to the ability of large numbers of nodes to suddenly come online and coordinate to attack a target. This occurs in much the same way as flash mobs do, as these nodes launch an array of distributed denial of service attacks, meant to disrupt the operation of a business. The hacktivists also have taken advantage of weak passwords, loose permissions, or misconfigurations in order to highjack the public-facing website of a company. In this way they can spread their own antigovernment, anticorporate message and in turn weaken the brand reputation of the company.

Countermeasures for Threats to the Financial Industry

To combat the hacktivism threat, some specific countermeasures have been effective.

The first countermeasure is to keep a low profile, if possible. Practice good operational security, which includes ensuring *all* publicly facing information regarding a company's web page is known. Employ cyber counterintelligence teams to review the digital footprint of an organization to see how it appears from an adversary's perspective. Have an information security program that reviews key information and publishes guidelines on what information can and cannot be posted publicly. This takes discipline and becomes increasingly difficult the larger and more international the company becomes. Additionally, the greater the number of business partners who are privy to sensitive information, the greater the chance that some of that information will be leaked. Some examples of information often publicly available and therefore accessible to those would-be hacktivists/attackers are:

- Job vacancy announcements: These often outline what architecture, software, or sometimes even which versions of software a company uses. This information can be used to craft targeted attacks.

- Requests for proposals or solicitations: Sometimes these provide entirely too much information publicly about an organization's structure and technology enterprise. For example, knowing the names of specific people and their job functions makes emails with Trojans or bad attachments seem much more believable and clickable by unwitting employees.

The second countermeasure is to conduct cyberthreat intelligence, both strategic cyber intelligence and tactical cyber intelligence. Tactical cyber intelligence needs to be real time. It must include live intelligence feeds that will actively help a company know exactly what is being targeted and how it is being coordinated.

Corporations also should establish and create an early indications and warning system. One highly effective system is Norse's solution. Norse's LIVE threat intelligence service, IPViking, offers highly impressive systems, providing more relevant and actionable intelligence than many other options available. Norse threat intelligence sensors are highly customized, configured, and adaptive, and include many sources, as well as a strategically deployed worldwide honey grid architecture with nexus points in cybercriminal underworld points, and cyber warzone points. With its large deployment area that is growing exponentially, Norse is able to create actionable intelligence faster through its ability to correlate and normalize global data sets through patented big data. Norse's complex proprietary collection methods are unknown to cyber adversaries, making it a model early warning system.

Finally, corporations need to make plans in the event of a cyberattack. This should include updating their continuity and disaster recovery plans, as well as corporate communications plans.

In the event of a DDoS attack, corporations must have a definitive plan in place for when the reliability and trustworthiness of a network is compromised. A playbook of possible scenarios and talking points must be readily available to combat any attack that might harm the company's brand reputation.

Key Specializations Needed by
Cybersecurity Professionals in the Finance Sector

As with all technical fields, there is a critical need for cybersecurity specialists in the financial industry. The atmosphere is ripe for a destructive attack against one or more of the world's financial institutions, making training a priority. As already discussed, one of the key areas of security is training all employees and making them aware of the risks inherent in their profession.

A specific need that must be addressed, however, is the involvement of more IT professionals holding security clearances. This will enable critical personnel to work more closely with government officials, as well as have greater insight into current threats on a global scale. Those individuals with experience with the Department of Homeland Security, the National Security Agency, the Defense Intelligence Agency, or the military will be in high demand due to their existing security clearances, as well as the host of contacts they bring with them to the industry. In fact, many organizations will be hesitant to hire someone without a security clearance, given the high cost associated with procuring one.

There are several key specializations important to the financial service sector, which include:

- Technology regulatory policy and international cyber law.

- Business continuity and disaster recovery.

- Enterprise risk management.

- Corporate communications.

- Cyber incident response and forensics.

In order to move forward and provide a secure financial system, it will be important for a company to have employees in place who fall under these specializations.

The State of the Cybersecurity Workforce in the Financial Industry

As previously noted, there is a lack of qualified individuals in the field of cybersecurity. There is often a tendency to outsource these positions and engage a third-party security company versus hiring in-house specialists. This is particularly evident in organizations without a true network operations center, leaving them without the starting capacity to establish a security operations center to monitor security alerts and events.

Outsourcing and offshoring present a significant risk for any company, but more so in the financial services sector due to the sensitive nature of data processed, the greater risk for monetary loss, and the potential for more insider threats.

Two ways that financial services firms can invest in their future are to partner with local universities to develop curriculum and to offer internships. In each of these circumstances it would be necessary to center the activities near the data center environments in which they operate. More security staff would benefit from this because most would be localized around data centers.

Regular training and exercises are necessary so that existing employees can maintain their proficiency and test company security policies and incident response plans.

In July 2013, the Securities Industry and Financial Markets Association conducted a cyber-training exercise. Quantum Dawn 2 involved more than five hundred individuals from many financial service firms and federal agencies. The exercise tested the response of specialists to three types of cyber-attacks intended to disrupt trading in the equities market (Vijayan 2013). Although the results of these exercises are not yet known, the continued use of such exercises will develop a skilled workforce capable of responding quickly to the growing threats in the financial sector.

Conclusion

This chapter sheds light on the nature of cybersecurity as it applies to the financial industry. The threat of cyber-attack on the financial industry could have devastating effects on a corporation, which could lead to destabilization within the host nation. We face an uncertain future, as legislation is slow to catch up to the demands of a rapidly changing cyberspace.

As cyber adversaries become smarter, savvier, and more technologically proficient, as our systems become more complex, and as society becomes more dependent on information technology, threats to the financial services sector will increase. As the threats grow, so too do the consequences of a successful cyber-attack. Our only hope lies in developing a talented cyber workforce capable of identifying threats and defeating what could be devastating attacks.

References

Bris, Arturo. 2007. "Managing Complexity in the Financial Services Industry." In *Managing Complexity in Global Organizations*, edited by Wolfgang Amann and Martha Maznevski, 103–118. Chichester, England: John Wiley and Sons.

Bureau of Consumer Protection Business Center. 2002. "In Brief: The Financial Privacy Requirements of the Gramm-Leach-Bliley Act." *Federal Trade Commission*. July. http://www.business.ftc.gov/documents/bus53-brief-financial-privacy-requirements-gramm-leach-bliley-act.

Claburn, Thomas. 2009. "Fannie Mae Contractor Indicted For Logic Bomb." *InformationWeek*, January 29. http://www.informationweek.com/security/management/fannie-mae-contractor-indicted-for-logic/212903521.

Department of Homeland Security. 2013. "National Infrastructure Protection Plan." Accessed August 13, 2013. http://www.dhs.gov/xlibrary/assets/nipp_snapshot_banking.pdf.

Espiner, Tom. 2010. "Cybercrime Reporting to get Government Boost." *ZDNet*, June 18. http://www.zdnet.com/cybercrime-reporting-to-get-government-boost-3040089275/.

Federal Financial Institutions Examination Council. 2006. "Information Security Booklet." *IT Examination Handbook Infobase*. http://ithandbook.ffiec.gov/it-booklets/information-security.aspx.

Federal Register. 2004. "Proper Disposal of Consumer Information Under the Fair and Accurate Credit Transactions Act of 2003." *Federal Register*, December 28. https://www.federalregister.gov/articles/2004/12/28/04-27962/proper-disposal-of-consumer-information-under-the-fair-and-accurate-credit-transactions-act-of-2003.

Federal Reserve Bank of St. Louis. 2002. "The USA Patriot Act Creates New Duties." *Central Banker*, Spring 2002. http://www.stlouisfed.org/publications/cb/articles/?id=924.

——. "The Gramm-Leach-Bliley Act." 2013. *Federal Trade Commission.* June 18. Accessed August 14, 2013. http://www.ftc.gov/privacy/glbact/glboutline.htm.

FFIEC. "USA Patriot Act." 2013. *IT Examination HandBook InfoBase.* Accessed August 14, 2013. http://ithandbook.ffiec.gov/media/resources/3356/con-usa_patriot_act_section_312.pdf.

FireEye. *Protecting Your Data, Intellectual Property, and Brand from Cyber Attacks.* White Paper, Milpitas, CA: FireEye, Inc., 2012.

Glenny, Misha. 2010. "Who Controls the Internet?" *Financial Times.* October 9: 1.

Gross, Grant. 2010. "CyberSitter Files Lawsuit Against China Over Green Dam." *PC World*, January 5. http://www.pcworld.com/article/185917/article.html.

Library of Congress. 2012. "H.R.3523—Cyber Intelligence Sharing and Protection Act." *Library of Congress.* May 12. http://thomas.loc.gov/cgi-bin/query/D?c112:4:./temp/~c112xT7XEx:.

Lynn, III, William J. 2013. "Defending a New Domain." *Foreign Affairs* 89:97–108.

Magnuson, Stew. 2010. "Malicious Firmware Could Sabotage Military, Security Systems." *National Defense*, February. http://www.nationaldefensemagazine.org/archive/2010/February/Pages/MaliciousFirmwareCouldSabotageMilitary,SecuritySystems.aspx.

Moore, Andrew, Marissa Randazzo, Michelle Keeney, and Dawn Cappelli. 2005. *Insider Threat Study: Illicit Cyber Activity in the Banking and Finance Sector (CMU/SEI-2004-TR-021).* Pittsburgh, PA: Carnegie Mellon University. http://www.sei.cmu.edu/reports/04tr021.pdf.

National Whistleblowers Center. 2013. "Senate Establishes 'National Whistleblower Appreciation Day.'" http://www.whistleblowers.org/index.php?option=com_frontpage&Itemid=71.

O'Murchu, Liam. 2013. "Last-minute paper: An indepth look into Stuxnet." *Virus Bulletin.* 2010. Accessed August 17, 2013. http://www.virusbtn.com/conference/vb2010/abstracts/LastMinute7.xml.

Smith, Dave. 2013. "International Business Times: Tech/Sci." *International Business Times.* April 12. Accessed August 14, 2013. http://www.ibtimes.com/cispa-2013-google-apple-top-massive-list-supporters-favoring-controversial-cybersecurity-bill.

Sourcefire. 2013. "Gramm-Leach Bliley Act (GLBA)." Accessed August 14, 2013. http://www.sourcefire.com/industry-compliance/compliance-solutions/gramm-leach-bliley.

Tendulkar, Rohini. 2013 *Cyber-Crime, Securities Markets and Systemic Risk.* Staff Working Paper, IOSCO Research Deptartment.

Thaw, David. 2013 "A Flexible Approach to Cybersecurity Regulation." *RegBlog.* July 9. Accessed August 14, 2013. https://www.law.upenn.edu/blogs/regblog/2013/07/09-thaw-cybersecurity.html

United States Department of Labor. 2010. "Consumer Financial Protection Act of 2010 (CFPA), Section 1057 of the Dodd-Frank Wall Street Reform and Consumer Protection Act of 2010, 12 U.S.C.A. §5567." *Occupational Safety and Health Program.* http://www.whistleblowers.gov/acts/dfa_1057.html.

Vijayan, Jaikumar. 2013. "Cyber Drills like Quantum Dawn 2 Vital to Security in Financial Sector." *Computerworld*, July 19. http://www.computerworld.com/s/article/9240920/Cyber_drills_like_Quantum_Dawn_2_vital_to_security_in_financial_sector.

Chapter 6

Cybersecurity and Utilities

Geoff Schwartz

Introduction

No sector of the nation's critical infrastructure is more important than major utilities—electricity, water, oil, and natural gas. An interruption of any utility can produce a significant cascading negative effect on every other sector, the economy, and the health and welfare of the affected public. In the past, the causes of utility interruption included natural events such as storms and earthquakes, equipment breakdown, fires, physical acts of war, and malicious physical damage. But as with other sectors, cyber-attacks have emerged in the past few years as a significant threat to the stability of utility operations. With the enormous growth in the use of computer networks to monitor and control these operations, there is now a very real threat of large-scale, extended interruption of utilities that would bring affected areas of the country to a literal standstill.

Utility operations involve essentially three major activities—the business operation of the utility company, the production (or generation) of the utility resource, and the transmission and distribution of the utility resource to customers. This chapter focuses specifically on the cybersecurity aspect of the second and third activities in regard to the nation's bulk electric power industry. Business network security is discussed elsewhere in this book, and the cybersecurity issues associated with electric power generation, transmission, and distribution are generally the same for other utilities.

Fundamentals

Electric Power Generation and the Use of Digital Monitoring and Control

Large electric generators are used in power plants to produce bulk electric power. A generator is constructed with two basic parts, a stator and a rotor. The stator is a fixed (nonrotating) hollow cylinder formed of wire wound around a magnetic material. The rotor is essentially a solid cylinder, also formed by wire wound around a metal core. The rotor fits inside the stator, and is mounted on a shaft so that it is free to spin around. When the rotor spins, the relative motion of the rotor and stator windings in the magnetic field created by the stator magnetic material causes electric current to be produced in the rotor windings. One end of the rotor also rotates inside slip rings. Wire brushes touch the slip rings as they rotate. Cables connected to the brushes allow the electric current to ultimately be transported out of the power plant (see Figure 6.1).

Compared with most other types of plants, nuclear power plants are capable of generating relatively large amounts of electric power in a single plant. A typical nuclear power plant can continuously produce one billion watts of electric power, which is enough to supply the daily needs of about two hundred thousand average homes. This is because a very small volume of uranium stores an enormous amount of energy. A nuclear reactor is a large, heavy steel vessel that contains uranium assembled in a manner that allows water to flow through the reactor vessel via pipes. As the water flows through the reactor vessel, energy in the form of heat is transferred from the uranium to the water. The heated water then can be used to produce steam to rotate turbines, which in turn rotate a generator to produce electric power (see Figure 6.2).

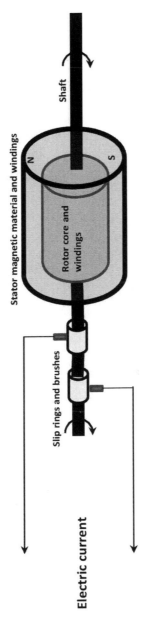

Figure 6.1. Simplified electric power generator (illustration by author)

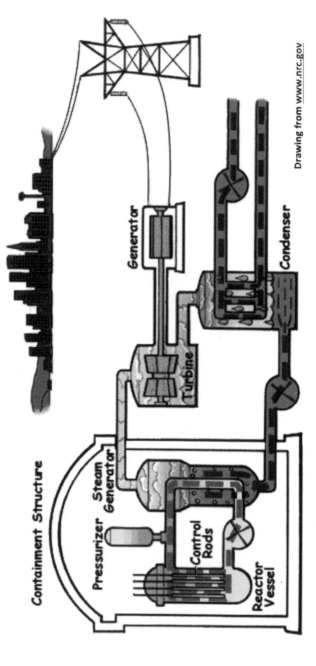

Figure 6.2. Simplified nuclear electric power plant (courtesy of U.S. Nuclear Regulatory Commission nrc.gov)

This description of a nuclear power plant is extremely simple. In fact, the plant consists of hundreds of complex mechanical, electrical, and digital systems that must interact and operate together to ensure that the voltage of the electricity being produced is stable, and that the plant is safe and physically secure and does not pose a risk to the health of the plant workers and the public. In order to accomplish this, the plant is continuously watched over by the operating and engineering staff, using a combination of analog and digital *monitoring systems*. The plant also contains hundreds of automatic *control systems* and devices, many of which are digital. It is the digital monitoring and control systems that present cybersecurity concerns.

Digital monitoring systems allow plant operators and engineers to understand the real-time state of the plant system *process variables*. There are many process variables. Several examples of the key process variables include the pressure, temperature, and flow rate of the cooling water circulating through the reactor, the voltage of the electric power produced by the generator, and the radiation level inside the reactor containment building. Let's look at how cooling water flow rate is monitored and how digital systems are involved. A small mechanical (analog) flow sensor is permanently installed inside the coolant system pipe at a particular location. The flow of water inside the pipe causes the sensor to generate a low-voltage electric signal. A wire connected to the sensor passes through a sealed penetration in the pipe wall, and then travels inside a conduit that runs several hundred feet to a computer room, where the voltage is converted from analog to digital and passed to a *process monitoring* server. The server uses the digital input from the converter to compute a flow rate based on a software program; it is connected to a network that displays the coolant flow rate at various workstation locations around the plant (see Figure 6.3).

Digital control systems are used to automatically operate mechanical and electrical equipment in the power plant. The same low-voltage analog signal produced by the flow sensor previously described also could be transmitted via a wire to a *controller* that converts the analog input to digital value. Simultaneously, the controller also can receive a separate low-voltage analog signal from a different sensor, which

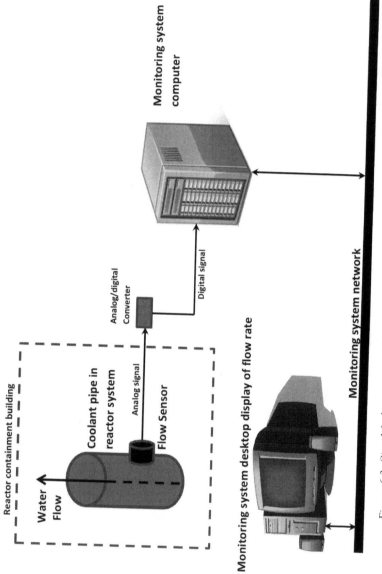

Figure 6.3. Simplified process variable monitoring of coolant flow rate (illustration by author)

measures the level of thermal (heat) power being produced inside the reactor. The controller similarly converts this voltage to a digital value. The two digital signals are then used as inputs to a microprocessor inside the controller. The microprocessor software program calculates the ratio of power over flow. The controller converts the digital ratio back to a low-voltage analog output signal. This signal is transmitted to a relay (basically an electric switch). If the voltage signal transmitted from the controller to the relay is above a set limit (also known as a set-point), the relay contacts open, causing the electrical power that keeps an electric breaker closed to be cut off, opening the breaker (a short discussion of breaker principles is contained in the next section). When this particular breaker opens, power is cut off to the equipment that withdraws the reactor control rods and holds them above the reactor core. The control rods then insert into the reactor core due to gravity and mechanical springs. As a result, the reactor automatically and quickly shuts down (see Figure 6.4).

Electric Power Transmission and Distribution and the Use of Digital Monitoring and Control

Power plants are connected to a transmission and distribution system commonly referred to as the *grid*. The grid is a network of heavy transmission cables, transformers, breakers, relays, substations, and distribution control centers. The electric generator in a large power plant might produce more than twenty million volts of electricity. This electricity is transported from the generator and out of the plant by heavy cable (also called the transmission "line"). The cables are connected to a transformer, which is designed to "step-up" this voltage to more than three hundred million volts. Transformers contain large stationary magnetic cores wound with wire. The stepping-up of voltage is produced by electromagnetic effects associated with the difference in the number of times wire is wrapped around each magnetic core. Large transformers also generate high levels of heat and are cooled by oil; the oil is itself cooled by fans. Breakers used in the grid are heavy-duty electric switches that pass current when they are closed, and cut current when they are open. Breakers allow parts of the grid to be disconnected for maintenance, or as a protective measure, such

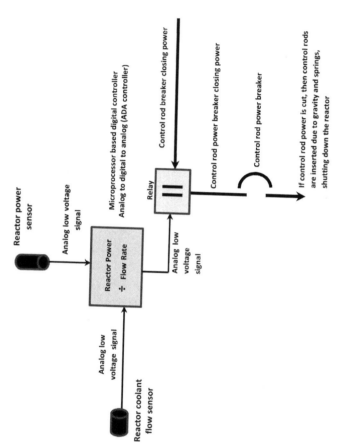

Figure 6.4. Simplified digital controller for reactor shutdown on high power to flow ratio (illustration by author)

as when electric demand is too high or too low. A breaker is usually built with an internal spring that supplies the force to keep the breaker contacts apart (i.e., to keep the breaker open). To keep the breaker closed, power is supplied to electromagnets in the breaker. The electromagnetic force is enough to overcome the spring tension and close the breaker contacts. Breakers can be opened and closed manually or automatically by a system of relays. Relays are switches much smaller than breakers that can control the power sent to the breaker contact electromagnets that keep the large breakers closed. Relays can be purely analog, or can use microprocessor based analog-to-digital-to-analog controllers, similar to the relay depicted in Figure 6.4. Substations essentially provide power branching points for the grid, where power is split and sent to different locations in the grid network. Substations generally contain breakers, relays, and transformers, as well as a small number of operating personnel.

Distribution control centers are used to monitor and control large parts of the grid, and keep electric power supply and demand balanced. Monitoring systems in distribution control centers are similar to those used in a nuclear power plant (as described in the previous section), but on a much larger scale. Digital monitoring systems present a cybersecurity concern for the grid. Personnel in distribution control centers can issue orders for substation breakers to be manually opened or closed, and for power plants to start up, raise power, lower power, or be shut down. Some distribution control centers can also remotely control parts of the grid by using a digital control network. The amount of digital control networks being used on the grid has grown dramatically within recent years, concurrent with the advent of the "smart" grid that uses large, complex distributed computer networks to automatically keep supply and demand balanced. These networks are a major cybersecurity concern as well.

Cybersecurity Threats

Digital monitoring and control systems used in power plants and the electric power transmission and distribution grid are faced with five cybersecurity *attack vectors* (also called threat vectors).

1. The wired communication pathway between the digital monitoring/control system and the Internet.

2. The wireless communication pathway between the digital monitoring/control system and the Internet.

3. The connection (authorized and unauthorized) of portable digital media and computing devices to the digital monitoring/control system.

4. Physical access (authorized and unauthorized) to the digital monitoring/control system.

5. The hardware/software supply chain.

Wired and Wireless Communication

Wired communication pathways between a power plant or grid monitoring or control network and the Internet (directly or via a business network), even with a firewall and encryption, place the monitoring or control network at risk of cyber-attack. Malware that breaches a firewall and/or wireless encryption and gives remote control of a business network to an adversary can also allow the adversary to take control of a digital monitoring or control network, if it is connected to the business network. The worst-case scenario is in a combined monitoring and control network, also known as a Supervisory Control and Data Acquisition (SCADA) network. An adversary with control over a SCADA network could cause a power plant or part of the grid to malfunction while simultaneously making operators initially believe nothing is wrong, delaying protective action by human intervention (Langner 2011).

Portable Digital Media and Computing Devices

Software updates and data downloads in digital monitoring and control networks are typically accomplished by connecting a portable storage device or laptop to the network via a USB port. This poses a significant risk for cyber-attack to the network, either intentionally or unintentionally, by the person connecting the portable device. The Stuxnet worm in 2010 infected a SCADA network in an enriched uranium fabrication facility outside the United States. It was deployed into the SCADA system by inadvertent insertion of a corrupt portable storage device to a SCADA USB port. The portable storage device had downloaded the malware either from another corrupt portable device, from an infected business network, or directly from the Internet. When the malware found its intended target, the control portion of the SCADA system malfunctioned and caused physical damage to centrifuges used in the enriched uranium fabrication process. Simultaneously, the monitoring system operated in a manner that prevented facility operators from initially discovering the malfunction and its cause.

Physical Access

Physical access to monitoring and control networks carries with it the risk for intentional or unintentional cyber-attack due to unauthorized or accidental alteration of software and hardware components such as switches, routers, servers, firewalls, and other defensive devices, as well as creation of unauthorized connections to external networks. The worst-case scenario is physical access by a knowledgeable insider. The knowledgeable insider is a trusted member of the utility organization, either with or without authorization for physical access to network components, and sufficient technical knowledge to either exploit weakly protected attack vector pathways, or to create an attack vector pathway, such as connection from the network to an undocumented workstation.

Hardware/Software Supply Chain

Utility companies purchase hardware and software from suppliers over which the utility typically has very limited control beyond contractual terms and conditions. This creates a challenging cyber-attack pathway through the supply chain, which is multiplied by secondary or subsuppliers to the utility's primary supplier. The supplier's fabrication and software development may occur far from the utility's plants and facilities that use the hardware and software (including in foreign countries), severely inhibiting the utility in performing ongoing monitoring of these processes.

Cybersecurity Laws and Regulations

Cybersecurity of digital monitoring and control systems owned by electric power utilities is primarily subject to laws and regulations that are administered and enforced by two federal regulatory agencies: the Federal Energy Regulatory Commission (FERC), and the Nuclear Regulatory Commission (NRC).

- Under FERC Order 706, FERC uses the North American Electric Reliability Corporation (NERC) to develop, monitor, and enforce a set of Critical Infrastructure Protection (CIP) standards for the cybersecurity of digital monitoring and control systems in nonnuclear power plants and the transmission and distribution grid.

- Under Title 10, Part 73.54 of the U.S. Code of Federal Regulations, the NRC monitors and enforces cybersecurity for digital monitoring and control systems inside nuclear power plants.

For those utility companies that own both nuclear power plants and parts of the transmission and distribution grid, the "bright line" of regulation between FERC/NERC and the NRC is the "downstream" side of the main electric power breaker through which the power from the plant generator flows to the transmission and distribution grid.

Basic elements of the cybersecurity programs required by FERC and the NRC include the following (North American Electric Reliability Corporation 2013; United States Nuclear Regulatory Commission 2013):

- Identification of the power plant and grid systems and components that are critical to safe and secure generation, transmission, and distribution of stable electric power to the nation.

- Identification of digital monitoring and control systems that are critical to the proper functioning of the above systems.

- Implementing established physical and digital protective measures to mitigate wired, wireless, portable media and device, and physical cyber-attack vector pathways to the critical digital monitoring and control systems identified above; physical measures must include facility access authorization for personnel.

- Developing and implementing controls to mitigate the cyber-attack vector pathway represented by utility suppliers of hardware and software.

- Implementing methods and programs to respond, mitigate adverse effects, and recover from successful cyber-attacks.

- Developing and implementing written cybersecurity procedures that utility company employees and contractors must follow, under penalties up to and including termination and prosecution.

- Developing and implementing formal work management processes requiring workers to be certified for the work they perform and to have authorization from plant and grid operators to perform the work, on a specified schedule, and using approved written work instructions that include cybersecurity measures.

- Developing and implementing cybersecurity training for utility company employees and contractors.

- Implementing programs to continuously monitor and mitigate emerging cybersecurity risks.

The Electric Utility Plant/Grid Cybersecurity Workforce

Workforce Adequacy, Skills Required, and Challenges in Building the Workforce

Today, most electric power companies have relatively few permanent employees involved in comprehensive oversight of cybersecurity for digital monitoring and control systems. This workforce role requires a very different skill set than the permanent staffing devoted to the company's information technology (IT) support and business network security. This is primarily because of the combined technical knowledge required in cybersecurity principles, engineering design, and operation of power plants and the grid. Presently, relatively few individuals possess such comprehensive knowledge. As a result, the use of contractors and teams of individuals with expertise in either IT or engineering is extensive. Additionally, it is not easy to turn an electric power engineer, even one with digital monitoring and controls system expertise, into a cybersecurity expert. Nor is it easy to turn an IT expert, even one with network security expertise, into a "power plant system knowledgeable" person. The power plant engineer who is insufficiently trained on cybersecurity may fall prey to preconceived, unrealistic notions about cyber-attack scenarios. The information security specialist with minimal plant/grid systems knowledge may default to thinking of a monitoring or control network as essentially identical to a typical business network. This presents a significant challenge for teams comprised of plant/grid engineers and information security specialists in staying focused on the correct tasks needed to develop and maintain an effective plant/grid cybersecurity program.

On the positive side, two considerations give us strong evidence that future employment opportunities for those interested in joining the electric power utility cybersecurity workforce are potentially very numerous. The current concerns in cybersecurity workforce adequacy are combined with a rapidly increasing demand for electric power and use of broadly networked SCADA systems in power plants and the grid, as well as exponential development of sophisticated malware designed to corrupt and even physically destroy electric power infrastructure.

Relative Ease of Hiring

Hiring personnel in the electric utility industry for jobs in monitoring and controls systems cybersecurity is currently a challenge, although compensation is attractive. According to the Bureau of Labor Statistics (2012), the 2010 median annual salary of information security specialists was approximately $75,000. For electrical, electronics, mechanical, and nuclear engineers, the median annual salary ranged from approximately $78,000 to $99,000. Although there is promise of substantial future income, this alone does not ease the difficulty of finding and hiring people, especially new graduates, who are the right fit to work in cybersecurity for electric power plants and the grid. In the past decade, colleges have started to expand degree programs in cybersecurity. However, as discussed in the previous section, an electric power plant/grid monitoring and controls systems cybersecurity expert generally has to be grown over a period of time in the workplace, by either training the information security specialist in plant and grid engineering, or training the engineer in information security. Additionally, the electric utility industry is a "24/7" business. Thus, there is high pressure to continuously maintain and operate generation, transmission, and distribution systems. Many new graduates may find this working environment less attractive from a quality-of-life perspective, making for greater competition for talent from companies that operate in a less-demanding operating environment.

Best Practices

Deterministic Isolation

Deterministic isolation of digital networks and components goes beyond the protection afforded by typical digital security measures such as firewalls and encryption. A digital network or component is deterministically isolated if it has no communication pathway, either wired or wireless, to it from the Internet.

Many digital monitoring and control components used in electric power plants and the grid are microprocessor based devices that are not digitally connected to a computer network; these take a low-voltage analog input, perform a calculation, and produce a low-voltage analog output. An example is as follows: Assume a system of piping, valves, and pumps is used to circulate cooling water through an air conditioning system in a power plant. The air conditioning is used to keep the plant environment habitable; therefore it is critical so that operation and engineering personnel can safely operate the plant. The system uses a pump to circulate the cooling water. A valve, called a temperature control valve, is also part of the system, next to the pump. This valve controls the flow rate of water through the system by opening slightly to allow more flow or closing slightly to allow less flow. A *digital controller* controls the opening and closing action, also called throttling. The controller contains a preprogrammed microprocessor that is not connected to a network. The controller receives a low-voltage analog electric signal from a thermometer in the plant. As air temperature in the plant increases or decreases, the analog signal into the microprocessor changes. The microprocessor performs a calculation based on the analog input signal, and sends a low-voltage output signal to the valve positioner. The positioner is a simple electromagnet that will move based on input voltage. The digital controller in this example is deterministically isolated.

Operators and engineers use monitoring networks to continuously receive information on process variables, such as pressure, temperature, and voltage. Although the monitoring network can be a closed (stand-alone or air-gapped) network, it is usually important to display this process variable information real-time for employees on the utility's business network. However, if such a connection passes through a firewall, the monitoring network is at risk through the cyber-attack vector pathway from the Internet because firewalls allow two-way communication and can be defeated. The best solution for this is a *data diode*. A data diode is a unidirectional communication device through which an electric signal can flow only in one direction. Using a data diode, process variable information can be sent from the monitoring network to the business network, but a communication pathway from the business network into the monitoring network does not exist (provided, of course, that the data diode is not deliberately or inadvertently bypassed). For SCADA systems, which combine monitoring and control in the same network, use of deterministic isolation by air gapping or a data diode is even more important than for a monitoring network. Corruption of a monitoring network can certainly disrupt plant or grid operation; however a worst-case scenario is an adversary obtaining remote control over plant or grid digital controls, allowing remote manipulation of equipment such as generators, breakers, and essential cooling systems.

Robust Physical Security

Best practices in physical security of power plant and grid digital monitoring and control systems and components include:

- Use of multiple independent physical structures, including reinforced concrete structures, locked and alarmed doors, and fencing with barbed or razor wire.

- Electronic surveillance and intrusion detection (cameras and motion detectors).

- Surveillance and intrusion detection and prevention by trained and armed security forces.

- Personnel access authorization, including background checks and psychological testing.

- Fitness for duty programs including random drug testing and behavioral observation.

- Facility entry control for employees and visitors, including electronic badging, biometrics (palm print, eye, and voice recognition), x-raying of personal items, and explosive detection.

- Electronic access badge coding that restricts access by trusted employees from facility areas they do not have a need to access in the course of their work.

Companies that own and operate nuclear power plants have had the above measures in place for many years. Companies that own non-nuclear power plants and grid assets are implementing these practices in response to the CIP requirements discussed earlier.

Portable Media and Device Control

Best practices in portable media and device control in connection with electric power plant and grid digital monitoring and control systems include multiple measures implemented simultaneously, including the following (Nuclear Energy Institute 2010):

- Locked and labeled USB port covers act as physical barriers to unauthorized insertion of portable media and devices.

- Disabling of "auto-run" capability in networks stops a network operating system from automatically downloading software from inserted portable media or devices.

- Network automatic detection and prevention software such as whitelisting will prevent the download of unrecognized software.

- Scanning of media and devices prior to connection will help detect viruses before USB insertion.

- Scanning programs should be heuristic, meaning scanning not only looks for known virus definitions, but also looks for patterns in coding that are typically indicative of viruses and malware.

- Scanning of portable media and devices should be accomplished using a dedicated computer for downloading antivirus updates from the Internet via the business network; the dedicated scanning computer should be physically secured, with controlled digital access, and should be separated from the business network with its own dedicated firewall.

- Central control should be established for quarantining of authorized portable media and devices.

- Authorized portable media and devices should be clearly labeled.

- Portable media and devices connected to digital monitoring and control should have wireless capability disabled.

Software and Hardware Supplier Control

As discussed earlier, electric utility companies are challenged to exercise direct cybersecurity control over software and hardware suppliers. However, there are practices that can be effectively implemented when used in concert with other best practices, such as portable media and device control. These practices include the following:

- Periodic inspections of supplier facilities.

- Demanding documentary evidence of personnel trustworthiness and cybersecurity training.

- Demanding that product development processes be deterministically digitally isolated from the Internet, and have robust physical protections.

- Demanding evidence that coding uses best practices for preventing creation of inherent cyber vulnerabilities in programs.

- Observing preshipping inspection and testing results.

- Demanding robust packaging in product shipment.

- Receipt inspection by the client utility.

- Preinstallation testing by the client utility, including virus checking and functionality testing.

- Demanding documentary evidence that the supplier demands cybersecurity measures for its own supply chain (subsuppliers).

Employee Awareness Training and Communication

Human error by employees and contractors can defeat the best practices described previously. Formal cybersecurity training programs for utility companies should not be limited to the security of business networks and sensitive information. Employees must be made aware that power plant and grid digital monitoring and control systems are subject to cyber-attacks that could have serious effects on the welfare of the public. Training should focus on the employee's role given the nature of their work responsibilities. This means there will be a wide spectrum of training for different employees, ranging from simple general awareness to detailed technical knowledge.

Cybersecurity Event Response and Recovery

Utilities must maintain an organization that is prepared to detect, respond to, and mitigate the consequences of a cyber-attack. The organization should contain a wide variety of skills, including general cybersecurity, plant and grid digital monitoring and control design, and comprehensive cybersecurity program details for power plants and the grid as described throughout this chapter. The incident response and recovery process must be governed by formal procedures on event recognition, forensics, and recovery from loss of system functionality. The U.S. Department of Homeland Security (DHS) includes both the U.S. Computer Emergency Response Team (US-CERT) and the Industrial Control Systems Cyber Emergency Response Team (ICS-CERT). US-CERT and ICS-CERT have resources at the ready to help utilities respond to and recover from cyber-attacks on power plant and grid digital monitoring and control systems.

Monitoring and Mitigation of Emerging Risks

New cyber-attack exploits are discovered daily, and the level of sophistication of the software code used by attacker(s) is experiencing dramatic growth. Personnel involved in cybersecurity for electric power plant and grid digital monitoring and control systems must stay aware of emerging risks and take prompt mitigating action. The North American Electric Reliability Corporation, US-CERT, and ICS-CERT websites are valuable resources that provide daily emerging risk updates.

Future Trends

This chapter has briefly described utility cybersecurity concerns and needs, focusing as a generic example on the electric power utility industry, which includes power generation, transmission, and distribution. The common characteristic of future trends in this industry is exponential growth: in power demand, in use of digital monitoring and control systems including SCADA systems, and in volume and sophistication of cyber-attacks. These will be the trends in the months and years ahead. Before 2010, cyber-attacks were commonly characterized as electronic theft of sensitive information and disruption of business processes. But in 2010, the Stuxnet code was used to corrupt a SCADA system and cause extensive physical damage. Now the possibility of "turning off the power" in wide areas for an extended period of time has moved to the forefront. This is expected to continue to be the case for the foreseeable future.

Sources of Further Information

The following websites are sources of free information on many elements of cybersecurity pertinent to utilities:

Industrial Control Systems Cyber Emergency Response Team. ICS-CERT.US-CERT.gov.
National Institute of Standards and Technology, Computer Security Division. CSRC.NIST.gov.
North American Electric Reliability Corporation. NERC.com.
U.S. Computer Emergency Readiness Team. US-CERT.gov.
U.S. Department of Homeland Security. DHS.gov.

U.S. Federal Energy Regulatory Commission. FERC.gov.
U.S. Nuclear Regulatory Commission. NRC.gov.

References

Bureau of Labor Statistics. 2012. *Occupational Outlook Handbook, 2012–13 Edition*. United States Department of Labor. http://www.bls.gov/ooh/home.htm.

Langner, Ralph. 2011. "Ralph Langner: Cracking Stuxnet, a 21st-Century Cyber Weapon." *Ted Conferences, LLC*. Video. http://www.ted.com/talks/ralph_langner_cracking_stuxnet_a_21st_century_cyberweapon.html.

North American Electric Reliability Corporation. 2013. "Standards." Accessed August 4, 2013. www.nrc.gov/reading-rm/doc-collections/cfr/part073/part073-0054.html.

Nuclear Energy Institute. 2010. *NEI 08-09, Revision 6, Cyber Security Plan for Nuclear Power Reactors*. http://pbadupws.nrc.gov/docs/ML1011/ML101180437.pdf.

United States Nuclear Regulatory Commission. 2013. "73.54 Protection of Digital Computer and Communication Systems and Networks." *NRC Library*. http://www.nrc.gov/reading-rm/doc-collections/cfr/part073/part073-0054.html.

Chapter 7

Cybersecurity in Education and Training

Ernest McDuffie

Introduction

Setting the Problem from Global to National to Regional to Local

Cyberspace has become a very real and important component of our global experience. From national security to identity protection, from banking to intellectual property protection, from critical infrastructure protection to social media, it all happens in cyberspace, and it all demands cybersecurity. President Obama declared that the "cyber threat is one of the most serious economic and national security challenges we face as a nation," and that "America's economic prosperity in the 21st century will depend on cybersecurity" (National Security Council 2013). To the extent that this same statement can be made about any country speaks to the global and national nature of the problem. At regional and local levels, the scale is smaller but the issues are the same. Particularly regarding education and training in the United States, most major decisions are made at the local level. The phrase "think globally and act locally" has never been truer.

The Stakeholders: Government, Industry, Academia,
the Public at Large

Thanks to its pervasive nature, cybersecurity is now everyone's problem and concern. Professionals working in the field, as well as everyday citizens, need to be aware of what is happening in this relatively new domain, how important it has become to our everyday lives, and what can be expected as the number of computers and computer networks continue to increase.

There are clear roles for all the stakeholders, but the dependencies and overlaps between them are the most important. The federal government's national security role requires that it lead the research and development (R&D) effort to ensure that the United States can defend its critical systems. Because of this important leadership role, the government must enable, develop, and nurture public–private partnerships with the other stakeholders. Eighty-five percent or more of the critical infrastructure in this country is controlled by the private sector. The U.S. Department of Homeland Security (DHS) has established sixteen critical infrastructure groups responsible for focusing on the various sectors that are so important to the safety and security of our country (Department of Homeland Security 2013a). In recognition of its effect on all of the sixteen sectors, recently a cross-sector group focusing on cybersecurity was established. These groups are designed to allow for the free exchange of information and ideas relevant to each sector between all of their members. Education and training become a topic of major importance as soon as we start to consider the workforce. The care and feeding of a cybersecurity workforce capable of defending critical systems, along with all the other related activities that comprise the breath of cybersecurity, starts with a solid educational background. Here academia has the lead role, but to be effective it must work closely with industry and government to ensure that the students are learning what they need to prepare them for a lifelong learning mindset. This is essential for a workforce that will require training and retraining on a regular basis.

Public–Private Partnership Approach to a Solution

Because cybersecurity is everyone's problem, strong public–private partnerships must be established. Three major stakeholder groups—government, industry, and academia—must form meaningful partnerships to address the ever-evolving issues that cybersecurity encompasses. Each of these stakeholder groups has diverse members of its own who can benefit from partnering internally. Examples and brief discussions of the nature of these internal partnerships are covered before we examine the external partnerships needed across the major stakeholder groups. It should not be inferred that these are the only important possible or needed relationships. The examples explored here simply represent the logical extension of the types of partnerships that have demonstrated value in terms of their ability to leverage resources and provide some economy of scale when attempting to reach a larger audience.

The National Coordination Office (NCO) for Networking and Information Technology Research and Development (NITRD) is an example of an internal partnership inside the federal government (Networking and Information Technology Research and Development Program 2013). The NCO for NITRD supports the planning, budget, and assessment activities for the federal government's NITRD program. The NITRD program, chartered by federal law, is the primary mechanism by which the government coordinates its unclassified networking and information technology (IT) R&D investments. Eighteen federal agencies, including all of the large science and technology agencies, are formal members of the NITRD program. Many other federal organizations also participate in NITRD activities. These agencies work together to develop a broad spectrum of advanced networking and IT capabilities to power federal missions, U.S. science, engineering, and technology leadership, and U.S. economic competitiveness. Their efforts increase the overall effectiveness and productivity of federal networking and IT R&D investments, leveraging strengths, avoiding duplication, and increasing interoperability of networking and IT R&D products. The more than 20-year history of this group demonstrates how effective it has been in the coordination of multiple federal agency activities resulting in accelerated progress and cost savings made possible by its efforts.

The Cybersecurity Credentials Collaborative (C3) is a partnership among cybersecurity certification companies that was formed to provide awareness of, and advocacy for, vendor-neutral credentials in information security, privacy, and related IT disciplines. The main mission of C3 is to advance the craft and practice of certification program development and to provide a forum to collaborate on matters of shared concern (Cybersecurity Credentials Collaborative 2013). These companies are working on vendor-neutral information security and privacy-related IT issues. Some of the activities they engage in include the following:

- Provide the industry with factual information on how C3 certifications accurately validate knowledge, skills, and abilities of the workforce.

- Where appropriate, promote a common IT certification message to legislators and government agencies and provide them with accurate information regarding the benefits of these certification programs.

- Identify opportunities for joint projects commissioning third-party research for the advancement of knowledge of vendor-neutral credentials in information security, privacy, and related IT disciplines.

The importance of credentials and training in cybersecurity highlights the need for academia to produce students who are ready to be trained. Later sections discuss this is some detail.

The Colloquium for Information Systems Security Education (CISSE) is an example of an internal partnership in the academic community. CISSE's goal is to work together to define current and emerging requirements for information assurance (IA) education and to influence and encourage the development and expansion of IA curricula, especially at the graduate and undergraduate levels. These are just three examples of internal partnerships.

The best example of an external public–private partnership is the National Initiative for Cybersecurity Education (NICE). This initiative has evolved from the Comprehensive National Cybersecurity Initiative, and extends its scope beyond the federal workplace to include civilians and students in kindergarten through postgraduate school. The vision of NICE, as stated in its strategic plan (http://csrc. nist.gov/nice/documents/nicestratplan/nice-strategic-plan_sep2012. pdf), is a secure digital nation capable of advancing America's economic prosperity and national security through innovative cybersecurity education, training, and awareness on a graduated scale that addresses the full spectrum of cybersecurity needs. Through NICE, twenty federal agencies are being coordinated in their efforts to have a positive effect on cybersecurity education, awareness, training, and workforce development. Like most of the other partnerships described here, NICE builds on the internal partnerships and then moves on to enable public–private partnerships with the other coordinating groups already working in this space. Together, the sum of the coordinated efforts is much greater than the individual organizations by themselves. By working together, these groups can more easily achieve their individual goals, leverage limited resources, reach a much larger audience, and achieve things that would have been impossible without their combined efforts. These types of collaborative activities have not been studied empirically; however, it is difficult to imagine the achievement of big goals without a meta-agency coordination function.

Measuring Success in Cybersecurity Education and Training

Questions about metrics related to cybersecurity education and training arise and must be addressed in terms of relevance to both the public good and the needs of the decision makers. Entire books can and have been written on the topic of effective education and training, but questions remain as to which educational pedagogies work best for which types of students. In the case of cybersecurity education and training, studies are under way to make this determination. It is clear already that a focus on hands-on training is important for a number of functional skills within cybersecurity. Much additional work is needed on this question.

A necessary first step is to produce a realistic mapping of an organization's current workforce, and what skillsets, and in what quality and quantity, are currently present. This baseline can then be used to conduct a gap analysis against the actual cybersecurity requirements of the company. In a real sense, this is the most basic metric that any organization can track. Using the National Cybersecurity Workforce Framework (NCWF) is a good first step to moving in this direction and understanding the different skills that make up the potential workforce (National Initiative for Cybersecurity Education 2013). The NCWF was developed by NICE to provide a common understanding of, and lexicon for, cybersecurity work. Defining the cybersecurity population consistently and using standardized terms is an essential step in ensuring that our country is able to educate, recruit, train, develop, and retain a highly qualified workforce.

There are a number of themes of importance that run through this section, such as critical infrastructure protection, the need for lifelong learning, and the ability to learn versus the skills to be learned themselves. These issues have particular importance for the field of cybersecurity that are discussed in some detail in later sections of this chapter.

Fundamental Issues that Are
Unique to Education and Training

Rapid Evolution of the Field Requires Near Constant Material Refresh and Update

Cybersecurity education and training has a particular challenge because of the rapid and ever-accelerating pace of change in this field. It is necessary that all providers of course material have plans in place for regular review and update of these materials. This produces a tension between the need to stay current and the practical matter of time and resources required to actually accomplish detailed updates.

It also becomes important to identify those core concepts that will not change significantly over time. This identification will help mitigate the refresh problem. A consideration of the specific skillset being updated will assist in determining the respective refresh cycle. A study of the thirty-one skills identified in the NCWF reveals that some of these skills are much more stable than others. A DHS report identified these mission-critical skills (Homeland Security Advisory Council 2012). The first recommendation of this DHS report was to "adopt and maintain an authoritative list of mission-critical cybersecurity tasks." That list of tasks is: system and network penetration tester, application penetration tester, security monitoring and event analyst, incident responder in-depth, threat analyst/counter-intelligence analyst, risk assessment engineers, advanced forensics analysts for law enforcement, secure coders and code reviewers, security engineers-operations, and security engineers/architects for building security. This is an example of the type of agency-specific analysis needed for the well-being of the cybersecurity workforce. Stability, mission priority, and limitations on resources are all important elements to consider when planning a refresh strategy.

After these considerations regarding course refresh, the distribution of these new materials must be considered. How will your plans affect the actual implementation of the new material in the classroom? Depending on the environment, the timing of the distribution could become an important factor for consideration. The importance of hands-on training for some of the cybersecurity skills also contributes to the unique difficulties of education and training in this field.

Need to Connect with a New Generation, Particularly
Underrepresented U.S. Groups

Digital natives are individuals who have grown up with the Internet and all things digital. They are comfortable in this continually evolving and increasingly complex environment. The heart of our future knowledge-based workforce will be formed by these digital natives. This is a very diverse group with interests as broad as the general population itself. In order to attract the numbers needed to fill the cybersecurity positions of today and tomorrow, particularly where U.S. citizens are required to fill jobs with security clearances, it is essential to do outreach with women and other underrepresented groups. Largely due to the historical and technical roots of cybersecurity in computer science, the field of cybersecurity suffers from many of the same problems in attracting underrepresented groups as computer science. These patterns can be tracked using large data sets from the National Center for Science and Engineering Statistics (National Science Foundation 2013b). An interesting phenomenon occurs when executing programs specifically designed to reach women and minorities; in almost all cases these programs have the same positive effect on majority populations. See the ongoing Women in Computing program at Carnegie Mellon University for an example of such a program (Carnegie Mellon University 2013). This results in a general overall uptick in interest and enrollment in programs that lead to professional positions in the field. Programs that focus on hands-on training, relating activities to improving the overall well-being of the community, and those that explore teamwork and team building to address large complex issues have been shown to be most effective in this space.

Need for Theoretical Knowledge and Hands-On Training

All academic disciplines cover a spectrum that runs from the most theoretical aspects of the field to the most practical. This continuum ranges from pure abstraction of the most fundamental concepts to actual physical demonstrations of functional skills that have been developed from the abstractions. All aspects of this spectrum are important and build on each other in interesting and not always straightforward and obvious ways. For the most part, four-year and graduate institutions focus on the theoretical end of this spectrum, with the actual degree program and level determining the functional skill development imparted. Training programs in industry and in the military often start at the functional skill development level and move in the theoretical direction only as needed. Most professional certification programs also reside in the functional end of the spectrum. Community colleges and other two-year institutions often provide a useful intermediate step between the two extremes. As a student (traditional or nontraditional), a displaced employee, or anyone simply interested in joining the field of cybersecurity, it is critical to understand this spectrum, identify the individual needs and the requirements of the field, and then decide how to engage the spectrum most effectively.

The field of cybersecurity requires theorists and practitioners on both ends of the spectrum. Those who would join the field must carefully consider the type of work they wish to accomplish, and pursue the education that is most appropriate for that career goal.

Including Traditional and Nontraditional Students when Developing the Cybersecurity Workforce

To have an effect on the overall workforce, individuals must understand what they can do if they are interested in becoming part of this growing field. Employers also will benefit from understanding the nature of these new proactive job seekers. As stated in the previous section, it is important to understand the nature of the education to training spectrum. After considerable evaluation of the student's current status and career goals, it is possible to generate individual student plans to achieve the career goals that have been established. This is an important activity for anyone in any field to pursue, but even more critical in new, emerging, complex, and rapidly evolving fields like cybersecurity. Once execution of the education plan has started, it is then important to continue to evaluate and assess the plan and the environment it is being executed in, and progress toward stated goals. Course adjustments will always be necessary, but by planning for them, the students become prepared for the unexpected while simultaneously constantly increasing the chances of achieving their goals.

Metrics to Measure Education and Training Progress

The question of metrics is of vital importance to any process or program. Identifying the proper metrics to determine the return on investment or simply measure progress toward specific programmatic goals can be useful. Effort is needed in this determination process to ensure that the agreed upon metrics meet these specific needs and are not just metrics for metrics' sake. In the cybersecurity education and training space, a simple count of the number of students completing a particular course or program is a necessary but not sufficient metric. Clearly a count is needed, but by itself it does not tell the complete picture. Measures of the skill level attained by graduates also must be quantified. Cost per student in terms of time and dollars is another important factor. There are several automated tools available to assist with this evaluation process in a rigorous and repeatable manner. Means to measure curriculum effectiveness also are being studied and would play a significant role in any comprehensive analysis of such systems (National Research Council 2004). Again, because of the relative newness of the cybersecurity field, a number of important metrics are still under development.

Cybersecurity Threats that Challenge Education and Training

Offensive versus Defensive Education

In any type of adversarial activity such as chess, football, or cybersecurity, the concepts of offense and defense are used. Aspects of both of the following statements are true: "the best offense is a strong defense," and its converse, "the best defense is a strong offense." The degree to which these statements can be applied largely depends on the actual activity being considered. For cybersecurity, there is a clear need for defenders to understand the mindset, tools, and techniques being used to attack the systems they are defending. The statement, "it takes one to know one," also comes to mind. The challenge for educators and trainers comes in the decisions around who should receive, and when, offensive education and training. Another related concern is how to mitigate the negative aspects of disseminating this potentially dangerous information to potential bad actors.

One fact to keep in mind when considering these issues is that a large amount of the offensive information already is publicly available. This fact makes it difficult, if not impossible, to ignore this field of study. Later in this chapter we explore the federal government program for recognizing academic institutions that have achieved a level of excellence in cybersecurity education and how it is handling this issue. A student's age, maturity, criminal background, and national origin all need to be considered. Even when these considerations have been satisfied, it is necessary that educators pay significant attention to ethics courses, policy implications, and security clearance regulations before making any deep dive into offensive cybersecurity operations.

Education for the Long Term versus Training for the Short Term

Tension naturally exists between education and training activities in most areas of intellectual endeavors. This is especially true for cybersecurity because of the importance of developing skills at both ends of the spectrum. The field has a real need for professionals who have deep knowledge of the fundamental principles that provide the foundation for the cybersecurity field of study. It is essential that this knowledge is used when making policy and regulatory decisions, as well as strategic analysis of critical systems and adversaries. At the other end of the spectrum, operational experience and hands-on abilities that manifest as skillsets only after years of training and real-world experience are a must for the professional cybersecurity operator. Between these two end points are many cybersecurity professionals who require aspects of both education and training balanced appropriately to produce the functional skillsets needed for the particular tasks they are responsible for performing.

Industry often calls on academic institutions to produce job-ready graduates. However, most companies operate systems and tools that are developed in-house, or change so rapidly that no academic institution can stay current. Industry has historically had on-the-job training and other in-house training and education courses to bring new employees up to speed. What it really needs from academia is students who are ready to be trained by their employers. Higher education should produce students with a broad understanding of the theoretical background and fundamentals of the systems and tools they will eventually master during their employment. There really is no clear-cut line between these two activities of education and training. Aspects of both are incorporated into the most successful programs, whether they are labeled "education" or "training."

Key Cybersecurity Risk Factors in Education Settings

The academic environment for cybersecurity has a number of risk factors, both internal and external to the institutions, which need to be addressed. We have already looked at offensive versus defensive operational education and the need to attract a diverse student population. Financial and other student data must be protected regardless of the field of study selected by the student. This is the same challenge that all institutions face when they collect Personally Identifiable Information on customers or students. This compliance requirement actually provides the opportunity for real-world experience and training for students while still in the academic environment, which can be beneficial to both the institution and the student.

An example of the external risks are the challenges to employment and human resources (HR) departments who are attempting to evaluate the education, training, and work experiences of these cybersecurity students. They may be at a loss on how to determine what type of activities or experiences are equivalent to which degrees or certifications. Making these determinations is a key factor in the proper development of the cybersecurity workforce. The rapid evolution of the field compounds the problem. The terms and concepts are mostly new to HR professionals, and these terms and concepts themselves are changing at a rapid rate. Specific training for HR professionals in how they deal with cybersecurity is often indicated as a mitigating strategy.

Funding for New Programs at the Federal, State, and Local Levels

There is a natural tendency in any complex enterprise to prioritize limited resources. Logic dictates that temporal considerations dominate this prioritization process. Near-term problems, particularly those that threaten the enterprise's existence, must be adequately supported, else longer-term and more damaging issues result. Education and training are "pay me now or pay me later" choices. Some large organizations benefit from investments made in the long-term availability of an appropriately trained and educated workforce. As worldwide competition for workers with technical and knowledge-based skills continues to increase, the education and training process for such a workforce becomes increasingly more essential. Cybersecurity carries the dual role of critical infrastructure protection and enabler of the entire Science, Technology, Engineering, and Mathematics (STEM) enterprise. Try to imagine any STEM enterprise without any computers or networks of computers. As we move deeper into the twenty-first century, this will become even more obvious. Both STEM activities and national security systems are built on these systems and will become even more dependent on them in the future. None of these systems can function properly without significant cybersecurity in place. To a large extent, the future economic and national security of any country will be affected by the quality and quantity of its cybersecurity workforce. The dynamic of these relationships should be well considered by decision makers.

These issues affect all levels of government, academia, and industry. A collaborative approach is required to provide a comprehensive response. Any response will need to be coordinated broadly and in a sustainable manner. NICE is the federal government's response to these complex issues.

Cybersecurity Laws and Policies Relevant to Education and Training

Distinctions between K–12 and Postsecondary Sectors

A main distinction between K–12 and postsecondary/higher education is that K–12 curricula are controlled at the state government level, whereas higher education in general is independent of this type of control. The federal government is prohibited by law from dictating

K–12 curricula. The interaction between government and industry with the K–12 and postsecondary sectors of education reflects government policy and the roles each play in the labor market. From a federal government viewpoint, the funding of research at universities through grants and other funding plays the major role in higher education. On the other hand, state and local governments have the most impact on grant programs for the K–12 sectors. The K–12 role is broad and regulated. By law, the entire population is affected by various mandates regarding topics to be covered during K–12 education. It is generally very difficult for any new topic to receive significant exposure. In the case of cybersecurity, some would argue that the fundamentals of computer science should be the higher priority. However, there are aspects of cybersecurity that are independent of computer science; by using a modular approach, concepts from both fields can be implemented across a K–12 curricula. A more formal approach can be taken in higher education with degree programs and the use of major and minor fields of study.

There is an important role for outreach from the postsecondary sector to K–12 in terms of attracting new students to STEM fields. When industrial partners collaborate with both academic sectors to ensure a pipeline and deep talent pool for their future workforce needs, resources can be leveraged to great effect. Government partners can enable such partnerships to complete the public–private partnership picture. This model harnesses the best aspects of these three major stakeholders and can be replicated on any scale anywhere across the United States.

Federal versus State Role in Laws and Policies

In reality, there is more of a shared responsibility between federal and state laws and policies. The issues faced by both groups are largely the same except in terms of scale. The sharing of information about new and persistent threat vectors is vital. States play a direct role in establishing curricula for their K–12 systems. In some states, the county government role is even more significant for K–12 due to internal structural differences between the state systems. These K–12 cybersecurity education challenges require both state and local government action. Articulation agreements between K–12 and postsecondary institutions can be managed and facilitated by the government. These agreements make the transition from K–12 to community colleges to four-year universities more predictable. They facilitate students wanting to accelerate their academic careers and provide flexibility of pathways from one type of institution to the next. Both state and federal offices and agencies can provide internships for cybersecurity students at various levels of education. These experiences would help attract new students while broadening their skillset, and strengthening the workforce pool.

Critical Infrastructure Protection across all Sectors Requires Relevant Education and Training

Presidential Policy Directive 21 (PPD-21) states, "the Nation's critical infrastructure provides the essential services that underpin American society. Proactive and coordinated efforts are necessary to strengthen and maintain secure, functioning, and resilient critical infrastructure—including assets, networks, and systems—that are vital to public confidence and the Nation's safety, prosperity, and well-being" (White House 2013). This statement from the president reinforces the idea that cybersecurity is the underlying enabler of both STEM enterprises and national security systems.

The nation's critical infrastructure is diverse and complex. It includes distributed networks, varied organizational structures and operating models (including multinational ownership), interdependent functions and systems in both the physical space and cyberspace, and governance constructs that involve multilevel authorities, responsibilities, and regulations. Critical infrastructure owners and operators are uniquely positioned to manage risks to their individual operations and assets, and to determine effective strategies to make them more secure and resilient.

The White House has weighed in on this issue, releasing the *Presidential Policy Directive: Critical Infrastructure and Resilience* (PPD-21). Specifically, PPD-21 outlines the coordination that should occur among agencies, with the intent of "facilitating initiatives to incentivize cybersecurity investments and the adoption of critical infrastructure design features that strengthen all-hazards security and resilience" (White House 2013). To address these and other issues detailed in PPD-21, the DHS has established sixteen critical infrastructure sectors along with their sector-specific agencies as follows:

1. Chemical: DHS

2. Commercial Facilities: DHS

3. Communications: DHS

4. Critical Manufacturing: DHS

5. Dams: DHS

6. Defense Industrial Base: Department of Defense

7. Emergency Services: DHS

8. Energy: Department of Energy

9. Financial Services: Department of the Treasury

10. Food and Agriculture: U.S. Department of Agriculture and Department of Health and Human Services (HHS)

11. Government Facilities: DHS and General Services Administration

12. Health Care and Public Health: HHS

13. Information Technology: DHS

14. Nuclear Reactors, Materials, and Waste: DHS

15. Transportation Systems: DHS and Department of Transportation

16. Water and Wastewater Systems: Environmental Protection Agency (Department of Homeland Security 2013b).

These committees meet regularly to share information and best practices with industry partners and appropriate government officials from several agencies. Recently, DHS organized an additional Cross-Sector Cybersecurity group to focus on the common issues in cybersecurity that cross sectors. Education and training of the current and future workforce is a focus of this group, and it has formed a subgroup to advance the cybersecurity-related aspects in a coordinated fashion. Through this subgroup the academic community can have a voice as well. DHS provides web-based information available to everyone that describes how one can engage with these groups.

The State of the Cybersecurity Workforce in the Education Sector

A recognized group of community colleges and universities is currently producing significant numbers of new graduates with the skillsets needed for all levels and areas of the complex cybersecurity workforce landscape. As of May 2013, there were 166 schools in the United States that had been given the status of a Center of Academic Excellence in Information Assurance Education (CAE/IAE) by the National Security Agency (NSA) and DHS (National Security Agency 2013a). In early June 2013 at the 17th Annual CISSE meeting, more than thirty other schools were added to that list. These institutions, along with others that have similar capabilities, and the various training and certification organizations, form the core of the pipeline for the cybersecurity workforce. It is difficult to determine the total number of students being prepared by the current system or the actual capacity represented by these groups in terms of total possible throughput. What *is* known is that the number of jobs currently available for qualified workers is much greater than the number of students being generated (Cyber Technology and Innovation Center). Industry often reports skillset mismatches in some graduates, or a general lack of hands-on experience. As we begin to describe the workforce with a common language in terms of functional skills, we are for the first time building a baseline of knowledge about the current workforce and the requirements of the labor market it supports.

*Common Language for Ground Truth: The National Cybersecurity
Workforce Framework*

This NCWF was developed by the NICE team in consultation with
subject-matter experts from throughout the federal government with
input from academia, industry, and the general public. This was done
"to provide a common understanding of and lexicon for cybersecurity
work. Defining the cybersecurity population consistently, using standardized terms is an essential step in ensuring that our country is able
to educate, recruit, train, develop, and retain a highly-qualified workforce" (National Initiative for Cybersecurity Education 2013). The
federal government is using this document to map its cybersecurity
workforce and begin a detailed gap analysis to guide future workforce
decisions. Federal contractors, other related industries, and academia
are likewise using the framework for workforce planning and curriculum development. It is critically important that this framework remain
a living document and represent, as closely as possible, the reality of
the present day cybersecurity environment. Developers of the framework are starting work on its next version with the goal of publishing
a new and improved version in early 2014. A regular refresh cycle of
every three years is being implemented and institutionalized for the
long-term sustainment of this effort. As always, public comments will
be requested during the drafting of this new version.

*Need, and Therefore Opportunity, Exists at all Levels
and in all Locations*

The global reach of cyberspace means that there exist both needs
and opportunities for cybersecurity everywhere. There is not a sector of society or a country on the planet that does not share in this
global phenomenon. For the past ten years, DHS has run a national
awareness campaign for cybersecurity. October has been designated
Cybersecurity Awareness month, with October 2013 marking the
tenth anniversary (Department of Homeland Security 2012). As this
grassroots effort continues to grow, the increased awareness of the
problem and surrounding issues will accelerate job growth in all sec-

tors. An improving economy is in part caused by better cybersecurity, and helps to generate new cybersecurity jobs. A very positive cycle of innovation and expanding capabilities is occurring at the intersection of STEM and cybersecurity. Much of the growth experienced during the latter part of the previous century and well into this one can be attributed to activity in this dynamic intersection. Serious attention must be paid to the educational infrastructure in this country if we are to maintain and expand the historic leadership role we have enjoyed.

Workforce Definition Needed for Proper Gap Analysis and Follow-Up Actions

The NCWF is a good first step in defining the cybersecurity workforce landscape. As necessary as this step is, it is not sufficient to complete the task at hand. The required follow-up activity of applying these definitions to the current workforce as broadly and quickly as possible must be accomplished. To this end, the U.S. Office of Personnel Management has produced an *Interactive How-To and Implementation Guide* to help federal agencies move forward with this process (National Initiative for Cybersecurity Education 2012). Once these definitions are established, the work of empirical gap analysis can began in earnest. Employers should be encouraged to pursue their own efforts both independently and in partnerships to establish the pipelines that they require to support their particular workforce needs. Effort is required in both bottom–up and top–down approaches.

Recommendations for Cybersecurity Best Practices in Education and Training

There is a growing interest among the community of educators, trainers, and cybersecurity professionals in applying the teaching hospital model from the medical profession to cybersecurity. The New York State Center for Information Forensics and Assurance and the University at Tulsa both have established examples of this program (New York State Center for Information Forensics and Assurance 2013;

University of Tulsa 2013). Within the scope of such a model, all the currently agreed upon best practices could be applied in a coordinated, cost-effective, flexible environment with systematic assessment and continual improvement. Like a teaching hospital, the activities of a cybersecurity teaching hospital (CTH) model enterprise would extend into the community where the partner organizations are located. One component of a CTH model is a major university granting degrees at the BS, MS, and PhD levels in multiple fields. In addition to a specific cybersecurity program, computer science, engineering, mathematics, and a selection of other related disciplines would be present to provide a well-rounded educational opportunity. Beyond the normal degree programs, intensive internships focused on the development of hands-on skills and operational experience would be available. These internships would be designed in part to enhance the critical infrastructure of the partner organizations of the model enterprise. These organizations would include area community colleges and K–12 systems. University-led outreach and articulation agreements would attract new students to the field by reaching them early in their academic careers. Local industry would partner to provide case-study opportunities that would improve their internal critical infrastructure while providing real-world hands-on experience for the students. A well-coordinated comprehensive model would provide an excellent learning environment for students, lifelong learners, and current professionals.

The Role of Mentorships and Internships in Cybersecurity

Internships are a key step on the path of career transition from academia to the workforce. They provide opportunities for both students and employers to get to know each other without making a full long-term commitment. Experience and understanding of a work environment are critical for the student's development and the employer's deeper understanding of what the student brings to the table, and can assist in the final employment decision. Many scholarship programs, as well as a number of comprehensive degree programs, require internships. In the federal space, these opportunities can sometimes be used to jumpstart the lengthy security clearance process, which is a key barrier to entry into the cybersecurity workforce.

Mentorships have long been recognized for their value in guiding students and new employees through the maze of obstacles often presented by institutions of higher education and new work environments. Institutionalized mentorship programs make the best use of limited resources in an organization by having top–down support and well-defined expectations for both the mentor and the mentee. It is important to note that mentorship relationships are not restricted to one-on-one situations. An individual may need more than one mentor to help with different aspects of the transition process and should be encouraged to seek out the type of support needed, regardless of the number of people that may involve. Mentorships are of general importance, but have particular significance for the field of cybersecurity because of its complex nature and the need to combine practical and theoretical knowledge.

Grade Level Appropriate Curriculum

Curriculum content is totally dictated by the target grade level. K–12 curricula are determined by state laws, whereas curriculum content in higher education is more a function of the marketplace. Lower-level graduates must take care that necessary simplifications do not interject an erroneous view of the deeper concepts, particularly when dealing with technical topics like cybersecurity that build on other more fundamental disciplines. As the grade level and the sophistication of the material increase, a solid curriculum will provide easy references to lower-level work to facilitate remedial work if needed. Pointers to advanced material also are important for the gifted student looking to move forward at his or her own pace. The main challenge here is the size of the curriculum versus the time available to teach it. In K–12 and postsecondary schools, these are real and often difficult constraints. When a new important topic like cybersecurity comes along, it presents a challenge as to how space can be made in already full curriculums. One approach is to modularize the content so that it can be spread across other topics and courses, adding value and breadth without the need to disrupt the big picture.

For a while it was thought that most of the concepts of cybersecurity were too advanced for younger students (say K–8); however, when proper context, language, and classroom techniques are used, students as early as grades 3 and 4 are able to comprehend the basic concepts that are sometimes referred to as computational thinking. For an example of computational thinking in education, the article, "Research Notebook: Computational Thinking–What and Why" by Jeanette Wing (2011) is helpful. Using cybersecurity as a way to introduce other STEM disciplines is another method for infusing the topic across the curriculum.

*Cybersecurity as the Underlying Enabler of the
Entire STEM Enterprise*

Try to imagine any STEM field with no computers. To do this, just think back to the pre-1950s time frame and the state of education in any STEM field. Look to the future and try to imagine any STEM field where the dependency on computers will be decreasing. This thought experiment quickly shows the important role that computers have and will continue to play in the advancement of science and innovation. Cybersecurity is needed wherever computer networks are involved. The information moving across these networks must be secure, reliable, and accurate while remaining user-friendly and available. The capabilities these systems of computers bring to the STEM enterprise are extremely valuable and necessary for continued growth and advancement. STEM is a global activity that depends more and more on reliable Internet connectivity and the security and privacy of the information moving through these systems. Cybersecurity is the enabler of all of this activity, even privacy. Proper cybersecurity policies and implementation are the keys for solid privacy programs and strong resilient STEM enterprises.

Future Trends in Cybersecurity Education and Training

Computer-Aided Classroom Instruction

All of academia is being affected by the new computer-aided tools. Everything from intelligent tutors to automatic test generators, graders to plagiarism detectors, are having an effect on how things happen in the classroom and beyond. The goal here should not be to replace teachers with computers, but rather to enhance teaching capabilities by giving them powerful computer-based tools to free them to do what teachers do best. The human interaction that takes place between student and teacher will not be replaced by any computer in the near future. It is important that we free teachers from tasks that can more easily and efficiently be handled by computer systems, so that they can spend valuable quality time with their students. Tasks like grading papers and tests, delivering subject content, and taking attendance can easily be automated. There is no replacement for direct interaction between student and teacher to inspire and motivate student achievement to its highest level. Cybersecurity will play a critical role here in terms of enabling privacy, as well as tailoring basic level instruction to specific student learning styles that are determined through student interaction with the machine. Cybersecurity enables privacy, a necessary but not sufficient step. Intelligent tutors are also needed to automate the determination of individual learning styles. Providing this information to the teacher can also inform the teacher of the techniques he or she should employ during the human-to-human interactions with the student that the teacher would not previously have had the time or resources to identify. This can lead to an accelerated and more efficient learning experience. Additional capacity also will be realized by adding computer power to the basic skillset of the teaching professional.

Massive Open Online Courses

A new type of course is now possible due to the Internet and computer-based assistant tools that extend teacher capabilities. Massive open online courses (MOOCs) represent a trend that could eventually bring quality education to massive numbers of people who have never before had access to the quality or quantity of information and educational courses now available. Experiments have been conducted with MOOCs at a number of first-class universities like MIT and Stanford with hundreds of thousands of students participating. Business models need to be developed, along with effectiveness studies to ensure that the learning experience meets the standards of other distance learning environments. The potential to reach billions of people around the world with world-class educational opportunities is a game changer at many levels. People often tell stories about that one gifted teacher in their academic career who had some profound effect on the rest of their lives. Imagine how different the world would be if this type of teacher was the rule instead of the exception. MOOCs, computed-aided classrooms, and other technology advances represent steps in that direction. These tools will give power to more teachers to be that gifted educator who has a profound effect on students. With education comes opportunity, progress, and advances in the quality of life for everyone.

Cybersecurity Challenges and Competitions

Over the past decade cyber-challenge competitions of various types have proliferated. They play a number of important roles by attracting new students, providing a platform for individuals and teams to demonstrate their knowledge and cybersecurity skills, and giving event sponsors a close look at new talent and potential new employees. U.S. Cyber Challenge Camp (National Board of Information Security Examiners 2013), the National Collegiate Cyber Defense Competition (2013), the U.S. Air Force Association's CyberPatriot National High School Cyber Defense Competition (Air Force Association 2013), and the Global Cyberlympics (Global Cyberlympics Organizing Committee 2013) are all examples of current cybersecurity competitions and challenges open to students of various age groups. These competitions have different formats and target different age groups. They are being used by students and potential employers alike. Employers sponsor these events to get a close firsthand look at new talent, and often make job offers on the spot to a strong team or individual performers. High school-age and even younger students are being attracted to the field by these competition activities. There are ongoing efforts to unify aspects of these competitions into a single league. The goals would be to institutionalize these activities, provide a stable environment for students to practice and develop their skills, and evaluate whether the status and popularity of these events could expand the interest and pool of potential workforce in the cybersecurity arena.

Expanding Centers of Academic Excellence in Information Assurance Education Program

NSA and DHS jointly sponsored the CAE/IAE, IA 2-Year Education and Training (CAE/2Y), and IA Research (CAE/R) programs. The goal of these programs is to reduce vulnerability in our national information infrastructure by promoting higher education and research in IA and producing a growing number of professionals with IA expertise in various disciplines (National Security Agency 2013b). Bishop and Taylor, in an article entitled "A Critical Analysis of the Centers of Academic Excellence Program," presented an analysis of this program, which was established in 1999. The introduction of this paper contained the following history:

> In 1997, the academic keynote at the NCISSE called for more and better academic information assurance and computer security programs to educate students in this area. To help fill this need, in 1998 the National Security Agency began a program to recognize those institutions working in this area. The institutions were designated "Centers of Academic Excellence in Information Assurance Education." The original goal of this program was to increase the number of students educated in information assurance, to create centers of computer security knowledge for education, and to provide a resource to which the nation could turn in order to improve the state of computer security and information assurance. Faculty at the centers would then perform outreach to surrounding institutions in an advisory capacity or as visiting faculty. The importance of this program was recognized by the Department of Homeland Security's becoming a co-sponsor of the program when that

Department was created. Now, 11 years later, the need for graduates from computer science programs to be educated in information assurance, and the faculty to teach them, is stronger than ever. (Bishop and Taylor 2009)

The CAE/IAE program has been under way for more than a decade. During that time the number of schools receiving this designation has grown steadily, with about two hundred recognized schools at this time. This is the only such program existing in the area of cybersecurity education that has national reach and federal government backing. In the past few years the program has expanded in response to the growing needs and complexities of the cybersecurity field. Two-year schools or community colleges have a critical role to play in terms of education and training for both traditional and nontraditional students. Their cost and easy accessibility make them ideal for displaced workers, returning veterans, and others who need more flexibility than is normally available at four-year institutions. For programmatic details on the CAE/IAE program for two-year schools, see the article, "National Centers of Academic Excellence in IA Education (CAE/IAE) Criteria for Measurement," which lists eight areas that are the metrics for the program (National Security Agency 2012). The areas include outreach and collaboration as well as specific guidelines around qualities of the academic program, including research, student, and faculty criteria. These metrics are a good example of best practices for academic programs operating in this space.

Recently, the need to start doing offensive cybersecurity operations education has prompted the program to establish a new track focused on this topic. A number of schools with classified facilities and other essential capacities in place have been awarded status to teach courses in this very sensitive area. Participation in the CAE/IAE program also allows a school to compete for Scholarship for Service funding provided by the National Science Foundation (National Science Foundation 2013a). The CAE/IAE schools form a core of academic institutions that are producing the talent needed for the cybersecurity workforce of today and tomorrow.

Sources of Further Information

FCC Small Biz Cyber Planner 2.0. http://www.fcc.gov/cyberplanner.

National Initiative for Cybersecurity Careers and Studies. http://niccs. us-cert.gov/.

National Initiative for Cybersecurity Education. http://www.nist.gov/ nice/.

Stop.Think.Connect. from the Department of Homeland Security. http://www.dhs.gov/stopthinkconnect/.

References

Air Force Association. 2013. "CyberPatriot National High School Cyber Defense Competition." Accessed August 8, 2013. http://www.uscyber patriot.org/Pages/default.aspx.

Bishop, Matt, and Carol Taylor. 2009. "A Critical Analysis of the Centers of Academic Excellence Program." *Proceedings of the 13th Colloquium for Information Systems Security Education*, Seattle, WA June 1–3, 2009.

Carnegie Mellon University. 2013. "Women@SCS." Accessed August 7, 2013. http://women.cs.cmu.edu/.

Cybersecurity Credentials Collaborative. 2013. "Mission Statement." Accessed August 7, 2013. http://www.cybersecuritycc.org/.

Cyber Technology and Innovation Center. (n.d.). "Cyber Jobs Report" http:// www.ctic-baltimore.com/report.html.

Department of Homeland Security. 2012. "National Cyber Security Awareness Month." http://www.dhs.gov/national-cyber-security-awareness-month.

———. 2013a. "Critical Infrastructure." http://www.dhs.gov/critical-infrastructure.

———. 2013b. "Critical Infrastructure Sectors." Accessed August 7, 2013. http://www.dhs.gov/critical-infrastructure-sectors.

Global Cyberlympics Organizing Committee. 2013. "Global Cyberlympics." http://www.cyberlympics.org/.

Homeland Security Advisory Council. 2012. "CyberSkills Task Force Report." https://www.dhs.gov/sites/default/files/publications/HSAC%20 CyberSkills%20Report%20-%20Final.pdf.

National Board of Information Security Examiners. 2013. "U.S. Cyber Challenge." Accessed August 8, 2013. http://www.uscyberchallenge.org/.

National Collegiate Cyber Defense Competition. 2013. "National Collegiate Cyber Defense Competition." Accessed August 8, 2013. http://www. nationalccdc.org/.

National Initiative for Cybersecurity Education. 2012. *The National Cybersecurity Workforce Framework: Interactive How-To and Implementation Guide.* October 1. http://csrc.nist.gov/nice/framework/national_cybersecurity_workforce_framework_interactive_how_to.pdf.

———. 2013. *The National Cybersecurity Workforce Framework.* http://csrc.nist.gov/nice/framework/.

National Research Council. 2004. *On Evaluating Curricular Effectiveness: Judging the Quality of K-12 Mathematics Evaluations.* Washington DC: National Academies Press.

National Science Foundation. 2013a. "CyberCorps: Scholarship for Service (SFS)."Accessed August 8, 2013. http://www.nsf.gov/funding/pgm_summ.jsp?pims_id=5228.

———. 2013b. "National Center for Science and Engineering Statistics (NCSES)." Last modified July 16. http://www.nsf.gov/statistics/.

National Security Agency. 2012. "National Centers of Academic Excellence in IA Education (CAE/IAE) Criteria for Measurement." Last modified August 12. http://www.nsa.gov/ia/academic_outreach/nat_cae/cae_iae_program_criteria.shtml.

———. 2013a. "Centers of Academic Excellence Institutions." Last modified February 21. http://www.nsa.gov/ia/academic_outreach/nat_cae/institutions.shtml.

———. 2013b. "National Centers of Academic Excellence." Last modified January 10. http://www.nsa.gov/ia/academic_outreach/nat_cae/index.shtml.

National Security Council. 2013. *Cybersecurity.* http://www.whitehouse.gov/administration/eop/nsc/cybersecurity.

Networking and Information Technology Research and Development Program. 2013. "Welcome to the NITRD Program." Accessed August 7. http://nitrd.gov/.

New York State Center for Information Forensics and Assurance. 2013. "CIFA Fosters Information Assurance and Forensics Activity at UAlbany." Accessed August 7, 2013. http://www.albany.edu/cifa/.

University of Tulsa. 2013. "Cyber Corps Program." Accessed August 7, 2013. http://www.utulsa.edu/academics/Centers-and-Institutes/cyber-corps-program.aspx.

White House. 2013. *Presidential Policy Directive: Critical Infrastructure Security and Resilience.* http://www.whitehouse.gov/the-press-office/2013/02/12/presidential-policy-directive-critical-infrastructure-security-and-resil.

Wing, Jeannette M. 2011. "Research Notebook: Computational Thinking—What and Why?" *The Link* 6: 20–23. http://link.cs.cmu.edu/files/11-399_The_Link_Newsletter-3.pdf.

Chapter 8

Cybersecurity in the International Arena

KAI ROER

Introduction

This chapter looks at the cybersecurity workforce from an international perspective. Formal research on how different countries organize, educate, and train their cybersecurity workforce is scarce. Therefore, this chapter draws from interviews with cybersecurity leaders from around the world as well as other sources to examine how different countries use cybersecurity as part of their information warfare strategy and how this affects their focus on the development of a cybersecurity workforce.

Laws and regulations, particularly privacy regulations, offer one international challenge. Another challenge is the problem of attributing an attack or security breach to the responsible parties. Additionally, different countries and regions have varying perspectives, goals, and philosophies relating to the economic and political balance of the world, and whether and how they use information warfare.

This chapter also discusses some of the standards-setting organizations around the world. There are currently no international standards for cybersecurity education, and few countries except China and the United States have a clearly defined strategy where academia plays a part in creating a workforce that can be used in information warfare.

One possible scenario is the establishment of regional hubs of cybersecurity competence; these hubs could become magnets for global cybersecurity talent that may result in draining talent from other regions. From a global workforce perspective, it is also relevant to consider how different cultures affect our communication and understanding of each other, and possibly interfere with our goals and strategies.

Fundamental Issues in International Cybersecurity

Cybersecurity is a global issue. In cyberspace, borders are almost completely removed and data travels freely. Where separate nation-states used to exist, blocks of cooperating nations now emerge. As new alliances form, old ones are either strengthened or deteriorate due to changing interests.

Whereas national borders, and to some extent multinational organizations, used to determine who was interacting with each other and why, technology now allows for all sorts of new alliances to form. Cyber threats can originate from any location around the world; someone can be located in the Ukraine and hack banks in the United States. This poses a very important challenge for national lawmaking, as American laws have no jurisdiction in the Ukraine. This means the law enforcement forces that are supposed to catch the criminals attacking their citizens no longer are able to effectively do their job.

Cyber threats come from many types of adversaries. At the Norwegian Armed Forces Cyber Command, Maj. Gen. Roar Sundseth (2013) divides cyber threats into three general categories: criminals, activists, and nation-states. No matter how you choose to divide your adversaries, two challenges are evident. The first is that a large number of attacks represent noise, either created by automatic systems and bots to determine low-hanging fruit, or as a backdrop to hide activities the adversary does not want you to discover (Sundseth 2013).

The second challenge is one of attribution. Attackers can easily hide their activities among hacktivists and criminals simply by piggybacking on others' attacks. It is also easy to hide the source of an attack using bots and remotely controlled computers, rendering it practically impossible to gather conclusive evidence that one particular computer or network was behind any particular attack. Groups or countries use the attribution challenge to create plausible deniability. China and Russia are two examples of countries that apply this tactic (Hagestad 2012; Prince 2009).

Competence and Training

Higher education is a key factor in innovation and human capital development. According to a report published by the Organisation for Economic Co-operation and Development, tertiary education has gone through massive and dramatic changes worldwide over the past fifty years (Tremblay, Lalancette, and Roseveare 2013).

Countries like China, Russia, and the United States recognized early the potential in using computer technology in information warfare. China has been studying how both Russia and the United States used information warfare in conflicts since the 1980s (Hagestad 2012). In China, universities have developed cybersecurity workers at least since 2001, and cybersecurity training has been part of China's military for even longer. Russia is equally versed in cybersecurity education, although there it falls under the country's computer science and mathematics departments. One challenge Russia is facing is the transition from the Soviet-era structure of education, and the strict division between education and research. When these two are merged, Russia is likely to have the ability to create higher quality education, research, and direction (Nag 2013).

A cybersecurity workforce requires more than just operational and technical training. In the increasing complexity that is cyberspace, workers need to be creative and to understand complex and abstract concepts where nontechnical aspects like interpersonal communication, culture, and motivation play an important role (Sundseth 2013). Education and training are vital in preparing the cybersecurity workforce for the challenges they will meet. As the complexity increases, educational institutions must alter and increase their curriculum to face the new needs.

In Norway, the Gjøvik University College (2013) is spearheading a curriculum codeveloped with the major security sectors in Norway. The initiative is called the Center for Cyber and Information Security, and is sponsored by major actors in both the public and private sectors. Some of the largest private companies in Norway are part of the initiative, as are the Norwegian National Security Authority, the Police Security Service, the Norwegian Armed Forces Cyber Command, and the Norwegian Defense Research Establishment, to name a few.

Cross-sector educational initiatives like the Center for Cyber and Information Security may prove effective in creating a broader understanding of the challenges cybersecurity poses on the international level.

In addition to cross-sector education, it is important to include cross-topic education as well. Cybersecurity workers must understand the inner workings of organizations, both the economic and managerial sides and the political side. Likewise, top-level management, boards, and politicians must be aware of the principles of cybersecurity. Adding cybersecurity at a strategic level to existing leadership education is recommended.

Legal Challenges

A challenge in the international cyber domain is the jurisdiction and applicability of laws. In cyberspace there are no real borders; without borders, there is no clear jurisdiction or sovereignty. Where we used to be able to draw a line on a map, or set up a border control post, we now need to find clear and concise rules and definitions to govern the cyber domain.

If a Ukrainian hacker steals credit card information from a U.S. clearinghouse, who should investigate, prosecute, and judge the criminal? The United States would prefer to handle the matter itself. The challenge arises when it comes to charging, apprehending, and extracting a foreign citizen in a foreign country. No country is allowed to enter another country to fetch any individual for any reason without permission. As soon as the crime crosses borders, the nation-state must adhere to international law, and use international bodies of policing like Interpol.

Organizations and nations are growing tired of being under constant attack in the cyber domain. Whereas some argue about retaliation and the right to "hack back," other groups focus on establishing a common legal ground through international cooperation and policing.

There can be no doubt that breaking into a computer is a crime, no matter who owns it. Legal principles also must apply in cyberspace. If we accept a culture of civil retaliation, where victims take it on themselves to hack back, no matter the motive, we move away from a system governed by law into a "wild west." From an emotional standpoint, it is tempting to endorse the "eye for an eye" viewpoint. However, if we allow ourselves to analyze the challenge from an intellectual point of view, we soon discover that a system based on retaliation is a short-term solution at best.

A workable, long-term solution must be developed based on the principles of human rights, a modern legal system, and respect for the global society. Over the coming decade, politicians and diplomats must find solutions that enable economic growth, a free flow of information, and a sense of control over the cyber domain.

As of 2013, the question of jurisdiction over the Internet is still an early and ongoing debate. There is a growing understanding that regulation is needed, and a growing concern for privacy and human rights as cyber surveillance increases.

Principles of Privacy

In the European Union (EU), there is a long tradition of privacy protection. The concern for privacy is a historic legacy coming from the demand for openness and trust after World War II. Privacy in Europe is considered the right to protect any and all information that relates to you as a person; the idea is that any information that relates to you should be yours to control.

In the 1980s, the EU examined privacy regulations concerning information used, transferred, or stored on computers and computer networks. There was a concern that computers made it easier to collect and analyze vast amounts of data, and that the collection, use, and storage of such needed a strict control.

The Data Protection Act (currently under revision) was implemented in 1995, and created clear and concise regulations for how organizations were to handle data tied to individuals (European Parliament 1995). A selection of the principles implemented includes the following:

- A division between sensitive and nonsensitive data.

- A clear definition of sensitive data (seven data types are considered sensitive).

- A clear set of rules as to how an organization can use, transfer, and store said data.

- The determination that each organization must have a risk assessment plan in place before said data can be used.

- Guidelines for deleting all personally identifiable data within a certain amount of time.

Privacy of information as implemented by the EU is built on the belief that any information that can identify you is personal information, and thus should be treated accordingly under the Data Protection Act (Carloan 2011).

Treatment of privacy of information varies from country to country. In the United States there has been little concern or interest in this topic until very recently. Only when news broke about the National Security Agency (NSA) tapping into Google, Facebook, and other companies did U.S. citizens and lawmakers start to realize cyberspace was an extremely powerful tool for collecting, storing, and analyzing data in the interest of profiling terrorists and criminals. In this light, it also is important to note that privacy is now a major concern and area of focus in the U.S. *International Strategy for Cyberspace*. One of its foundational principals is valuing privacy: "Individuals should be protected from arbitrary or unlawful state interference with their privacy when they use the Internet" (White House 2011).

Paradoxically, in both the EU and United States, users seem to trust cyberspace with their information, and willingly share details of their lives. Observing users in countries like Russia and China, it appears that people are less likely to share anything on publicly available networks. Users in countries with less freedom of speech and trust in their governments seem to be more wary of giving up their privacy online.

An interesting trend is the growth of social media use to communicate during civil unrest. What initially was a way to invite your friends to join you in a peaceful rally for or against a topic of interest has quickly become a powerful tool to organize civil unrest. A widespread use of social media during the Arab Spring helped spread the news about the revolution, reaching user groups that might not have caught on to the political change without such tools.

This kind of explosive spread of information, seemingly out of the control of the existing government, has proved a challenge for modern rulers to handle. A political demand is starting to request more control on how information forms and spreads over social media during a crisis.

Status of the Workforce

The cybersecurity workforce and its status varies from region to region, and country to country. In developed countries, the cybersecurity workforce is educated and highly skilled, even as many countries are not able to fill the demand for more trained cybersecurity workers.

The demand for cybersecurity workers has created a large number of new educational programs worldwide. You can study cybersecurity to various degrees in most countries, although the level and quality of the education varies. NATO countries, spearheaded by the United States, are working actively to increase the quality of the workforce, as well as the available education. All countries recognize the need for cybersecurity competence—locally, nationally, and internationally.

Legislation, Governance, and Standards Relating to International Cybersecurity

Standards-Setting Bodies

There are a number of standards-setting bodies that relate to cyber-space. However, there are currently no international cyber workforce education standards. Many countries outside of the United States are developing cybersecurity education programs, usually within their established computer science programs. In the United States, the National Security Agency (2012) works closely with universities and higher educational bodies to develop and implement a cybersecurity curriculum. This kind of direct intervention from the government security agencies to form and control cybersecurity education is not equaled outside of the United States.

Most developed countries have programs and education for information security and information and communication technologies (ICT) security within their computer science programs. Some of these countries are now developing laws and regulations to enhance the security competence. However, it appears that various regions focus on different aspects of security, if they consider it at all. As an example, the EU and South Africa focus more on privacy, whereas Russia tends to concentrate on computer science and mathematics, and China aims toward a general heightening of tertiary education as a whole.

On an international level, the International Organization for Standardization (ISO) and the International Electrotechnical Commission (IEC) also should be mentioned. The ISO/IEC organization has been issuing a growing set of standards within security and information security. One challenge of standards from ISO/IEC is a relatively high cost of implementation and certification.

The International Telecommunications Union (ITU), the UN agency for telecommunications, is developing strategies, regulations, and legal documentation related to cybersecurity. Russia and China have proposed more control of information in telecommunications, whereas leaders within the United States and the EU believe the current conventions already implement the needed controls, and thus oppose the changes. A notable effort by the ITU is in developing and distributing a set of legal documentation for its developing country members. If implemented by the members, this would be a major step toward a global understanding, and legal practice on cybersecurity will be put forth.

It is also important to look at efforts by NATO to create a manual on cyber warfare. The Tallinn Manual (Schmitt 2013) discusses the applicability of traditional international law to cyber warfare. The manual defines a set of rules and explains how each rule would be used in a cyber war. The manual has received opposition, especially by Russia, which argues for making all cyber warfare illegal. In examining these organizations, we can see that in cyberspace, there is no way around legal and regulatory compliance (Roer and Lakhoua 2011).

ISO/IEC

ISO/IEC is an international organization providing standards for business and government organizations. Their standards are not enforced, but are considered voluntary. ISO was started in 1947, and today consists of 163 member countries. The standards provided by ISO cover topics ranging from quality management to corporate social responsibility. A large number of standards are related to ICT, from standards on vocabulary to definitions of data types. For cybersecurity, the ISO27000 family of standards has been established. Another relevant ISO standard for security in general is the ISO31000 series, which covers risk and risk management.

The ISO27002 standard and its determination of best practices is widely used in both private and governmental organizations worldwide. From a risk management point of view, the standard offers a set of best practices that enables a quick and adaptable approach for each organization to assess and mitigate risk. Even organizations not certified under the ISO27001 tend to use the risk management best practices offered by the standard.

One challenge of an ISO certification is the cost of implementation. Due to the process of certification, the documentation requirements, and the organizational changes required to apply a standard, many smaller organizations find it a challenge to become certified. Their incentives are usually tied to customer requirements, as both the public sector and many private sectors increasingly require their suppliers to be certified.

The International Telecommunications Union

The International Telecommunication Union (ITU) is the UN's specialized agency for ICT. With 193 member countries and more than seven hundred private-sector entities and academic institutions as members, ITU is a global forum with focus on international cooperation between governments in the field of ICT. In the global scene, ITU seems to have more power and impact in developing countries than in the United States.

One of the cybersecurity efforts of ITU (2009) is its cybercrime legislation toolkit. The toolkit aims to help developing countries understand national and international challenges regarding cybercrime, and provides a set of example legislation. The ITU argues there is a need to create a common understanding and international legislation related to cybercrime. As long as cybercrime is treated differently in different countries, there is always a risk that some countries may provide safe havens for criminals and other unlawful activities.

A recent criticism against ITU is a concern that it may become a new regulatory body where the members can apply regulations, surveillance, and border control technology on their own national Internets (Weissman 2012). Such regulations would be considered to be UN-sanctioned, meaning that they would be considered a legalized measure from an international point of view (Weissman 2012). Interestingly, this right to stop, control, and inspect telecommunications at the border is already a part of the ITU Constitution (International Telecommunication Union 2011), and has been so since the establishment of the first ITU Constitution in 1865. Relevant ITU programs for the cybersecurity sector include the ITU-IMPACT (International Multilateral Partnership Against Cyber Threats), the Child Online Protection initiative, and educating member states on the need for skilled cybersecurity workers.

Other Standards

There are a number of other standards related to cybersecurity. It is helpful to divide these into two groups:

1. Voluntary programs where one may choose whether to implement the standard or best practice. This group includes ISO/IEC, Common Criteria, NIST, and Cobit and ITIL.

2. Multilateral/bilateral agreements where countries agree to adhere to certain standards. EU, NATO, and BRICS are example of such agreements. These kinds of agreements often come with requirements to which each party agrees to accept and adhere.

NATO and the Tallinn Manual

Few international laws exist when it comes to regulating cyber warfare, as discovered by NATO when it analyzed the situation in 2009 after the 2007 Tallinn cyber-attack. The United States and its allies in NATO set out to write a code of conduct where it defined different kinds of cyber-attacks and rules on how to respond to each one (Schmitt 2013).

The Tallinn Manual states that cyber warfare should follow the laws and practice of war and, as such should follow the UN charters. The United States embraces the *Tallinn Manual*, as is evident in the presentation State Department Legal Adviser Harold Koh made at a USCYBERCOM sponsored conference in 2012 (Schmitt 2012).

Outside the United States, the *Tallinn Manual* has received mixed responses. As of June 2013, very few entities inside NATO seem to have adopted it, and controversy comes both from within and outside NATO itself. However, the NATO defense minister is taking cybersecurity seriously, and it is likely that NATO countries will follow the U.S. lead and apply the manual. Russia remains a country to watch, as its skepticism of the *Tallinn Manual* has been well documented (Chernenko 2013).

BRICS

The BRICS countries consist of Brazil, Russia, India, China, and, since 2010, South Africa. What started as a multilateral coalition to align common goals and provide a negotiating body to promote the member's economic interests in the World Bank and the International Monetary Fund, has quickly evolved into other areas. According to Rasmus Reinvang (2013), the BRICS countries are responsible for the creation of the G20 forum, the world's twenty largest economies acting as a global economic security forum. The G20 forum replaced the G7 forum, which up until 2009 had been considered the driving force behind global economic growth.

Although the BRICS countries have different agendas and goals in many multilateral areas, they are becoming an important political factor. They exercise that power already; for example, through their blocking of votes in the World Trade Organization (Reinvang 2013).

Cybersecurity is not yet (as of this writing) a part of the common discussion and multilateral scope of BRICS. Considering the quick expansion of its scope since it was established in 2009, it will be important to follow the BRICS countries closely in the coming years. All BRICS countries are members of the ITU, as well as the UN.

Of the BRICS countries, China and Russia seem the most active in cybersecurity, both operatively and diplomatically. These two countries are also members of the UN Security Council, and as such, they may have a different focus than the rest of the BRICS countries. It is worth mentioning that South Africa has a long tradition of cybersecurity, both in academia and in private industries.

A Great Divide

Different regions and countries have very different perspectives on cybersecurity. Some countries, like the United States, clearly demonstrate an ability, willingness, and power to be in the forefront of cybersecurity. The National Initiative for Cybersecurity Education (NICE), the National Initiative for Cybersecurity Careers and Studies (NICCS), and the aforementioned NSA certification program for tertiary education are all enabling the United States to develop and maintain a skilled and resilient workforce with an understanding of cybersecurity.

Another indicator of the United States' development is the Stuxnet worm, which at the time of its development and deployment was far beyond any other threat (Kerr, Rollins, and Theohary 2010). It is also necessary to realize the importance of the actual deployment of Stuxnet. Suddenly, ideas that had so far only been discussed as possibilities became true. More importantly, the concept of a state-sponsored, targeted attack with potentially physical implications became a reality.

Few other countries are at the same level as the United States. Israel was an early adopter of cybersecurity technology, and has a thriving environment for developing cybersecurity technology. Tight relations with the United States ensure a steady stream of competence and information flowing both ways. Most other countries are currently unlikely to be at the same level as the United States, but more research is needed in this area. One possible area of future research would be to measure the cybersecurity maturity level of different countries. To my knowledge, no such research exists on a global level today.

Challenges and Opportunities in Building the Cybersecurity Workforce

The most important challenge in cybersecurity is the gap between the available competencies and the needed competencies. This is not only true in the United States, where NICCS and NICE have developed the "Best Practices for Planning a Cybersecurity Workforce" (National Initiative for Cybersecurity Education 2013), but globally.

The speed with which computer technology develops quickly surpasses the ability of society to stay up to date. In Europe, computer classes are introduced in primary school. In countries like Norway and Denmark, pupils in elementary school use iPads as part of their learning experience. The rationale is to create a more interesting learning experience, and to prepare children for a future filled with devices and cyber technology.

Universities in Europe and Asia offer many courses of study with a focus on cyber technology; increasingly their emphasis has shifted to security. In Africa, governments are developing university programs offering master's degrees and doctorates. Globally, the race is on as to who can develop the most knowledgeable cyber workforce first.

From a global perspective, the cybersecurity workforce is likely to become a scarce resource. All nation-states and multinational corporations will compete for the brightest minds. A combination of increasing demand and decreasing resources makes it likely that cybersecurity professionals will become a highly sought after resource. This will increase the cost of employment, effectively leaving companies and countries with fewer resources and greater vulnerability.

The increased demand for cybersecurity specialists will also create a level of workforce volatility, where human capital is likely to be drained from some regions and to regroup in others. Consider the segregation model developed by Schelling (1969), which we can apply to cybersecurity education. According to Schelling, when the threshold of some individuals is reached, they will move out of the area, to an area where they are comfortable. In this case, think of each individual's threshold as a measure of his or her interest in cybersecurity. The higher the interest, the more likely the person is to seek out similar environments, moving into areas (both geographical and in terms of employment) where the interest can be honed and harvested. In this perspective, it is likely that common interest and education, combined with common work tasks, will create international hubs where cybersecurity professionals are more likely to be found. Using Schelling's model, we can foresee that a scarce resource like cybersecurity professionals is likely to seek out others to create competence hubs. We can expect the competence war to be fought by creating the best possible environment for our cybersecurity professionals to thrive locally, nationally, and internationally.

Creating such environments becomes increasingly important. Most nation-states and multinational organizations recognize this challenge, and are making plans to deal with it. Individual organizations will also need to put in motion a strategy to identify and attract highly skilled cybersecurity workers.

Employee Sourcing

Employee sourcing strategies vary from region to region and country to country. Different organizations and industries also have different strategies and practices. Because cybersecurity talent is employed in a broad range of industries across many domains, both public and private, it may be worth taking a closer look at employment sourcing strategies.

Multinational corporations have a different palette of tools available than do local organizations. The private sector is usually less restricted in its talent hunt than the public sector is. A local organization sources its talent locally or nationally; only rarely does it cross borders in the hunt for talent. This may be due to economic restrictions, lack of vision, or local requirements. For example, a local manufacturer may not have the resources to source and relocate talent from abroad. Due to its small size, this type of organization may have a local base of talent it can pick from without cannibalizing its resource pool. A multinational corporation may have outgrown its local or even national pool of available talent, forcing it to look outside the country's borders. Multinationals are, by definition, already operating in several countries, exposing them to cultural differences, legal requirements, and legal opportunities.

Let's assume that a local manufacturer decides to employ a foreign worker. It offers her the job, and only too late realizes the visa and work permit requirements are far tougher than they initially thought; then add to that the other possible challenges in language differences and cultural background. For a local manufacturer with no prior experience, this may turn out to be a daunting task. The situation for the multinational corporation is different. It is well versed in cultural differences, politics, and the legal aspect of a global workforce. A multinational also has the option to employ new workers locally, where they already live, a luxury the local manufacturer usually does not have.

The private- and public-sector sourcing strategies also vary. In many countries, the public sector is forced into restrictions that the private sector need not follow. For example, many public offices choose employees based on legal requirements, forcing them to choose a candidate with more seniority (even when one is not needed), or not allowing them to employ a great operational talent without a formal degree. The private sector usually is less restricted and can employ whomever it chooses.

Location, Location, Location

We need to view the cybersecurity workforce as a global resource pool; as such, there is a constant battle for the best talent. Hubs develop in some areas, creating a draw for talent. The United States is one such hub, attracting workers from all over the world. For the United States and similar hubs, this trend helps source the best talent in a global pool of cyber workers. This does not mean that anyone with cybersecurity competence is welcome to move to any hub of their liking, as many countries have strict rules when it comes to employment visas. Another possible challenge with using a global workforce lies in the need for background checks and security clearances.

For organizations that are not located in or nearby such a talent hub, a growing challenge arises as local talent moves to places where opportunities for growth and development are perceived as better. This drain on the local workforce is likely to create weak spots where cybersecurity may be prioritized at a lower level than in the hubs, leaving these areas less secured technically, operationally, and strategically. In other words, such segregation of the talent pool may also create *low-hanging fruit* more likely to be victimized.

A higher level of available cybersecurity talent creates a higher level of understanding, increasing the overall cybersecurity competence of the country and making it more attractive for cybersecurity talent to go there for work. A positive spiral is created. Of course, the flipside of this upward spiral is the impact on the cybersecurity competence of a less-attractive country. With its cyber talent being drained, that country becomes less attractive to others in the workforce.

Culture

Opposing cultures can create challenges in a global workforce. One example of a cultural impact on security is found in the research done by Joseph Bonneau (2012), comparing password strength on a global scale. His findings show that the language you speak is a predictor of the strength of your password. Germany and Korea are the two countries with the strongest passwords.

Culture also affects the way we communicate, how we interact, and what we do. Our culture also affects our actions, goals, and targets. Understanding the culture of your workforce is as important as understanding the culture of your adversaries.

Educating the Workforce

Cybersecurity education and its scope vary widely from region to region and country to country. As mentioned before, in Russia and former Soviet countries, cybersecurity education seems to be based in advanced mathematics and engineering, with a focus on abstract models. South Africa follows Europe more closely, focusing on a general understanding of computer science, where security is one of several topics. Both China and India have been known to send students to other countries, most commonly to the United States. In the 1990s, Indian students attended many computer science classes, and today many foreign students are Chinese.

From a foreign perspective, it makes sense to send students to other countries for study. Developing countries can educate their workforce to a higher level than they might be able to internally, and without having to develop the required infrastructure first. As is evident in India, and is beginning to show in China, sending students to a country with well-established educational systems not only provides said students with competence and credentials, but when the students return home, they can help spread and refine the knowledge locally. One strategy is to use the returning students to create higher-quality tertiary education. It seems like China has employed this strategy successfully, unlike India. As shown in Table 8.1, India has only one university on the World Top 500 University list (Center for World-Class Universities 2013). China has twenty-eight universities on that same list, more than half of which are rated as the same or better than the Indian university. The United States has 150 universities on the list.

Table 8.1. Number of Universities a Country Has on the
World Top 500 List

Country	Number of Universities on World Top 500	Population in Millions
United States	150	311
China	28	1,344
Japan	21	127
Brazil	6	196
Norway	4	5
Russia	2	142
India	1	1,241
South Africa	No data available	50

Adapted from Center for World-Class Universities 2013.

By comparison, tiny Norway, a country with some five million inhabitants, has four universities, twice as many as Russia in this ranking.

There are several other university rankings available, including the Times Higher Education World University Rankings. The purpose of Table 8.1 is to demonstrate that the size of a country does not correlate to the number of highly ranked universities.

Such rankings do not tell us all there is to know (Marginson and van der Wende 2009). There are, for example, large cultural differences between these countries. China and India are similar in terms of population, yet China has an economy almost three times as large.

Economic theory alone does not conclusively explain the economic growth of Asia, and the subsequent economic growth of China (Sarel 1996). It also is important to consider the historic background of higher education in China and India (Altbach 2009). Both countries have a long tradition and experience in educating their workforce, and more recently, both were heavily influenced by Western higher education. In India, a British educational model replaced the traditional one. The traditional Chinese model was first systematically replaced by a Soviet model, and later totally removed during the Cultural Revolution.

It appears that political strategy and priorities are a more likely explanation for the growth, and rise in quality, of tertiary education in China. Knowing that China has a deeply rooted tradition of long-term strategies, and taking into account its philosophical perspective on war (Tzu 2010), one conclusion is that China has a clear and long-term strategy to create world-class universities to compete with Western universities. Such universities may become a resource pool for the global market.

From a sourcing point of view, it makes sense to pay close attention to how regions and nations develop their workforce. As long as the cybersecurity workforce is in growing demand, and the resources are scarce, organizations and countries must educate their own population while also attracting foreign talent.

Abstract Thinking versus Operational Skills

Some countries lack technically advanced equipment like modern computers and networking environments for students. This is true in Romania, formerly part of the USSR. In the former Soviet Union, education was an important part of building the country, enabling Soviet advances and creating a workforce that was highly skilled in the hard sciences (Medynsky 1944; Rosen 1980). Romanian citizens, like those in many other former Soviet countries, are well versed in mathematics and science. Even without advanced technology, Romania educates some very skilled cyber workers, many of whom find computer-related work abroad. Even without the availability of highly advanced technology, some countries are able to train and educate a cyber workforce. This leads to an interesting question: What is more important in cyber education: technical competence or abstract thinking?

In a phone interview in 2013, former White House CIO Carlos Solari described a class at a university where he lectures. The class was a high-level, master's degree course; the students had great technology skills. Yet, he had to spend a large amount of time explaining the basic cybersecurity concept of confidentiality, integrity, and accessibility (CIA).

The concept of CIA is an abstract one. To understand it requires a certain level of abstract thinking, and the ability to relate abstract concepts to real-world scenarios. CIA is not directly related to bits and bytes, nor is it connected to ICT; it relates to information itself, regardless of the method of transport that information uses. Solari ended up with the same question as presented earlier—What is more important in cyber education: technical competence or abstract thinking?

Technical competence is a skill that can be easily learned, whereas abstract thinking requires a different approach and longer training. It would be interesting to see research in this area, to compare the usefulness of abstract thinking in cybersecurity with the focus on operational skills currently prevalent in the Western world. However, this is a topic that is more related to educational studies, psychology, and cognition than it is to cybersecurity itself. From a cybersecurity workforce education point of view, it makes sense to understand how both abstract thinking and technical training (skills) relate to the effectiveness and education of the cybersecurity workforce.

Future Trends

Cybersecurity is still a young profession. As such, it is very hard to predict future trends with much confidence. Adding in the complex global nature of cyberspace, one may predict that less mature countries are likely to evolve and develop their competence to higher levels than today. The principles of information security will remain the same (Swanson and Guttman 1996). As cybersecurity education and workforce requirements continue to evolve, a saturation of the competence requirements is expected (Allen 2013). In addition to purely technical competence, there is an increased need for skills in communication, leadership, and risk management.

It is also possible that cybersecurity will develop a whole new set of international rules and laws governing data, privacy, and surveillance. The most current trends in cybersecurity from an international perspective include political concerns, and for private organizations, leadership concerns. What used to be considered an ICT-specific area is quickly becoming a boardroom matter. Another trend is the focus on creating laws and legislation without a comprehensive understanding of what cybersecurity is, the complexity of international law, and the implications regulations may have on the free flow of information.

As it becomes clear to countries and organizations alike that an ungoverned cyberspace is impossible to maintain, and unlikely to be in the best interest of its users, many people continue to advocate for an Internet where everyone can share anything, in full anonymity. Companies and countries implement laws, regulations, and policies to control the kind of information and activities they consider acceptable. Not everyone likes that, but can we expect a society—even a virtual one—to exist without regulation?

Sources of Further Information

There is not much formal research on how different countries develop and train their cybersecurity workforce. Practices vary widely, opening the topic to debate and speculation. There are many areas where more research would be beneficial, including:

- Cybersecurity maturity levels of regions and countries.

- Cybersecurity maturity levels of companies and organizations. On this topic, The World Economic Forum announced a *Partnering for Cyber Resilience* initiative in 2012. More information can be found on their website at http://www.weforum.org/issues/partnering-cyber-resilience-pcr.

- Security culture, and matching social sciences with security behaviors, needs, and expectations (Da Veiga and Eloff 2010).

- How different educational systems effect cybersecurity.

The article series "The ITU and the Real Threats to the Internet," by Dwayne Winseck (2012) is worth a read. Its criticism is well balanced, with references and links to material relevant to the ongoing discussion on International Telecom Regulations.

One of the challenges in cybersecurity is the relative immaturity of the field. There are many ideas, thoughts, and hypotheses about where the cybersecurity sector is heading; some are fueled by the expectation for profits, some are fueled by political agendas. Some are based on misconceptions, and some show an understanding of the complexity and frailty that the field of cybersecurity will continue to display until the sector has matured and found its place in society.

To broaden one's horizon on cybersecurity in general, topics like organizational psychology, motivational theory, and cognition may be great areas to explore. Ultimately, cybersecurity is about people, so understanding how the human mind functions may help create better defenses, as well as a better understanding of adversaries. One may also benefit from looking into sociology and anthropology. Understanding how humans interact, how groups form and function, and how different groups have different rules may help improve cybersecurity strategies and tactics. Because the role of cybersecurity is to support and secure organizations' operations, understanding organizations, business, and politics is also critical to succeeding in the field.

References

Allen, Julia H. 2013. "Security is not Just a Technical Issue." *Build Security In, Carnegie Mellon University*. Last modified May 13. https://buildsecurityin. us-cert.gov/articles/best-practices/governance-and-management/ security-is-not-just-a-technical-issue.

Altbach, Philip G. 2009. "The Giants Awake: The Present and Future of Higher Education Systems in China and India." In *Higher Education to 2030: Volume 2, Globalisation*: 179–203. Centre for Educational Research and Innovation.

Bonneau, Joseph. 2012. "The Science of Guessing: Analyzing an Anonymized Corpus of 70 Million Passwords." In *2012 IEEE Symposium on Security and Privacy*, 538–52. San Francisco, CA: IEEE.

Carolan, Eoin. 2008. "The Concept of a Right to Privacy." In *The Right to Privacy: A Doctrinal and Comparative Analysis*, with Hilary Delany, 1–30. Dublin: Round Hall. http://papers.ssrn.com/sol3/papers.cfm?abstract_id=1889243.

Center for World-Class Universities. 2013. "2013 Academic Ranking of World Universities (ARWU)." Shanghai Jiao Tong University. Accessed August 15, 2013. http://www.shanghairanking.com/ARWU2013.html.

Chernenko, Elena. 2013. "Why Russia is Taking on the West over Cyber Warfare." *Kommersant*. Accessed June 11, 2013. http://worldcrunch. com/world-affairs/why-russia-is-taking-on-the-west-over-cyber-warfare/ russia-nato-un-cyber-attack-tallinn-manual/c1s12151/.

Da Veiga, A., and J. H. P. Eloff. 2010. "A Framework and Assessment Instrument for Information Security Culture." *Computers & Security* 29:196–207. doi:10.1016/j.cose.2009.09.002.

European Parliament. 1995. "Directive 95/46/EC of the European Parliament and of the Council of 24 October 1995 on the Protection of Individuals with Regard to the Processing of Personal Data and on the Free Movement of Such Data." *EUR-Lex*. October 24. http://eur-lex.europa. eu/LexUriServ/LexUriServ.do?uri=CELEX:31995L0046:en:NOT.

Gjøvik University College. 2013. "HiG—Høgskolen i jøvik." http://www.hig. no/nyheter/historisk_forskningssatsing.

Hagestad, William T., II. 2012. *21st Century Chinese Cyberwarfare*. Ely, United Kingdom: IT Governance Publishing.

International Telecommunication Union. 2009. "Legislation." http://www.itu. int/en/ITU-D/Cybersecurity/Pages/Legal-Measures.aspx.

———. 2011. "Constitution of the International Telecommunication Union." In *Basic Texts of the ITU*. http://www.itu.int/net/about/basic-texts/index. aspx.

Kerr, Paul, John Rollins, and Catherine A. Theohary. 2010. "The Stuxnet Computer Worm: Harbinger of an Emerging Warfare Capability." Washington, DC: Congressional Research Service. http://www.fas.org/ sgp/crs/natsec/R41524.pdf.

Marginson, Simon, and Marijk van der Wende. 2009. "Europeanisation, International Rankings and Faculty Mobility: Three Cases in Higher Education Globalisation." In *Higher Education to 2030: Volume 2, Globalisation*: 109–44. Centre for Educational Research and Innovation.

Medynsky, Eugene. 1944. "Schools and Education in the U.S.S.R." *American Sociological Review* 9:287–295.

Nag, H. 2013. "Direction of Russian Higher Education." *QS Intelligence Unit*. Accessed August 30, 2013. http://www.iu.qs.com/2013/05/ direction-of-russian-higher-education/.

National Initiative for Cybersecurity Education. 2013. "Best Practices for Planning a Cybersecurity Workforce." http://niccs.us-cert.gov/sites/ default/files/documents/files/Best%20Practices%20for%20Planning%20 a%20Cybersecurity%20Workforce_062813_v4.2_FINAL_NICE%20 branded_0.pdf.

National Security Agency. 2012. "NSA Announces New Program to Prime College Students for Careers in Cyber Ops." *Press Room*. May 21. http://www.nsa.gov/public_info/press_room/2012/new_college_cyber_ ops_program.shtml.

Prince, Brian. 2009. "Cyber-attacks on Georgia Show Need for International Cooperation, Report States." *eWeek*, August 18. http://www.eweek.com/c/a/Security/Cyber-Attacks-on-Georgia-Show-Need-for-International-Cooperation-Report-States-294120/.

Reinvang, Rasmus. 2013. "BRICS—Gimmick or Political Reality?" *Internasjonal Politikk* 71:175–93.

Roer, Kai, and Mourad Ben Lakhoua, eds. 2011. *The Cloud Security Rules: Technology is your Friend and Enemy; A Book about Ruling the Cloud.* Drammen, Norway: The Roer Group.

Rosen, Seymour M. 1980. *Education in the U.S.S.R.: Current Status of Higher Education.* Washington DC: U.S. Government Printing Office.

Sarel, Michael. 1996. *Growth in East Asia: What We Can and What We Cannot Infer. Economic Issues, No. 1.* Washington DC: International Monetary Fund Publication Services.

Schelling, Thomas C. 1969. "Models of Segregation." *American Economic Review* 59:488–93. doi:10.1126/science.151.3712.867-a.

Schmitt, Michael N. 2012. "International Law in Cyberspace: The Koh Speech and Tallinn Manual Juxtaposed." *Harvard International Law Journal*, 54. http://www.harvardilj.org/wp-content/uploads/2012/12/HILJ-Online_54_Schmitt.pdf.

Schmitt, Michael N., ed. 2013. *Tallinn Manual on the International Law Applicable to Cyber Warfare.* New York, NY: Cambridge University Press.

Sundseth, Roar. 2013. "Cyberoperasjoner—Utfordringer i Cyber." Oslo Militære Samfund. February 18. http://www.oslomilsamfund.no/oms_arkiv/2013/2013-02-18-Sundseth.html

Swanson, Marianne, and Barbara Guttman. 1996. "Special Publication 800-14: Generally Accepted Principles and Practices for Securing Information Technology Systems." National Institute of Standards and Technology Administration. http://csrc.nist.gov/publications/nistpubs/800-14/800-14.pdf.

Tremblay, Karine, Diane Lalancette, and Deborah Roseveare. 2013. "Assessment of Higher Education Learning Outcomes: Feasability Study Report; Volume 1—Design and Implementation." *Organisation for Economic Co-operation and Development.* http://www.oecd.org/edu/skills-beyond-school/AHELOFSReportVolume1.pdf.

Tzu, Sun. 2010. *The Art of War: Spirituality for Conflict.* Mumbai: Jaico Publishing House.

Weissman, C. G. 2013. "ITU responds to criticism about the upcoming International Telecommunication summit." *Herdict Blog.* Accessed June 15, 2013. http://blogs.law.harvard.edu/herdict/2012/06/27/itu-responds-to-criticism-about-the-upcoming-international-telecommunication-summit/.

White House. 2011. *International Strategy for Cyberspace: Prosperity, Security, and Openness in a Networked World.* http://www.whitehouse.gov/sites/default/files/rss_viewer/international_strategy_for_cyberspace.pdf.

Winseck, Dwayne. (2012). "The ITU and the Real Threats to the Internet." http://news.dot-nxt.com/2012/11/28/itu-and-real-threats-internet.

Chapter 9

Cybersecurity in
Small Businesses and Nonprofits

GREGORY P. KEELEY

Introduction

The Internet provides customers with the opportunity to locate and purchase a wide variety of items, including unusual and unique products not readily available from large retail stores. The Internet also allows for the widespread distribution of information related to non-profit causes and activities. As a result, the explosion and advancements of the Internet have spurred growth in the small business and nonprofit sectors over the past decades. Markets and customers that were geographically out of reach or limited in their offerings are now but a click away. However, as often is the case, with opportunity comes individuals who are ready and willing to take advantage of the new advancements for their own personal gain. With the growth of small and nonprofit businesses, the Internet has served to deliver new "customers" to a wave of opportunistic cybercriminals who are free of geographic boundaries or barriers.

Recent reports indicate that cybercriminals regard small businesses and nonprofits as easy targets for cyber-attacks. The recorded number of attacks on these two sectors is surging at an alarming rate.

Attacks on the small business sector alone rose by a startling 42 percent between 2011 and 2012 (JZ Analytics 2012). In 2012, many of
these criminal forays—31 percent of the total—hit businesses with
less than 250 employees. This represents the highest growth in cyber-
attacks for any specific sector (Symantec Corporation 2013).

Small businesses and nonprofits are particularly vulnerable to
cybercriminals. In most cases they "do not have the resources to imme-
diately rectify security breaches, resulting in extended down-time, limited access to company and customer information, and the cost of
cleaning up damaged data and hardware" (Jennex, Walters, and Addo
2004). One particularly disturbing statistic is that, of small businesses
targeted by cybercriminals, approximately 60 percent close within six
months of a cyber-attack (JZ Analytics 2012).

Perhaps even less understood or reported is the Trojan horse
infiltration, where small businesses and nonprofits are used as gateways
to gain access to clients, business partners, donors, and prime contractors. This type of activity is in need of more attention, research, and
analysis because the threat posed by this backdoor method of attack
must not be underestimated.

This chapter considers and analyzes cybersecurity within the
small business and nonprofit sectors. It examines the fundamental
issues regarding cybersecurity in this underprotected and underreported
sphere and examines the cyber threats faced by small businesses and
nonprofits. It also is important to review laws and policies relevant to
small businesses and nonprofits, provide a broad analysis of the cybersecurity workforce needed in these two sectors, and appraise recommendations for cybersecurity best practices within the small business
and nonprofit sectors. We conclude by examining future cybercrime
trends that will affect these sectors and assess how these challenges
will affect their workforce development.

A Brief Theoretical Note

This chapter examines security issues faced by both the small business and nonprofit sectors. However, the scope of research addressing

cybersecurity within the nonprofit sector is limited. As a result, this chapter primarily relies on data relating to the small business sector and applies that knowledge to the nonprofit environment. Nonprofits and small businesses have a number of similarities and overlaps in the establishment, management, and challenges they face grappling with cybersecurity and cybercriminals. Budget and resource constraints, management cultures, a focus on the day-to-day running of an organization, the growing use of technology and the Internet, and the lack of specialized information technology (IT) and cybersecurity staff all are issues faced in both small businesses and nonprofit organizations.

Some of the data referenced in this chapter probes "small organizations" (see Symantec Corporation 2013) rather than small businesses. This seemingly minor delineation allows us to broaden the scope of the research considered. The terms *small business*, *nonprofit*, and *small organization* are used interchangeably as a majority of available research tends to deal with small and medium businesses as organizations with similar characteristics and cybersecurity trends. The term *small business* or *small organization* has been used to describe businesses with as few as one hundred employees or as many as one thousand. The U.S. Small Business Administration uses a definition of fewer than five hundred employees as the dividing line, but this definition varies by industry (Ironman 2011). For our purposes, a small business/organization is defined as having between 1 and 250 employees.

Fundamental Issues in Cybersecurity in Small Businesses and Nonprofits

The use of the Internet for commerce, funding, and distribution of information in the small business and nonprofit sectors is surging. Research conducted by Symantec and the National Cyber Security Alliance (NCSA) in 2012 found that 87 percent of small businesses used the Internet every day for commerce, with 71 percent dependent on the Internet for day-to-day operations, and 46 percent maintaining their own website. Small businesses use the Internet for activities varying from sales, social media, marketing, and research, to managing financials, accounting, and communicating with customers. Websites have been embraced by both small businesses and nonprofits as a means to reach customers and donors globally, allowing the purchase of products and services, the solicitation of donations, and to provide information about products and causes (JZ Analytics 2012). The importance and rapid growth of the Internet as an integral business tool for organizations within the small business and nonprofit sectors will most certainly continue to flourish.

There are a number of fundamental issues that influence and affect the cybersecurity strategy, or lack thereof, for small businesses and nonprofits. Arguably the most critical point is that organizations in these sectors are not simply smaller versions of large businesses or organizations (Jennex, Walters, and Addo 2004). Small business and nonprofit organizations have a number of unique characteristics related to how they operate within the cybersecurity space. In many cases, these individualities challenge the ability, and in some cases desire, of the organizations to secure themselves against cyber threats, which in turn makes them uniquely vulnerable to cyber-attacks.

Small, centralized management teams, often focused around the owner, generally characterize small organizations. In most cases, there is a lack of specialized staff, limited planning, and inadequate control systems. Small organizations usually are more focused on the day-to-day operation of the organization rather than a proactive or long-term approach to protecting assets, planning ahead, or developing control systems. Financial resources also often are limited (Jennex, Walters, and Addo 2004). These factors significantly affect the security of the organization and create an environment that is characterized by a number of factors:

1. Small organizations often have "a relaxed culture and a lack of formal [cyber]security policies" (Singleton 2002). A study published by Symantec and the NCSA in 2012 found that 87 percent of small and medium-sized businesses have "no formal cybersecurity plan" and 69 percent "do not even have an informal Internet security policy for employees" (JZ Analytics 2012). Additionally, cybersecurity within the small business and nonprofit sectors is sometimes ignored in favor of other more pressing matters, such as day-to-day operations, which exacerbates the relaxed and vulnerable cyber environment.

2. In many cases, small organizations are simply ignorant of the extent of the security threats and the consequences of lax security countermeasures. They may not know how to develop and implement cybersecurity policy or how to develop a response strategy to cyber-crime threats. Lack of knowledge or experience dictates that small organizations often fail to implement sophisticated cybersecurity software or applications and are less likely to employ complex security solutions (Jennex, Walters, and Addo 2004). Low knowledge levels regarding the importance of cybersecurity inevitably result in a sub-stantial deficiency of technical skills in their employees. Despite the rise in cyber-attacks on small business and nonprofit organizations in 2012, and the absence of effective cybersecurity within the sectors, 86 percent of small businesses "are satisfied with the amount of security they provide to protect customer or employee data" and 83 percent believe they "are doing enough or making enough investments to pro-tect customer data" (JZ Analytics 2012). This belief persists despite the lack of proper cybersecurity policies in small organizations. Addition-ally, notwithstanding the high failure rate among small businesses that experience a data breach, 47 percent of small business owners believe a data breach would have no effect, and 66 percent say they are not concerned about external or internal threats (JZ Analytics 2012).

3. Small organizations generally do not have a dedicated IT staff or security training (Singleton 2002). The NCSA/Symantec survey found that 69 percent of small business websites were being man-aged in-house, with 90 percent of small business owners not having an internal IT manager "solely focused on technology-related issues." The result is that 66 percent of owners and operators of small busi-nesses and nonprofits are personally responsible for cybersecurity (JZ Analytics 2012). Small businesses and nonprofits therefore are forced to depend on advice from vendors and consultants, restricting their capacity to implement "sophisticated software or applications" due to limited in-house expertise (Jennex, Walters, and Addo 2004).

4. Small businesses often have limited funds and security is rare-ly considered a priority. "Scarce investments in security technologies" due to limited resources, limited knowledge regarding the importance of cybersecurity, and failure to prioritize cybersecurity are fundamen-tal issues within small organizations (Singleton 2002). This includes

investment of time and resources (Jennex, Walters, and Addo 2004).

5. "A lack of either business continuity or disaster plans" characterizes small organizations (Singleton 2002). In 2012, 59 percent of small businesses did not have "a contingency plan outlining procedures for responding and reporting data breach losses" (JZ Analytics 2012). This is a serious shortcoming and likely contributes to the high number of small businesses that fail as a direct result of a data breach.

A critical issue within the small business and nonprofit sectors is the disconnect between the current cybercrime challenges and the inadequacy of cybersecurity practices and controls. This is due to the flawed perceptions small businesses and nonprofits have regarding cybercrime and their security vulnerabilities. Despite the poor cybersecurity environment prevalent within the small business sector, 77 percent of small businesses surveyed in 2012 viewed their company as "safe from cyber threats" and 66 percent were "not concerned about external threats . . . or an internal threat." Additionally, 47 percent believed that "a data breach incident would have no impact on their business and it would be treated as an isolated incident," whereas 18 percent "would not know if their computer network was compromised" (JZ Analytics 2012). This demonstrates the well-defined fissure between the perceptions of those in the small business sector and the reality of the cybersecurity hazards they face.

Threats that Challenge the Cybersecurity of Small Businesses and Nonprofits

As discussed earlier in the chapter, the small business sector is increasingly at risk from cyber threats and organized crime, with a marked growth in cyber-attacks between 2011 and 2012. Cybercriminals have migrated from the more robustly defended large businesses and organizations down the chain to prey on the weaker, more susceptible smaller organizations. It is important that we appreciate the upsurge of attacks on small businesses and nonprofits and also understand the motives and methods of the cybercriminal predators.

Cyber-attacks are often the result of opportunity. The 2012 Data Breach Investigations Report presented by Verizon found that 75 percent of cyber-attack victims were simply opportunistic and that 96 percent of attacks were fundamentally basic. This demonstrates that many cybercriminals focus on targets of opportunity rather than strategic objectives, and that the majority of cyber victims possessed "an (often easily) exploitable weakness rather than because they were pre-identified for attack" (Verizon 2013). Implicit in the data is that cybersecurity defenses within the small business and nonprofit sectors often are limited and ineffective, particularly when compared with larger organizations that are able to implement more robust cybersecurity countermeasures. For example, lower levels of knowledge, limited resources, and inexperience can affect the design, configuration, and implementation of hardware such as routers, switches, and networking gear. Poor hardware controls such as default passwords and irregularly updated security settings will result in increased vulnerabilities to cyber-attacks. Additionally, lower levels of knowledge regarding cybersecurity can lead to reckless use of Wi-Fi hotspots, hotel networks, portable devices, and reckless web surfing by employees (Pinzon 2008). All these activities have the potential to bring malware into the organization's network. Additionally, there is the risk for insider attacks such as employees stealing data and proprietary information. Evidence suggests that this risk is low in small organizations; however, it is still present. In 2012, cybercrime targeting small businesses and nonprofits as "victims of opportunity" rose markedly, and this trend is likely to continue in the future (Symantec Corporation 2013).

Hackers and cybercriminals target small businesses and nonprofits for a multitude of reasons and disparate goals. As noted by Symantec (2013), "money stolen from a small business is as easy to spend as money stolen from a large business." There is a smorgasbord of valuable offerings for criminals to steal from small businesses, including customer information, intellectual property, and the information-age version of cold hard cash. Although the rewards from targeting small businesses and nonprofits might be limited in comparison to pursuing larger organizations, the comparative ease with which small business and nonprofit organizations can be attacked makes cyber-attacks on organizations in these two sectors worthwhile to cyber criminals.

Ransomware, a malware that locks a computer unless a release fee is paid to the attacker, was used more regularly against small businesses in 2012, with "one group . . . attempting to infect 500,000 computers over an 18-day period" within the small business sector (Kopelke 2013). There also was an escalation in reputational attacks in the small business sector in 2012, with virtual copies of the websites and emails of organizations replicated by hackers in order to steal the personal details of clients and customers (Kopelke 2013). With more small businesses and nonprofits using the Internet as a fundamental pillar of their business process, the prospects for cybercriminals preying on organizations in the two sectors will continue to escalate.

Although cybercriminals are increasingly besieging small businesses and nonprofits as targets, small organizations also are attacked as an end to other purposes, such as providing a gateway to other organizations. Small organizations often conduct business with a variety of partners and enterprises, and customers use their websites for any number of transactions. These smaller company websites are being used as backdoors into larger organizations through cyber-attacks known as "watering holes" (Symantec Corporation 2013). This attack occurs when cybercriminals target easily accessible websites, such as those run by small organizations, which are accessed frequently by the ultimate quarry. When the targeted organization accesses the compromised website, "a targeted attack payload is installed on their computer" (Kopelke 2013). In this way, "attackers leverage weak security of one entity to defeat the strong security of another" (Symantec Corporation 2013). This is similar to the attack focused on gaining access to data and information stored electronically within smaller organizations that have relationships and share data with larger organizations. The smaller organizations can be used to leapfrog and gain access to the larger enterprise. In these ways, the lower levels of cybersecurity controls evident within small business and nonprofit organizations affect and threaten the security of associated organizations that access their websites and/or share information, clients, or customers. Ensuring that cybersecurity of small businesses and nonprofits is improved is therefore vital for organizations that have business relationships with small businesses and nonprofits in order to safeguard their data, information, and access.

Cybersecurity Laws and Policies Relevant to Small Businesses and Nonprofits

There are two key policy areas directly relevant to organizations within the small business and nonprofit sectors. The first is workforce development. There is a significant skills gap shortage within the U.S. IT community, indeed in the whole country, as it relates to cybersecurity. The skills gap shortage within the cybersecurity workforce uniquely affects small organizations that are competing with larger organizations and the federal government for skilled personnel. As noted by Shapero (2013), who testified to the House Subcommittee for Small Business, "There are a lot of great opportunities that come with working for small and medium size companies that you cannot get in a larger institution, but we simply cannot compete with the recruitment dollars that are spent by the bigger names." The skills shortage therefore is a fundamental reason for the low levels of cybersecurity in small organizations. The Computer Technology Industry Association (CompTIA) suggests that one way of addressing workforce shortages is to focus on industry-recognized certification. CompTIA argues that this "will encourage others looking to enter the cyber workforce to focus on certifications as an entry point and help close the skills gap" (Shapero 2013).

The second policy area related to small organizations is an understanding of the importance of cybersecurity, the risks faced by small organizations, and the steps that small organizations need to take to secure and protect their IT infrastructure. As we have discussed, the majority of cyber-attacks are a direct result of opportunity and a lack of awareness of effective security controls. This can be addressed somewhat via education and the implementation of cybersecurity policies and systems. This shift would not only benefit small businesses and nonprofits, but also the overall U.S. IT ecosystem (Shapero 2013). As has been demonstrated here, poor cybersecurity threatens the particular organization that is targeted, as well as their customers, donors, clients, and business partners. Therefore, it is incumbent on broader U.S. business, government, and IT ecosystems to encourage, educate, and assist small organizations to ensure that they have satisfactory cybersecurity protocols.

Legislation as it pertains to cybersecurity must be addressed or reformed to assist small businesses and nonprofits. Data breach notification (DBN) laws are one such piece of legislation that needs swift attention in Congress. The DBN "establish the circumstances under which a consumer must be notified when a breach of their personally identifiable information (PII) has occurred" (Shapero 2013). This is important legislation; however, under its current guise, it creates unnecessary challenges and difficulties for small organizations because "the majority of cyber-attacks create exposure across state lines'" (Shapero 2013). There are currently forty-seven state DBN laws in America, which differ on when consumer notices must be provided. Some DBN laws require a consumer notification when the company is made aware of the data breach, whereas others only require a consumer notice should the data breach be likely to result "in consumer harm to the consumer" (Shapero 2013). The patchwork of DBN laws results in a tremendous burden on smaller organizations, including duplicative costs, and undermines the ability of smaller organizations to meet DBN compliance obligations. The complexity of the current system requires small organizations to expend large amounts of resources "to track down the various compliance obligations" (Shapero 2013). CompTIA suggests that the complexity of current DBN laws and the burdens on smaller organizations could be reduced by "the creation of a national framework for data breach notification [which] can go a long way towards reducing costs and eliminating barriers to entry" for smaller organizations (Shapero 2013). It will also "serve as an incentive toward the expansion of IT service across state lines" (Shapero 2013).

The sharing of threat information between the commercial sector and government is another important legislative initiative requiring immediate attention. Dr. Phyllis Schenk (2013), vice president and chief technology officer for the public sector at McAfee, notes two possible ways of facilitating this. The first is through an information-sharing bill, as was introduced by House Intelligence Chairman Mike Rogers and Ranking Member Dutch Ruppersberger. The bill, the "Cyber Intelligence Sharing and Protection Act," would facilitate information sharing between government and the private sector with "liability protections for private entities sharing cyber threat information in good faith" (Schenk 2013).

Information Sharing and Analysis Centers (ISACs), endorsed by the government and established by the private sector, "provide a specific mechanism for sharing cyber threat data" (Schenk 2013). However, small businesses are not able to participate in ISACs in their current guise due to the limited budgets of small organizations and the lack of cybersecurity experts in their workforce. Small organizations, therefore, are not able to contribute or benefit from information sharing with regards to cybersecurity. As noted by Schenk (2013), "We need to find a way to include small business in our nation's security paradigm—and that includes information sharing."

Status of the Cybersecurity Workforce within Small Businesses and Nonprofits

There is a dearth of qualified cybersecurity professionals in the marketplace, with the majority of them either working for large corporations, specialized intelligence and security groups, the military, or the federal government. Even these sectors, which are traditionally hyperselective in hiring, are faced with challenges in recruiting a cybersecurity workforce. Federal agencies that no longer offer the job security of past generations and provide lower compensation packages than commercial alternatives are faced with a cyber workforce that is aging and facing shortages (Wait 2013). Fifty-six percent of federal government departments and agencies say they do not have enough security staff (Wilson 2013).

The supply-and-demand principal as it relates to cybersecurity recruitment is a great impediment to small businesses and nonprofits when it comes to employing knowledgeable and skilled cyber professionals. Competition with large companies and the federal government for specialists results in increased hiring and operating costs. Small organizations are reluctant to hire specialized cybersecurity personnel based on a limited understanding of the importance of cybersecurity, the smaller and generalized workforces within the sector, a scarcity of experienced practitioners, and the cost.

According to the study referenced earlier by NCSA/Symantec, 69 percent of small business websites are managed internally and 66 percent of small business owners and operators surveyed were solely responsible for their online and cybersecurity. Eleven percent of businesses interviewed said that no one was responsible, whereas 9 percent rely on an IT-savvy employee. The report also found that only 8 percent used an outside IT consultant (JZ Analytics 2012). The pool of available, specialized cybersecurity professionals within the small business and nonprofit sphere is therefore extremely limited. The result is that nontechnical workers are pressed into technical positions, resulting in lost productivity and greater vulnerability to cyber threats. This is directly attributed to the lack of skilled cybersecurity workers. Research by Microsoft found that "small businesses are losing more than US$24 billion in productivity each year when nontechnical employees . . . are responsible for their companies' IT security. This loss stems from [the employees] being removed from core business activities" (Microsoft 2013). This report used the definition of a small business as one having less than one hundred employees. Other key findings from the research found that:

- Thirty percent of involuntary IT managers (IITMs) felt that IT management was a nuisance.

- Twenty-six percent of those interviewed felt they were not qualified for the job.

- Sixty percent wanted to simplify technology solutions to simplify their job.

- IITMs lost an average of six hours per week on managing the organization's IT (Microsoft 2013).

Here, an IITM is defined as someone who is pushed into the position of being an IT manager without being qualified or without it being included in his or her job description. This Microsoft study exemplifies the effect a scarce and expensive cybersecurity workforce has on small organizations. One alternative to combat the deficiency in qualified cyber professionals is by using outside solution providers and cloud services. However, this solution may be prohibitive from a cost and resource perspective, and may ultimately require the small organization to implement cybersecurity policies on its own premises.

Recommendations for Cybersecurity Best Practices in Small Businesses and Nonprofits

Small businesses and nonprofits can take a number of practical steps to protect their data and systems from cybersecurity attacks. This is especially important due to the current low levels of cybersecurity knowledge and controls within the small business and nonprofit sectors. Issues that need to be addressed quickly include the lack of policies governing internal Internet usage, usage of client information, poor application of security solutions, and low knowledge levels with regard to cybersecurity, crime, and the threat in general.

The first and simplest step for small businesses and nonprofits is to understand that they are at risk from cybercriminals and the nature and shape of the risks. Vulnerabilities on both the human and technical sides of cybersecurity need to be addressed using some basic security principles, as follow:

- Know what you need to protect (Kopelke 2013). A small business must understand how its information is used, stored, and ultimately how to protect it. This is a core cybersecurity tenet and is a crucial element of any strategy that includes making use of cloud providers.

- Ensure total information integrity (Kopelke 2013). "Near enough" is no longer good enough. A 99 percent solution will still leave a small business or nonprofit vulnerable to attack.

- Implement robust password policies (Kopelke 2013). Strong access controls are key to establishing security. Employees should use passwords of at least eight characters, including numbers, symbols, and letters.

- Disaster planning. Most small organizations do not have a disaster strategy, despite the significant risk for data loss and the potential effects on the operation of the organization. Kopelke (2013) argues that small enterprises should identify critical resources, employ security and redundancy solutions to archive important files, and keep disaster plans current.

- Encryption. Encryption is sometimes overlooked, yet is an important security tool. Encryption should be done on all devices to ensure the validity of internal as well as client data (Kopelke 2013).

- Deploy a reliable security solution (Kopelke 2013). This is perhaps the easiest yet most important cybersecurity step a small organization can take. A proven security solution to scan email and other files can prevent the introduction of spam and viruses into the organization.

- Keep updated (Kopelke 2013). An out-of-date security solution is ineffective due to the regularity with which new viruses, Trojan horses, worms, and malware are created.

- Employee education and training (Kopelke 2013). Employees must understand the threats posed to the organization, actions to take if machines are infected with malware, how to protect information, and general Internet safety. The benefit of educating employees regarding cybersecurity is borne out by CompTIA research, which found that after remote workers were trained regarding cybersecurity,

92 percent of organizations reported fewer major security breaches (Pinzon 2008).

- Develop procedures and policies for Internet and email usage, customer and employee information privacy, and Wi-Fi, public network, and portable device usage (Pinzon 2008).

- Ensure that all networked devices are correctly installed and configured, and ensure that default passwords and settings are changed and upgraded. If possible, perform an automated audit scan, for example a penetration test, and gain assistance from consultants. Correctly installing networked devices and changing default settings and passwords is critical, and relatively simple (Pinzon 2008).

- Improve the overall cybersecurity culture within the organization (Dojkovski, Lichtenstein, and Warren 2007).

- Purchase affordable cybersecurity insurance to help mitigate the damage and consequences of cyber-attacks (Shapero 2013).

- Use service providers who understand the needs of small businesses and nonprofits and are able to assist in the implementation of cybersecurity.

- Education is especially important when migrating to the cloud. The cloud offers small organizations a number of benefits, including saving capital outlays and time, and the opportunity to focus on the day-to-day running of the organization. However, the migration to the cloud must be assisted by professionals. As noted by a provider of cloud solutions, "The large telecommunications and large cloud-only providers do a great job serving enterprise businesses with big IT staffs who know exactly what they need" (Weber 2013). However, smaller organizations who want to use the cloud are faced with a challenge, as "they don't have the IT staff to help them with their migration to the cloud and the big cloud providers are not set up to help them" (Weber 2013). Therefore, it is important to use service providers who understand the needs of small organizations.

Cobb (2013) suggests a catchy six-step plan for small organizations. There is a significant commonality with Kopelke:

- Assess your assets, risks, and resources;

- Build your policy;

- Choose your controls;

- Deploy your controls;

- Educate employees, execs and vendors; and

- Further assess, audit and test.

Cybersecurity professionals working with small business and nonprofit organizations must be cognizant of the cybersecurity challenges faced by these organizations. As noted, a majority of small businesses view an effective cybersecurity infrastructure as critical for their business and their reputation. As a whole however, there is a minimum of understanding among small businesses that a cyber-attack can have grave, adverse repercussions on their organization, despite abundant and readily available evidence to the contrary. While viewing cybersecurity as important, the majority of small businesses have almost no strategy or execution plan with regards to simple issues such as Internet usage policies, privacy policies, and effective security solutions.

Interestingly, despite the barrage of news and commentary surrounding the apparent ease with which cyber criminals can violate seemingly secure networks, small business owners and nonprofit managers often consider their ineffective, limited, and sometimes nonexistent cybersecurity protocols sufficient to counter cybersecurity threats and criminals. Cyber professionals working in this space must understand this lack of awareness and grasp the importance of educating the small business and nonprofit sectors regarding the importance of enhanced cybersecurity solutions. The threat faced by small organizations cannot be overstated. The loss of data, the potential effect on productivity, the impact on profit/loss, and terminal reputation damage are potentially crippling when considered individually, let alone together.

Small business and nonprofit entities must expand the role they play in protecting customers, clients, business partners, donors, volunteers, and large organizations through improved cybersecurity protocols. Additionally, clients and donors who interact with small business and nonprofit organizations should be wary and skeptical when smaller organizations think that they have enough cybersecurity. Another challenge for cybersecurity experts is the potential "unfamiliarity, lack of knowledge, comprehension of vendor advice, security, payments and technical details" (JZ Analytics 2012) when working with small businesses and nonprofits. This is due to the lack of specialized staff and due to the majority of cybersecurity measures being implemented by untrained, unqualified, and untested employees or volunteers. It is essential that cybersecurity specialists operating in the sector communicate with nontechnical clients and guide them through the process of establishing and managing cybersecurity.

Future Trends in Small Business and Nonprofit Cybersecurity, Including Workforce Development

Small businesses and nonprofits are likely to see cyber-attacks and cybercrime targeting them to continue to trend upward. With smaller organizations more often relying on the Internet to transact business, the opportunity for exploiting security vulnerabilities will continue to fall on less-prepared targets. Smaller organizations will be targeted as an end in themselves, and then used as a means of pursuing their clients, customers, donors, and business partners.

There is no silver bullet with which to stop the criminal attacks on cyber networks. The increasingly vulnerable small business and nonprofit sector must be educated regarding the importance of cybersecurity, the threats faced by their organizations, their vulnerabilities and the potentially catastrophic results of a successful attack. Amid the trend of progressively sophisticated and potent cyber-attacks, the interrelatedness of organizations, clients, donors, and customers via the Internet increases the risks and consequences of cybercrime substantively. It is in the interest of the wider business community and the federal government to assist small organizations in understanding the necessity of cybersecurity, and the need to take urgent measures to reduce their susceptibilities.

A consequence of shoring up the cyber culture in small businesses and nonprofits would be an increased demand for cybersecurity specialists. Ensuring that the trained and qualified cybersecurity workforce grows substantially is central to improving cybersecurity within the small business and nonprofit sectors. Increased education may also encourage small business and nonprofit organizations to deploy cloud services and cybersecurity solution providers who can assist in automating services and processes to increase productivity.

References

Cobb, Stephen. 2013. "Cyber Security Road Map for Businesses." *We Live Security.* May 14. www.welivesecurity.com/2013/05/14/cyber-security-road-map-for-businesses/.

Dojkovski, S., Sharman Lichtenstein, and Matthew Warren. 2007. "Fostering Information Security Culture in Small and Medium Enterprises: An Interpretive Study in Australia." In *Proceedings of the 15th European Conference on Information Systems,* 1560–1571. St. Gallen, Switzerland: University of St. Gallen.

Ironman [pseud.]. 2011. "How Many People are Employed by Small Business?" *Townhall Finance.* October 5. http://finance.townhall.com/columnists/politicalcalculations/2011/10/05/how_many_people_are_employed_by_small_business/page/full.

Jennex, Murray E., Aaron Walters, and Theophilus B. A. Addo. 2004. "SMEs and Knowledge Requirements for Operating Hacker and Security Tools." In *Innovations Through Information Technology,* edited by M. Khosrow-Pour. Hershey, PA: Idea Group Publishing.

JZ Analytics. 2012. "2012 NCSA / Symantec National Small Business Study." *National Cyber Security Alliance* and *Symantec.* www.staysafeonline.org/download/datasets/4389.

Kopelke, S. 2013. "A Primer on SMB Cybersecurity." *Business Spectator.* May 28. www.businessspectator.com.au/article/2013/5/28/technology/primer-smb-cyber-security.

Microsoft. 2013. "Small Businesses with 'Involuntary' IT managers Lose US\$24 Billion in Productivity Annually, According to AMI-Partners Study." April 22. www.microsoft.com/en-us/news/Press/2013/Apr13/04-22InvoluntaryITManagerPR.aspx.

Pinzon, S. 2008. "Top 10 Threats to SME Data Security." *WatchGuard Technologies.* www.watchguard.com/docs/whitepaper/wg_top10-summary_wp.pdf.

Schenk, Phyllis. 2013. "Protecting Small Businesses against Emerging and Complex Cyber-Attacks," *House Small Business Subcommittee on Healthcare and Technology.* March 21. http://smbiz.house.gov/Uploaded-Files/3-21-2013_Schenk_Final_Testimony.pdf.

Shapero, Dan. 2013. "Protecting Small Businesses against Emerging and Complex Cyber-Attacks." *House Small Business Subcommittee on Healthcare and Technology.* March 21. http://smbiz.house.gov/Uploaded-Files/3-21-2013_Shapero_Revised_Testimony.pdf.

Singleton, Singer. 2002. "Consultants can Offer Remedies to Lax SME Security." *TechRepublic.* February 6. http://www.techrepublic.com/article/lock-it-down-consultants-can-offer-remedies-to-lax-sme-security/1031090.

Symantec Corporation. 2013. *2013 Internet Security Threat Report.* vol. 18. http://www.symantec.com/security_response/publications/threatreport.jsp.

Verizon. 2012. "The 2012 Data Breach Investigations Report." http://www.verizonenterprise.com/resources/reports/rp_data-breach-investigations-report-2012-ebk_en_xg.pdf?r=58

Wait, Patience. 2013. "Federal Cyber Workforce Is Getting Older." *InformationWeek.* April 9. www.informationweek.com/government/security/federal-cyber-workforce-is-getting-older/240152537.

Weber, William. 2013. "Protecting Small Businesses against Emerging and Complex Cyber-Attacks." *House Small Business Subcommittee on Healthcare and Technology.* March 21. http://smbiz.house.gov/Uploaded-Files/3-21-2013_Weber_Testimony.pdf.

Wilson, Tim. 2013. "Businesses Feel Impact of IT Security Skill Shortage, Study Finds." *Dark Reading.* February 25. www.darkreading.com/management/businesses-feel-impact-of-it-security-sk/240149286.

Chapter 10

Future Directions for Educating a Cybersecurity Workforce

James H. Jones, Jr.

Introduction

Determining how to educate a cybersecurity workforce has much in common with educating workforces for other domains, past and present. For example, education in the early twenty-first century changed to satisfy the workforce needs of the technology boom in response to emerging gaps between the workforce and industry. These gaps were frequently only recognized when the existing workforce became inadequate. A delayed process then occurred to adjust education in order to close the gap, and we often overshot our targets. The chapters of this book assess the cybersecurity workforce needs of various domains and industries, identify emerging or future workforce gaps, and propose approaches and programs to eliminate those gaps before they are fully realized. The education of a cybersecurity workforce has some unique characteristics, such as the cross-domain and ubiquitous nature of cybersecurity, national security implications, and the lack of a well-defined scientific discipline of cybersecurity. In this concluding chapter, we aim to summarize the common and sector-specific needs of a cybersecurity workforce, and to propose a way forward that will close the emerging and future gaps and meet the growing need that we expect to continue for the foreseeable future.

Common Cybersecurity Workforce Needs

Understand the Technological Underpinnings

Certain technical aspects of cybersecurity are the same regardless of industry or application. For example, multinational banks and small businesses use the same underlying digital hardware, software, and communications technologies. The bank's computers and networks might be faster and more robust, but they are still processing zeros and ones with the same logic chips, execution environments, and network protocols as the small businesses. The cybersecurity workforce needs to understand these underpinnings to some degree if it is ever to perform beyond pushing a series of buttons. When an unusual event or failure occurs, it is the underlying knowledge that permits a person to reason through the novel event or troubleshoot the failure. This requirement to understand the technical foundations of cybersecurity is not as daunting as it first appears, as the foundational knowledge is a much smaller set of knowledge than the applications and tools that rest on that foundation. Furthermore, foundational knowledge serves the short- and long-term goals of the workforce and those who employ them; a worker with the underlying knowledge is better equipped to deal with the challenges of today, and is better prepared to add knowledge to that foundation in the future.

Understand the Tools

Just as a master carpenter must understand woodworking tools, a cybersecurity worker must understand the tools of the cybersecurity trade. However, where the carpenter's toolbox is relatively small and static, the toolbox of the cybersecurity worker is large, growing, and constantly changing. New security applications, algorithms, and hardware emerge daily. It is unrealistic to expect a cybersecurity worker to know every tool available, but understanding a subset of these is necessary and there are educational approaches to accomplish this. For example, the strong technical foundation mentioned previously provides a basis to more quickly grasp new tools, group similar tools, and apply existing knowledge. Additionally, gaining competence with a set of core tools, like network sniffers, instrumented execution environments, and rudimentary scripting or programming environments is analogous to a carpenter's use of the hammer, saw, and drill; such tools are used frequently and they form the basis for additional skills.

Understand Vulnerabilities, Threats, and Risks

The history of computer viruses, worms, and cyber-attacks is full of examples that simultaneously affected corporate, government, and individual users. Because we use common technology, and the attacks and attackers are frequently indiscriminate, this is not surprising. Therefore, a fundamental understanding of vulnerabilities, threats, and corresponding risks is necessary for any cybersecurity worker. Risk assessment and mitigation, built on an understanding of possible events and their implications, is the foundation of nearly every good cybersecurity decision, whether related to technology, process, or people. Specific vulnerabilities, threats, and risks are unique to industries and organizations, but the framework for understanding them is common to all.

Understand the Unique Environment

All cybersecurity workers need to understand the environment in which they are operating. Ensuring the security of an air traffic control system is different than building websites for home businesses. Both have security aspects and failure in either has costs, but the technical nature and scope of consequences are quite different. Understanding an organization's mission and operations is key to making solid security decisions. Measuring risk is key to these good decisions, and organization-specific input is necessary to accurately assess risk. Of the common cybersecurity workforce requirements outlined here, this final one is perhaps the most difficult to satisfy. Whereas a common curriculum or training program can address the first three requirements, this final requirement is necessarily industry-specific. Historically, these workers have been created organically, starting with either a cybersecurity-trained person or an industry-experienced person and educating them on the missing half. This is a costly approach that does not scale well, and we can afford neither the high cost nor the lack of scalability. In our recommended path forward, outlined later in this chapter, we propose cross-sector and cross-topic education that will begin to address this shortcoming.

Sector-Specific Cybersecurity Workforce Needs

Government

Cybersecurity services in the government domain, whether international, national, regional, or local, often are delivered by commercial organizations using commercial tools. It is neither cost-effective nor practical for government organizations to create their own staffs and products, so the commercial sector fills the government's needs. On the one hand, this is very efficient, as the free market drives and pays for most innovation while governments benefit from that progress at a fraction of the cost. Furthermore, workers frequently cross the blurry line between government and commercial organizations, serving to cross-pollinate and maintain state-of-the-art solutions on both sides. On the other hand, governments often have special requirements stemming from their unique missions of public service and public security. The cybersecurity workforce, whether employed directly by a government or by a contractor providing services to a government, must understand these missions and the associated regulatory and legal considerations.

Military

Cybersecurity in the military environment shares the challenges of government cybersecurity and has the added challenges of recruitment and retention. Accepting a military cybersecurity job provides training and an entree to the cybersecurity world, but typically entails a multiyear commitment, a highly structured work environment, lower pay, service-specific training and work not related to cybersecurity, career advancement dependent in part on time in service, and little say in the nature or location of assignments. Compare this with commercial technology and security workers who may frequently change employers and locations in order to advance their careers, and advancement that mostly depends on success, even if short-term and short-sighted. These drastically different environments and success formulas produce cybersecurity workers trained to different standards, processes, and operations. Although crossover from the military to the civilian sector is common, it most often is successful when the commercial organization provides services to the military, for example, to protect military information technology assets or conduct offensive cyber warfare on behalf of the military. Military cybersecurity workers crossing into non-military commercial organizations have a significantly longer and steeper learning curve. Training military and commercial cybersecurity workers to a common set of underlying cybersecurity principles and knowledge would significantly reduce the gap between the two workforces, and would enable a smoother, more effective transition between the two.

Health Care

Cybersecurity in the health-care industry is struggling to deal with two related issues: the digitization of health records and increased privacy concerns, legislation, and regulation. Digitization of health records has created an explosion of data and legitimate requests for access to that data, yet all of that data is also more accessible to unauthorized parties and by law must be protected. Cybersecurity workers in the health-care sector must understand the laws and regulations specific to health-care data and systems. The high cost of failure, such as a health-care data breach or a negative effect on patient safety, means they also must maintain cutting-edge knowledge and remain ahead of the attacker community as much as possible.

Telecommunications

Cybersecurity work in the telecommunications sector contains a higher technical component than most other sectors. To oversimplify, the business of telecommunications is driven by throughput. Pushing bits and bytes reliably from point A to point B, and the cost of doing so, continues to fuel technological innovation in response to voracious public, commercial, and government appetites for bandwidth. As a result, the technology of telecommunications is complex and dynamic, requiring cybersecurity workers with advanced engineering or technical degrees, knowledge, and experience. Another unique aspect of the telecommunications sector is that workers are on the front lines of information sharing and privacy debates. As the carriers of information for and between all other sectors, telecommunications companies and workers are uniquely positioned to collect and analyze that information. This broad access enables sharing of critical security information across sectors, from which all have benefited. However, such access is technically unbounded and has only ethical and legal limits, which history has shown to be inadequate. The telecommunications cybersecurity worker is in the midst of this debate, required to implement the best security controls possible while satisfying access requests of which affected users or the public may not be aware.

Finance

To paraphrase the over-quoted Willie Horton, people rob banks because that's where the money is. Similarly, cyber-attackers target financial institutions because that's where the digital money is. Given the perceived high payoff of a successful cyber-attack against a bank, cybersecurity workers in the finance sector face the most talented, persistent, patient, and best-funded cyber-attackers. Workers in this sector must be similarly qualified, and must be willing to keep up with the ever-changing threat landscape. Lagging behind the attackers by days or even hours can be the difference between thwarting a cyber-attack and falling victim to it. The financial sector cybersecurity worker also must understand the complex nature of underlying financial systems. Such systems are complex, robust, self-checking, and designed to resist attacks from within and without. However, understanding that complexity is necessary to defend it. On the other side, the attacker need not understand the underlying systems, and may only need a single vulnerability to perpetrate a successful attack.

Utilities

The utility sector leads other industries in the deployment of cyber physical systems, specifically the control of physical systems using computers. Power generation, oil refining, water treatment, and similar processes are increasingly complex and require the speed, sensitivity, capacity, and throughput of digital devices to measure, monitor, and optimize these processes. The resulting requirement for cybersecurity workers in the utilities sector is to have more engineering knowledge that includes the underlying processes and the systems and equipment that control them.

Education and Training

Ubiquitous bandwidth and mobile computing present tremendous opportunities for the education and training sector. Faculty and learning content once expensive and inaccessible are now generally available to anyone with a device and Internet access, even freely available as massively open online courses. Offering interactive, hands-on, remote courses for credit is now feasible and affordable, providing a boon for both providers and students. Cybersecurity workers in the education and training sector must deal primarily with authentication, privacy, and content refresh issues. Reliable authentication will ensure that the student receiving credit for a course or training is the same student doing the work. Currently, this is a problem only partly solved by a mix of online mechanisms (e.g., cameras and lockdown browsers) and traditional approaches (e.g., proctored tests at central locations). Cybersecurity workers in this sector also must protect student information. Although regulations for student data protection are not as cumbersome as those in the health-care industry, some jurisdictions have enacted laws with substantial penalties (e.g., Family Educational Rights and Privacy Act in the United States). Ensuring that only authorized users see student information, especially when dealing with a globally distributed student body and possibly a distributed and cloud-based delivery, content, and record-keeping system, will require cybersecurity workers with specific skills. Finally, education in the dynamic cybersecurity field requires frequent content updates. Fortunately, this challenge is somewhat mitigated by the use of digital content, which is easily altered, and digital delivery, which drastically shortens the time for new content to reach students.

International

Cybersecurity as a scientific discipline is still evolving, and this is most apparent when working internationally. Different countries have widely differing views of what cybersecurity is, how to educate the cybersecurity workforce, and what qualifies one to work in the cyber-security field. Different nations and jurisdictions allow and prohibit different elements of cybersecurity, with hacking, offensive cyberwarfare, and encryption being three of the most notable areas of differences. Operating in this potentially conflicted environment requires deep understanding of the local laws and regulations, even of the local culture. Development and adoption of a common set of cybersecurity standards, both operational and to qualify the workforce, would encourage cross-domain movement of people, technology, and knowledge, enhancing cybersecurity for all.

Small Businesses and Nonprofits

The implementation of cybersecurity carries both fixed and variable costs. Unfortunately, these fixed costs can be significant and may encourage small businesses and nonprofit organizations to invest inadequately in cybersecurity. Only after a detrimental event are the costs apparent, at which time the damage may be too great for the organization to recover. Delivering cybersecurity services in the small business and nonprofit sector requires cross training, enabling an employee to perform multiple functions, one of which is cybersecurity. Standardizing cybersecurity knowledge and qualifications will facilitate the cost-effective delivery of such training. Optionally, larger organizations already offer "security as a service" to cost-effectively deliver cybersecurity services to multiple smaller customers. As with cybersecurity qualifications, standardization in the cybersecurity domain will allow potential customers to better evaluate potential service providers and the quality of their work.

Next Steps for Educating a Cybersecurity Workforce

In this section, we present next steps toward educating tomorrow's cybersecurity workforce. We first discuss relevant trends in the cybersecurity and education domains, then we combine these trends with our assessment of general and sector-specific cybersecurity workforce gaps and discuss specific next steps.

Trends

STUDENTS AND COURSES MOVING ONLINE

Universities, training providers, and even high schools are consistently moving course content and delivery online. Course delivery is both synchronous and asynchronous, and there exists a wide range of delivery mechanisms and quality, but the common feature is that students are asking for online courses and providers are delivering them. Successfully educating the future cybersecurity workforce will leverage online learning, and will develop new delivery and learning methods that exploit the unique aspects of online education.

Emerging Need for Specialization

For the first 20 years or so of cybersecurity, say 1970 to 1990, most everyone in the business was both an expert and a generalist. Most people in the workforce came from technical backgrounds; there were only so many aspects to cybersecurity; and there were a limited number of products available. Today, each of the subareas of cybersecurity (e.g., forensics, networks, programming, etc.) is complex and deep, each worthy of a lifetime of study and practice. It is no longer feasible to be an expert in more than a handful of these subdomains, any more than a medical professional can be an expert in both brain surgery and cardiology. Although there is a common body of underlying knowledge for cybersecurity (just as organic chemistry and anatomy underlie medicine), future cybersecurity workers will need to specialize in a limited number of subdomains.

Cyber–Physical Systems

The virtual world of computers and the physical world are becoming increasingly connected. Whether it is the valves and pumps of a chemical processing plant, a computer-controlled prosthetic limb, or an autonomous aircraft or car, digital logic is exerting control over physical elements of our world, and in general doing a better job than a human ever could. For the cybersecurity workforce, this means increased training and knowledge of engineering and physical systems to ensure the security of such systems is maintained.

Increasing Availability of Big Data

Big data is a simple concept with complex and far-reaching consequences. In short, we are awash in data, so much so that we cannot possibly process or store it all. The research community is actively developing algorithms, methods, and systems to derive useful information from big data. For the cybersecurity workforce, some of these advances will directly benefit system security, enabling such capabilities as predictive defense and adaptive traffic control. Cybersecurity workers will need a basic understanding of data analytics and data management, and they will need to understand how these algorithms and systems work, their limitations, and their weaknesses.

Increasingly Sophisticated Adversaries

Our adversaries are becoming smarter and more skilled over time. The incentive to commit cybercrime or engage in cyber warfare continues to increase, so we expect our adversaries to continue their growth in terms of skills and resources. Collecting intelligence on adversary behavior, tools, and tactics is a massive undertaking, currently performed in a distributed and uncoordinated manner by various commercial and government entities. An individual cybersecurity worker must monitor a daunting array of sources to keep up. A solid technical underpinning and continuing education will enable the cybersecurity workforce to process, incorporate, and apply new information quickly.

Asymmetry Between Attacker and Defender

In general, it is easier to break into a cyber system than to defend it, mostly because the defender must block every attack vector and the attacker only has to find one unaddressed vulnerability. Add to this the fact that cyber-attacks are cheap to execute and hard to trace, and the attackers' advantage is clear. This is not likely to change anytime soon, so tomorrow's cybersecurity workers will need to be creative as well as proficient, looking for ways to erode the attackers' advantage. Flash systems, replicated execution, non-deterministic processing, and deception are emerging ideas that will contribute to this effort, but that also require additional training and knowledge for the cybersecurity worker.

Next Steps

Standardize the Cybersecurity Discipline

As a scientific discipline, cybersecurity is still relatively new. Efforts have been made over the years, increasing recently, to standardize the practice of cybersecurity and the education of its workforce. However, these standards remain fractured and in some cases divergent, the product of unique environments, goals, and constraints. A concerted effort to enumerate the core, common elements of the cybersecurity domain will facilitate a corresponding standardization of cybersecurity education and credentialing.

Track, Test, and Adopt New Delivery Methods Enabled by Online Technologies

Online technologies are more than vehicles for distributing recorded classroom lectures. Such technologies open up educational delivery options that do not exist in a face-to-face environment, including options we have yet to explore. By combining these technologies with the underlying goals of education, rather than simply pushing existing methods online, we will open up possibilities and education to a world of students eager to learn.

Develop Interdisciplinary Programs

Cybersecurity is a crosscutting domain, borrowing from various scientific disciplines and applicable to even more. As such, a competent cybersecurity workforce will be best educated in a cross-disciplinary manner. Educators should seek to develop interdisciplinary, collaborative programs between departments, schools, and even different universities and organizations. Such programs are more challenging to develop and manage, and they do not fit the traditional university model, but recent successes in other disciplines (e.g., information technology, applied math, etc.) demonstrate their feasibility and value.

Incorporate Practical Experience and Real-World Tools, Data, and Intelligence

Educating a cybersecurity workforce requires more than classroom time and solving simple and simulated problems in a lab environment. Exposing students to the tools, data, and intelligence of real problems in real environments better prepares them to skillfully contribute quickly after graduation. Such exposure may be gained through internships, collaborative arrangements with industry and government, academic licenses for commercial software, guest lecturers, real problems in the classroom, and access to data feeds from industry.

SUPPORT RESEARCH INVESTMENT

Students remain great, untapped resources for creative thought and problem solving. If we present real, unsolved cybersecurity problems to students, they may only solve a small fraction of them, but they will learn from all of them. Students can gain a sense of the challenges facing the industry, faculty are able to direct and execute funded research, and schools gain positive exposure. Structured public–private partnerships would ensure a steady stream of problems for students and faculty, and would facilitate reliable job placement for students and graduates.

Conclusion

Cybersecurity education has emerged and evolved in response to a complex set of needs, environments, and priorities. The resulting system has satisfied some industries particularly well (e.g., finance), whereas others (e.g., utilities) have been left borrowing and adapting from others to deliver "good-enough" solutions, while students struggle to learn what they really need to know on the job. In this book, we outlined the unique nature and requirements of nine industry sectors with significant cybersecurity requirements. The resulting gap analysis led us to propose a way forward for cybersecurity education based on standardization, embracing technology and interdisciplinary approaches, and active engagement with industry. This way forward promises to educate a cybersecurity workforce with solid core skills and industry-specific knowledge to secure cyberspace in the short term, and to deliver graduates with the mental tools to continue learning and securing cyberspace for years to come.

About the Contributors

Editor

Jane LeClair, EdD, has had a long and distinguished career in education, technology, and the energy industry. She is currently chief operating officer of the National Cybersecurity Institute at Excelsior College in Washington, D.C., whose mission is to serve as an academic and research center dedicated to increasing the knowledge of the cybersecurity discipline. Dr. LeClair served as dean of the School of Business and Technology before assuming her current position.

Before joining Excelsior College, Dr. LeClair held numerous positions in education, technology, and energy. After earning her doctorate, she brought her teaching energies to Syracuse University and numerous other colleges, lecturing in their education and management programs. Paralleling her career in education, she also had a career in the nuclear industry, serving in various management positions with leading energy organizations and authoring numerous energy-related works. Her work in the energy industry brought her to the attention of the International Atomic Energy Agency, with which she continues to collaborate on an ongoing basis.

Dr. LeClair also has been actively involved in a variety of professional organizations. She is well known for being a vocal advocate for attracting and retaining more women in the fields of nuclear energy and cybersecurity, as well as other technology areas.

Contributors

Melody Balcet, BA, MA, has served the public sector in various capacities over the past seventeen years as a federal employee and consultant, including more than two years living in a felt tent on the Mongolian steppe while volunteering with the Peace Corps. Ms. Balcet is a service area manager and certified senior managing consultant with IBM's Public Sector Cybersecurity and Privacy practice where she serves clients mostly within the major federal agencies and the Department of Defense (DoD). Currently, Ms. Balcet is an advisor on DoD-wide FISMA activities under the DoD deputy chief information officer for cybersecurity. She serves as an officer on the Board of Directors for the ISACA National Capital Area Chapter and volunteers with a number of local organizations. Ms. Balcet holds Certified Information Systems Security Professional (CISSP) and Certified Information Security Manager (CISM) certifications.

Anthony Bargar, BS, MA, is an experienced cybersecurity industry professional, and has served as an executive for two firms, as well as in senior positions within the U.S. DoD, Intelligence Community (IC), and global financial services sector. He now leads a team of trusted advisors to assist clients in thriving within today's highly contested cyber environment. During his public service tenure, he took a lead role in implementing information assurance (IA) and cybersecurity. He was the cyber policy and strategy advisor for DoD and served as deputy chief information security officer. He was on the White House team to develop the president's Comprehensive National Cyber Initiative, which unified security response/information-sharing policies across government, financial, and critical-infrastructure sectors. In the IC he managed the U.S. counterintelligence DoD IA insider threat program, overseeing counter-espionage cases to safeguard the privacy of U.S. classified information.

Mr. Bargar co-led an international research project on shared information infrastructure protection and defense with the National Defense University (NDU) and the Swedish National Defense College. He holds a master's degree in information and telecommunication systems for business from Johns Hopkins University. Additionally, he is certified as a chief information officer from the NDU, where he graduated at the top of a class of nearly fifty students.

Capt. Shana Kayne Beach, BFA, MA, graduated from the University of Kansas in 2007 with a BFA in industrial design with a concentration in cognitive psychology and an MA in communication studies. Her graduate studies centered on organizational communication, and her thesis analyzed organizational commitment in high-reliability organizations. Upon graduation, she earned a commission into the U.S. Air Force through the Reserve Officer Training Corps. She has served more than six years in the Air Force and has been stationed in Texas, Colorado, Maryland, and Washington D.C. She currently holds Network+, Security+, and Certified Ethical Hacker certifications.

Tom Connors has more than twenty-nine years of experience providing assurance and advisory services to many large clients in the technology, media, and telecommunications industry sectors. He specializes in the areas of governance, risk, and regulatory advisory services, including internal audit and controls assurance, IT security, cloud computing, and contract risk and compliance. He has held a variety of regional and national leadership roles, including national leader of Deloitte's Sarbanes-Oxley Advisory and Governance Risk and Compliance Services. He is a certified public accountant in the State of New York and a certified information systems auditor (CISA).

Kyle Foley, BA, MS, is a cybersecurity professional with more than twenty-five years of experience in the financial services and federal sectors. He is currently a senior managing consultant in IBM's Global Business Services Cybersecurity and Privacy Practice where he provides IA consulting services to organizations throughout the federal government. Before joining IBM, he was a senior analyst at the Board of Governors of the Federal Reserve System, an operations manager at the U.S. Department of the Treasury, and president of the Information Systems Audit and Control Association's (ISACA) National

Capital Area Chapter. He is a CISA, Certified in the Governance of Enterprise Information Technology (CGEIT), and Certified in Risk and Information System Controls (CRISC). He received his MS in business technologies from Marymount University and a BA in political science from Villanova University. The views presented in his chapter are his own and do not represent those of IBM.

James H. Jones, Jr., BS, MS, PhD, has been a cybersecurity practitioner and researcher for more than eighteen years. He is an associate professor for George Mason University, and was previously a principal scientist for SAIC, Inc. He earned his bachelor's degree from Georgia Tech in industrial and systems engineering, a master's degree from Clemson University in mathematical sciences, and a PhD from George Mason University in computational sciences and informatics. His professional, academic, and research interests are currently focused on digital forensics, data, and intelligence analysis; malware behavior and detection; and cyber warfare.

Gregory Keeley, BA, MA, is the principal and founder of Ariana Partners Inc., which operates in the defense, cybersecurity, intelligence, and homeland security spaces. Concurrently, he is chief strategy officer for Araxid Inc. and a Visiting Fellow at the National Cyber Institute.

He served in Afghanistan from 2011 to 2012 with the U.S. Navy, providing daily briefings to the commander ISAF/U.S. Forces and served as an official ISAF spokesman. He operated in 14 provinces.

He previously served in a number of senior roles in the U.S. House and Senate, including special advisor to the vice chairman of the House Armed Services Committee and the chairman of the Joint Economic Committee. He advised the chairman of the House Foreign Relations Committee on counterterrorism and emerging threats.

Mr. Keeley received his undergraduate degree from Curtin University and holds a master's degree in conflict and security from Deakin University. He is a graduate of the Royal Australian Naval Academy. He continues to serve the U.S. Navy (Reserve) as executive officer at Navy Expeditionary Combat Command, Combat Camera.

K. Maman, MSSE, MBA, is a director in the Security and Privacy Services Group of Deloitte & Touche's Enterprise Risk Services practice. He has more than twenty-five years of industry and client experience. He has been with Deloitte for more than fifteen years, and specializes in serving the telecommunications and financial services industries with information security and infrastructure consulting. Before joining Deloitte & Touche, he spent twelve years with NYNEX/Bell Atlantic, where his last position was director of Business Network Services and Program Management. While there, he supported the implementation of a new fiber-based 2.6-million telephone-line and cable TV network in Thailand.

He has written and presented on various papers for conferences and panel discussions and is the holder of a U.S. Patent on a security system. He earned a MSEE from the Illinois Institute of Technology and an executive MBA from Columbia University.

Ernest McDuffie, MS, PhD, is currently the lead for the National Initiative for Cybersecurity Education at the National Institute of Standards and Technology. He was previously the associate director of the National Coordination Office for Networking and Information Technology Research and Development. He has also held the position of deputy director of the Office of Naval Research–Science and Technology for America's Readiness initiative and the lead program director for the Federal Cyber Service: Scholarship for Service Program at the National Science Foundation. He served as an assistant professor at Florida State University. He also participated in software engineering projects for the U.S. Air Force, the National Center for Atmospheric Research, the Federal Aviation Administration, Lockheed Missiles and Space Company, Los Alamos National Laboratory, and the National Security Agency. Dr. McDuffie received his PhD and MS degrees in computer science from the Florida Institute of Technology in Melbourne, Florida.

Sean Murphy, BS, MS, MBA, is currently a vice president in Leidos (formerly SAIC) Health Solutions Group and serves as the organization's health information privacy and security officer. He is a health-care information security expert, with nearly twenty years of experience in the field, serving at all levels of health care from the hospital to an international integrated delivery system. Before joining SAIC, he was a lieutenant colonel in the U.S. Air Force Medical Service Corps. He has served as CIO and CISO, but his proudest professional accomplishment was his service as senior mentor to the Afghan National Police Surgeon General's Office in 2008–2009 in support of Operation Enduring Freedom. He has a master's degree in business administration (advanced IT concentration) from the University of South Florida, a master's degree in health services administration from Central Michigan University, and a bachelor's degree in human resource management from the University of Maryland. He is also an adjunct professor at Saint Leo University, a fellow at the American College of Healthcare Executives, board-certified by the Healthcare Information & Management Systems Society, and holds two certifications from the International Information Systems Security Certification Consortium. He is a past chairman of the HIMSS Privacy and Security Committee and currently serves on the Excelsior College Industry Advisory Councils for Information Technology and General Technology.

Kai Roer is a European information security practitioner. In 1994, he founded The Roer Group AS, a management consulting company focusing on communication, leadership, and security. The company is known for its groundbreaking work on security culture and developing the security culture framework. He is the author of *The Leaders Workbook*, and the editor of *The Cloud Security Rules*. He is a highly sought after speaker, trainer, and consultant, who works all around the world. He serves as the chairman of the board of The Cloud Security Alliance, Norway Chapter. He is a lover of good food, a caring father, and a devoted family man. Mr. Roer blogs at http://roer.com and tweets as @kairoer.

Geoff Schwartz, AB, MSM, MSME, is program manager of nuclear power plant cybersecurity for Entergy Corporation, a position he has held since 2007. He has thirty-eight years of nuclear power experience, including twenty-one years active duty as a naval officer in submarine operation, maintenance, and engineering. After his naval career, he entered commercial nuclear power. Since then, he has served as the engineering director at several nuclear power plants, and has also been a project manager for a number of large projects, including plant life extension, design and construction of an above ground spent nuclear fuel facility, plant decommissioning, and modernization of plant process monitoring system networks.

He is a member of the Nuclear Energy Institute (NEI) cybersecurity task force. He is a co-author of guideline NEI 08-09, "Cyber Security Plan for Nuclear Power Reactors," and guideline NEI 10-04, "Identifying Systems and Assets Subject to the Cyber Security Rule." He holds a bachelor's degree in mathematics from the University of California at Berkeley, a master of science in mechanical engineering from the U.S. Naval Postgraduate School, and a master of science in management from Rollins College.

Index

ABOUT HUDSON WHITMAN

Hudson Whitman is a new, small press affiliated with Excelsior College, which has administrative offices in Albany, New York.

Our tagline is "Books That Make a Difference," and we aim to publish high-quality nonfiction books and multimedia projects in areas that complement Excelsior's academic strengths: education, nursing, health care, military interests, business and technology, with one "open" category, American culture and society.

If you would like to submit a manuscript or proposal, please review the guidelines on our website, hudsonwhitman.com. Feel free to send a note with any questions. We endeavor to respond as soon as possible.

OTHER TITLES BY HUDSON WHITMAN

The Call of Nursing: Stories from the Front Lines of Health Care
William B. Patrick (print and e-book)

Shot: Staying Alive with Diabetes
Amy F. Ryan (print and e-book)

The Language of Men
Anthony D'Aries (print and e-book)

Courageous Learning:
Finding a New Path through Higher Education
John Ebersole and William Patrick (print and e-book)

Saving Troy:
A Year with Firefighters and Paramedics in a Battered City
William Patrick (e-book only)

N21—Nursing in the Twenty-First Century
A peer-reviewed mobile journal available as a free iOS app.